D1046289

WAKING UP MARRIAGE

WAKING UP MARRIAGE:
FINDING TRUTH INSIDE YOUR PARTNERSHIP

BILL O'HERRON, LCSW

atmosphere press

Copyright © 2020 Bill O'Herron

Published by Atmosphere Press

Cover design by Nick Courtright

No part of this book may be reproduced
except in brief quotations and in reviews
without permission from the publisher.

Waking Up Marriage
2020, Bill O'Herron

atmospherepress.com

"Whenever the essential nature of things is analyzed by the intellect, it must seem absurd or paradoxical."

— Einstein

Marriage is the ultimate source, mechanism and arena for sustained human friction. This book is a celebration and ode to this great challenge and discourse, and an entreaty to keep standing in the fire of your deep-seated emotions at the altar of marital friction. The stormier the clouds, the more beautifully intense the lightening.

I want to thank Jacalyn Burke for her tireless support. I dedicate this book to my wife Linda and three daughters Claudia, Natalie, and Miranda who blindly, bravely, and lovingly refused to stop asking me that noxious, six-word question, "When will the book be done"? This was always going to be for them.

To my exceedingly patient parents, sister, and brother who somehow never fully tired of their sometimes reckless and always restless youngest son and brother. There is no me without them. To Sunny, for always keeping me company.

CONTENTS

"Asking questions is the source of all knowledge."

— Thomas Berger

INTRODUCTION
COMMODITIES SALES-TRADER, MEET THERAPIST

"This moment now is not independent in time but part of a causal chain rooted deep in your inner history."
— Christopher Bache

One of my clearest memories was when I was nine years old, walking in my backyard on one of those dull, languid New Jersey summer days. The yard was a patch of grass walled in by overgrown hedges that separated our house from our neighbors on three sides. I would wander over the piles of discarded brush and grass clippings in the far corner.

The humidity rolled in on long, stifling waves, and the cicadas' hypnotic hum was louder than the cars passing nearby. I walked to the edge of the yard, stepping over low mounds of dead grass and stopped. In that moment, I sensed that I had been there before. I was standing where others had stood a long time ago.

I walked carefully, feeling that I was stepping on these peoples' bones and pottery, like I could dig a shallow pit and find jewelry from a people I somehow just left. More than that, I sensed these people were still here, whispering, chanting, lighting fires, sleeping or scouting rival tribes. Somehow, in Richard Nixon's early 70's, in my New Jersey backyard, time had dissolved and overlapped.

And then there were the dreams.

Three nights before an eighth grade overnight ski trip to North Jersey, I dreamed that I was standing on top of a slope, ready to go down. What was unusual was that the sky was dark and there were lights around the edges of the hill. I paused, confused about the dimness, wondering if I should go. Suddenly, like being pushed, I was off. The skis seemed to turn on their own, and I was effortlessly gliding and bouncing. It was the same feeling as bouncing on a trampoline, that glee of weightlessness, of being suspended in midair all the way down the mountain. I could feel the rotating movement of my legs in the dream. It was an otherworldly sensation that now felt real.

As it turned out, our overnight ski trip included a visit to New Jersey's first ever lighted mountain: an intermediate hill covered with soft snow. I had forgotten the dream right until we stopped at the edge of that run. As soon as we began, though, as my buddies raced down, that dream body sensation returned. It was like magic. My skis turned back and forth without me thinking about what to do, and that bouncing lightness was exhilarating.

Growing up I mostly felt like I was *here*: in my house, in my neighborhood, and schools. A part of me felt, though, that I was in another time and place. The worlds of my dreams and daydreams were too vivid not to exist somewhere nearby. As such, as a kid and later as an adolescent, I simply learned to walk between the two spaces.

A pivotal moment for me came after college graduation. One fall morning I sat in my parents' kitchen, in the house that I grew up in, just four months after college graduation. As everyone else was starting their school or work day, I gazed into the yard outside feeling confused, alone, and untethered to anything meaningful or constructive. It would be my first bout of adulthood.

What had I been doing over the last eight years, and where would I go from here?

I was exhausted from years of academic hard-lifting. I was even more jaded with the vacuous college lifestyle and its endless adolescent, drunken rituals. Don't get me wrong, my college days and nights are some of the best I will ever have. Nothing else compares to these days. But at this point I was totally burned out and wanted something new, anything that would bring a sense of building something.

I was just about to pick up the phone and call the New York educational department when a counterthought struck. *Maybe I need to put money in the bank first?*

I was broke, living with and off my parents' generosity. Everyone knew that new teachers didn't make much. I was ready to make serious money, have my own account and start building a foundation for all the work to be done down the road. This thought of financial freedom, of having something bigger to do, won out. I started my sales career on Wall Street that month.

The specifics of the job or role that I wanted, as the fall of 1986 rolled around, once I had determined to go make money, were inconsequential. I knew how to tell a story, I just needed subject matter to sell. My first job on Water Street, downtown New York, was to sell research and market commentary to bond and currency traders at banks and investment companies. No real training, just a phone, a territory, and a list of people at these types of firms throughout the city. Not rocket science, just desire and conviction. I knew if I let people talk, tell their story, I would be able to move them towards *my story*.

I remember one particularly lucrative moment nine

months into this role. My dad's friend was the manager of technology maintenance at Citibank. His job was to make sure that all the quote machines, all the computers sitting on the desks of their vast downtown trading floor, worked properly. He respected my father and was drawn to my youthful zeal and candor. He said he would help me in any way that he could.

After our third meeting, really with me just listening to his stories, I summoned the courage to ask him for a favor. I asked him if he would let me onto the trading floor. That was Shangri-La. No one at my firm or at any of our competitors had ever stepped onto that hallowed ground. But that was where all the high priests and high priestesses of finance sat, reckoned, and moved global finance prices. These were the great and good currency and bond traders of the 1980's. This was where the real manna was. All I had to do was go from computer to computer, trader to trader, and get them to read my firm's research. I just needed one to two minutes per person.

Reluctant at first, since he could get in trouble for allowing an unauthorized person onto the trading floor, my father's friend eventually lead me to one of the back doors of that infamous Citi trading floor. Before he unlocked the door, he politely but sternly reminded me that he trusted my father and was therefore willing to trust me to be respectful and mindful of the risks and authority that this access provided. I did not take this warning lightly.

Over the next three months, after spending those two and half hours literally tapping people's shoulders and politely describing my product, I earned over $19,000. For a twenty-three year old in 1987, who ten months earlier had $280 to his name, it was like winning the lottery. But it was not the amount of money that continually intrigued me, it was the process by which money could be made and the potential to make more. While on that trading floor, witnessing the intensity and focus needed to succeed in the money game, I realized I did not want to sell products to the money changers; I wanted to be one. "Render unto Caesar" like the radio's morning song, piped through my hair.

No other job would fully satisfy me. A family friend described this business as the hardest way to make an easy living. That was the sales-trading anthem. I wanted in.

A year later, through a friend, I found my way onto a small but very successful trading desk. From 7:00 a.m. to 5:00 p.m. the world of scheduled meetings, lunch breaks, sports highlights, taxicabs, family events, etc. disappeared. There were only three things that mattered during our brokering and trading day: the prices of all the financial instruments flashing across our screens, the news headlines and rumors that caused these prices to move, and whether we bought or sold these prices at the right time.

Every blinking number, every price of each commodity told a story, had a unique personality that was somehow linked to all the other financial instruments, that in turn were all connected to the global news and economies. Nothing happened in isolation.

It was an all-consuming role in which I realized that to be successful, you had to be prepared. You had to continually anticipate specific scenarios and understand the interrelationship between all the markets. The twenty-four-hour reporting of global economic news, political

7

results, and corporate and financial outcomes created patterns in stock, bond, and commodity price movement.

To try to stay in sync with these movements, you had to be a little bit of everything: historian, psychologist, salesman, economist, analyst, speculator, and risk manager. I was lucky enough, over my eleven years of trading, to work with not just the industry's best and brightest, but some of the world's all-time greatest speculators and money managers.

No other job compared to this one. And it was not long before I realized that there were two universal skills that every one of these renowned, profitable money managers had that others did not. The first was that the greatest traders *had the uncanny sense of recognizing patterns.* They studied every possible "if-then" scenario, how one event or a certain price movement impacted everything else.

What also made them good was that they were behaviorists.

"Every movement of importance is but a repetition of similar price movements...familiarize yourself with the actions of the past."
— Jesse Livermore, *How to Trade in Stocks*

What made these money managers great, though, was the second and more important attribute. They all understood and accepted the fact that it was not the actual price movements that they were battling, but their *own responses to market movements and subsequent actions that generated the profits.*

Learning these two facets of trading, of life, from these

clients mesmerized me. I filled countless notebooks over eight years with observations of my responses to prices. The markets became my lenses for watching my own insecurity, fear, knowledge, and trust of self.

"You must give up the life you planned in order to have the life that is waiting for you."

— Joseph Campbell

By 1996, exactly ten years after sitting at my parents' kitchen table after graduation, this charmed and materially abundant life that had found me, started feeling hollow, thin, and somehow not mine. The flashing prices on my trading screen began to look like random numbers again because my curiosity about the story they told was waning. I had become psychologically and emotionally exhausted. I'd just turned thirty-two and the experiment of seeking profit, for its own sake had simply lost its meaning

On a personal note, my love life held very little love in it. This was not due to a lack of wonderful women. I just could not figure out why every romantic relationship ended with me feeling an incipient ennui. I always ended up feeling that the current *she* was not the one to pour my uncontainable and totally unknowable feelings into. So, I would simply turn off my affection and retreat like a coward, like the boy I still was.

Despite the paychecks and the allure of my ex-patriot lifestyle in the world's greatest city, my heart had begun to shut down. I was lost in the linear world of work that had always made sense.

I started to become haunted by an other-worldly

longing, the same one that had spoken to me in my backyard summers as a boy. Again, I was straddling two worlds, but this time the gap between my inner and outer world was much wider. Ten years of nonstop action, rationalizing, and accumulating had created a callus around my heart. It was a decade of doing, with very little feeling. But a muffled heart will eventually come up for air. When our rational side does not pay enough attention to our emotional side, eventually things just get distorted.

Working on Salomon Brother's trading floor in London, the largest in the world at the time, did not help either. The sea of ringing phones and shouting salespeople only made me feel smaller, emptier. I realized I needed to stop for a week or two, to let this ache in my stomach and heart come up or just go away. I decided to fly back to the states, back to my parents' house, and retrace my steps. Returning to what was familiar would hopefully ease these unfamiliar and uncomfortable sensations.

That decision led to a fateful Sunday evening at my former college and an experience that changed my life forever. It would set in motion everything that still informs my thoughts and actions today, some twenty-two years later.

I flew home, back to New Jersey. It was March 1996. A couple of hours after I had arrived at my parents' house, I wandered over to a neighborhood park, one that I had been to a thousand times before. My dad ended up joining me.

The conversation in that park was the most candid, honest one we had ever had. I shared everything with him. I talked about how little I knew about his family, how we rarely talked about his parents and their lives.

As a tear welled up, I asked my dad what it was like for him when he was thirty-one. He said that he never really stopped to reflect or wonder back then. As he spoke, I got the sensation of the lowering of a moat bridge that separated me from him, me from all the fathers that had come before us and who had never spoken to *their* sons. Sitting on that bench with him, in that March sun, I knew there were some very old feelings from an unexpressed past that I was somehow a part of, and this past was becoming restless in me. That was how I was feeling at thirty-one years old.

The outside world seemed flat while my inner world was getting round, more complex and restless. In the middle of it all stood my father, my hero, my connection to my history, to our ancestors.

Realizing that I wanted to keep retracing my steps back to when I thought I knew myself better, I booked a flight to Vermont and decided to visit my old college. Having lived abroad for the last five years, I reasoned that it would be nice to return. I had no phone on me. I was single and had no unfulfilled obligations other than a well-paying job that could wait.

"Until you make the unconscious conscious, it will direct your life and you will call it fate."

— Carl Jung

I got to campus on Sunday afternoon. It was quiet: a few listless seniors and wayward freshman walked towards town as I headed up the steep sidewalk towards the cafeteria. I was a ghost, a stranger moving in the dusk.

I felt like a ghost because if someone asked me, *who I was and what I did*? I wasn't exactly sure what my answer would be. I'm Bill, class of '86 was all I could think of. Beyond geography, I was a thirty-something male who, at that point in life, could have easily just kept walking north into the woods and never come back.

Walking up to the center of campus reminded me of a scene in my favorite book in high school, Joseph Conrad's *Heart of Darkness*. Marlow, the main character, is about to begin his journey up the Congo River looking for the trading post commander stationed deep in the jungle and finds a note: "Hurry up." – "Where?" – "Up the river?" "Approach cautiously."

I was not sure why I was there, and it was a bit foreboding. But no other place made sense either.

Ten years out of school and I still recognized some of the faces in the black and white photos hanging outside of the cafeteria walls. I went into the cafe and got a bagel. None of the students actually noticed or gave me a second look.

On the bulletin board of upcoming campus events, there were signs for math tutoring, Red Cross training classes, a blood donation drive, and some music lesson sign-up sheets. At the very bottom was a flyer for a meditation class at 7 p.m. *A Sunday evening meditation class, really?* It kind of jolted me. I got nervous just thinking about it. Group sharing classes were not my thing. *I am not ready for something like this*, I thought, *hopefully I already missed it*" I checked the cafeteria clock: 6:53 p.m. *Oh man, no way, not me. I will just head in the general direction but not go in.*

Of course, I ended up gingerly walking into that class

and by the time I started figuring out my escape route, she walked in. It was too late. Christine, the instructor, had arrived. *Fuck.* I was more embarrassed about walking out than staying.

Christine was a woman with dark piercing eyes and thick black hair. She walked confidently, not wasting a single movement. She looked me up and down like I had two heads.

When she got to the center of the room, she simply said, "Welcome back, please get on your cushions with your legs crossed." She then asked us to briefly introduce ourselves. When I shared with the group that I was an alum just wandering through campus, she thanked me and said, "Before you leave tonight, Bill, we need to speak." *What's that about?* I thought. Now I really wanted to bolt.

What followed was a simple but powerful meditation practice, one that I still do and teach today. I will share it with you later in this book.

By the end of the meditation class, I had sunk into a heavy fullness. Hard to explain. If you have ever been on a boat heading east off the coast of Florida when it is calm, you can see the much darker waters of the gulf stream off in the distance. The continental shelf and its playful turquois water slowly gives way to the deep blue, formidable current of the mighty gulf-stream. The gulf stream is ominous; one million cubic feet of water flow past the shelf's edge every second, 2,600 feet deep in places. I felt like I had drifted to this edge and had touched an un-fathomable, slightly uneasy serenity just by sitting in this class.

I hadn't known it at the time, but a subtle interruption of all things linear and obvious to me had occurred.

"In moments of solitude you may become aware of some other streams of consciousness… hear words, see images that appear out of context with your own thoughts."
—Jane Roberts, *Seth Speaks*

And Christine knew, just by my body language, that there was more going on. She asked me my birthday, and as soon as I said November, she shook her head and said, "Oh boy, figures. I've dated a few Scorpios. You guys just start asking questions and refuse to give up; you have to just go all the way."

I had no idea what she was actually saying, but it felt like she was unwrapping me. Then she said, "Meet me downtown tomorrow at 10 a.m. at the bookstore. I have two books you need to buy. Do you even know," she paused briefly, "what you are doing here?"

I blinked. "Not really. I just saw the flyer and have been kind of aimless recently, not that happy. I think I'm just looking for some answers," I replied.

"Remember, Bill," she responded, "All Eastern thought is based on not knowing, on *I don't know*. Western thought is about defining everything with thoughts, about having an answer. The further you go into *I don't know*, the wobblier it gets." I had no answer, but was firmly in the grips of *I don't know*.

The wobbling had begun.

Unbridled, traumatic, enlightening, and extraordinary are adequate words to describe the ensuing twelve months after meeting Christine.

Ten days after flying back from this trip home and to my college, I finally got the courage to try sitting quietly alone in my Sloan Square apartment.

It was dusk. I put my pillow on the floor facing the chimney-lined skyline. I took a few deep breaths and started to relax and feel heavy. The squeaky breaks of those racing, London cabs kept doing what they always did, slicing another wet night. This night was different, though; as my neck and chest started to tense, and my arms started to get jittery. A few minutes more and my shoulders began to heave as if something was stuck and trying to exit my throat. Tears started to flow but there were no emotions, thoughts, or memories behind or connected to them.

I have never been choked, but my body seemed to know how to do it to itself. At the height of this tension, sitting on the floor, with a very faint voice of reason whispering "hang on" in the back of my head, I passed out in a pool of tears. I am not sure how long I was slumped over on the floor. But when I awoke and cautiously slid back onto the pillow, so I could figure out what just occurred, and I heard, "Welcome back!"

"Deep down below the surface of the average conscience a still, small voice says to us, something is out of tune."

— Carl Jung

I was wide awake, and even though I had just seemingly experienced being choked or hanged, I was completely relaxed. I thought I knew what my own thoughts and ideas sounded like inside my head. The tone of that "welcome back" sounded older though, a bit wiser and even playful. It jolted me. The hair raised on my neck. I was sitting on the floor in the dark, alone, in an apartment that I had lived in for five years, but there was a sense of not being alone.

I just kept sitting, waiting for something. I was timidly glancing around, almost nervous that maybe someone had come in while I was asleep. More chills down my back. And then just like a theatre set change, the scene shifted, and I felt like I was sitting in the middle of a circle of old, Native American women who were chanting. My eyes were open in the pitch dark, and they were sitting around me. As I close my eyes now, I can hear that same song, those haunting, deep tones.

There were no white lights or cosmic openings. It just felt like some knowable dreamscape had become three dimensional in my downtown apartment. Instead of glimpsing this other place in pieces or flashes when asleep, it was now a slightly uncomfortable reality. Uncomfortable because it was so foreign to sense it while awake. Instead of waiting to show up while I was unconscious during sleep, these singing women decided to very faintly materialize while I was still awake.

Joseph Campbell, the world's most renowned expert on mythology, explains why humans in every culture have been sitting quietly since the beginning of time: "You are released from the local system of illusions and put in touch with mysteries of the psyche itself which leads to wisdom concerning both soul and its world." He goes on to say that "The chief aim of all religious teachings and ceremony is to suppress the sense of ego and develop that of participation." This was *the* moment when my left brain, that part that organizes and rationalizes, stepped into the world of my right brain. This was when life truly opened up.

This is my sole purpose for writing this book: to get you, the reader, to use the excruciatingly difficult emotions that are whipped up in you and in your relationship with your partner as catalysts and motivation to push you into your silence. Recognize and gather all the old feelings that get stirred up in you and sit quietly with them, alone in a room.

The goal is to simply bring together that which you know, think, and feel with what you *do not* know and cannot understand. Sitting in silence and breathing, the most basic practice of yoga, is simply uniting your physical body with whatever it is connected to, non-physical or spiritual, whatever you want to call it. There is a whole other life stored in your feelings that you cannot see or touch. That is where the non-physical, the divine, dharma, Jesus, Yahweh, Allah, Great Spirit, Krishna, Jah, Buddha, the spiritual lives, in your feelings, intuition, and sensibilities. Those are all just word-symbols fastened and carved by us to express the ineluctable and sometimes painful sensation of physically releasing your emotions into your neck, forehead, midbrain and top of head via your breath. The breath-filled human becomes spiritual as that is the definition of the word. "To breathe" in Latin is *spiritus*. True unfettered awareness, spirituality, is the life-long process of continually introducing your analytical adult attention to your eternally unruly and incomprehensibly intelligent feelings, emotions, dreams, and perceptions, all the things of which our rational mind is wary.

Imagine that. The secret to your life has been there the whole time; you just had to wait for it to bubble up when sitting alone. And if you want to really complete your life, to fully create and finish your ninety-year (or so) life story, you will have to release *all* your feeling, non-physical world onto your linear, thinking world. The full intelligence of your life is stored in the intersection of these two sides of your body-brain, in between your thoughts and your feelings. But to get at them all, you need another person, I believe, to create more friction and collaboration. The more interaction with another, with your partner, the more and heavier the joy, frustration, love, anger and, hence, the friction. Your reactions to the other dredge up more of yourself. Without the other to fire you up, you do not go as deep, you won't finish it all up. *It* is your true life.

By sitting alone, you learn to recognize and embrace your true and irrationally brilliant self, but your partner brings out even more of it through the friction. It is not the outcome of the relationship you should focus on; it is your willingness and commitment to the growth it will bring you. If you stay with it for as long as you can, stay and sit with all the child-like feelings that come up in your everyday, in reaction to your partner, you will achieve your full potential. You will become the most emotionally intelligent and mature adult you could become this time around. Friction is the great bestower of the truth of your life that awaits you. Albert Szent-Györgyi says, "To regulate something always requires two opposite factors."

Exactly one year after that first meditation class with Christine in Vermont, and four months after this past-life session, I moved to Merida, Venezuela and enrolled in a six-hour a day Spanish immersion program. I was thirty-two, living in the home of a local Venezuelan woman and her two sons, none of whom spoke English. I guess I was getting an early jump on a midlife crisis, but enjoyed the fact that did not have to buy the red sports car or have sex with a secretary.

I went from steak tartare in South Kensington to local South American beans and rice, endless hours of language study, and long nights sitting in the dark. Nothing else made sense but to do this. The path that lead me from there, in Merida, Venezuela, to graduating from Columbia University's School of Social Work in New York six years later was filled with marriage, children, a return to the comfort and emptiness of suburbia, and a desire to materialize this deep-seated yearning to be of service to others.

After Linda and I got married in London, we moved back to the US with our four-month-old daughter. We bought a house in a bucolic Connecticut suburb to begin this next phase of our relationship. Bland pizza, a used mini-van, trying to make new friends, the uncut lawn, and broken dishwashers were all in the mix.

Linda and I continually challenged one another to communicate more about why we were reacting throughout all those tough, young-kids phase of marriage. We always took the time to stop after a big, fatigue-induced argument and look hard inside ourselves at what was coming up. Was the anger about an in-law staying two extra days at our house new, or were these feelings old, based on something from our childhood? We called it the *check-in.*

Yes—she threw a few plates at my head, and I ranted about her spending habits and mean-spirited comments, especially in those early days and months. Carl Jung reminds us that "The meeting of two personalities is like the contact of two chemical substances: if there is any reaction, both are transformed" and that "everything that irritates us about others can lead us to an understanding of ourselves." That is what I started to realize early on, that this arena called marriage could be my path to awareness.

Within months of moving into that first home in Connecticut, I was back working on a stock trading desk at one of the industry's largest and most successful hedge funds. I had to start making money again, and this was the only job that seemed to make sense and that could pay the bills.

Twelve of us traders sat elbow to elbow amidst stacks of computer screens, shouting over each other and into our phones nine hours a day. It was relentless banter, modern financial warfare, as we fought to own a single price on every transaction, buying and selling hundreds of millions of dollars' worth of stocks every day.

Every evening, though, once Linda and my daughters went to bed, I would change into my sweatpants and t-shirt and enter a completely different arena. I would bring my mediation pillow into the living room on that oriental rug and just sit. The house was quiet and the well-manicured lawns of this suburban dominion were now hidden below the night. I came to this spot on my living room for one reason: to try to find out who I was. I would wait for the waves of feelings and old emotions to arrive. They would often come like a storm as I breathed into my stomach. My chest would fill with a cacophony of sensations, like joy, frustration, and longing. As Joseph Campbell tells us, "The cave you fear to enter holds the treasure you seek."

Night after night, I knew exactly what was in store for me. I knew the physical unraveling that would take place, and how my body would literally cough up more stored memories and emotions. I would get images of being in battles during the Middle Ages. My body would contort while tears of joy and longing for things and places that I was not even sure of would flow. I would see faces of Native elders sitting around fires and hear whispers and insights about my family from relatives and ancestors I've never met. It was like a workout, with snot pouring out my nose and sweat forming from the muscle contractions.

Of all the thoughts and sensations that overwhelmed me on a nightly basis, there were three main themes that kept coming up. These three, I thought, would eventually form the base of all the work I would someday do as a counselor or therapist. If I thought I could help others better understand their joys and sorrows, rebuild their dreams, which became my life's mission, I knew I would have to help others understand and work with these three concepts.

The first concept: who you are and what you are living right now is an accumulation of experiences, both yours and those you grew up with. We are layered with all of these moments that are stored in our heart and stomach and limbic brain. As Christopher Bache says in *Lifecycles*, we are all an "aggregation of life experiences stored in your limbic body. This moment now is not independent in time but part of a casual chain rooted deep in your inner history".

The second: the emotions and feelings that you absorbed from your parents are the foundation of who you are and how you feel and react. You have to go back to the child that lives inside of you. It turns out that your relationship with your spouse started when we were seven years old because that is how and when you learned to relate to men, women, and yourself. You were formed in the *Space in Between* (*SIB*) your parents. During the first ten years of your life, your "nervous system acts as an 'antenna,' which is tuned to and responds to the electromagnetic fields produced by the heart of other individuals." Your parents transferred their world, their joys, sorrows, and longings via the magic of electrons. "When people touch or are in proximity, a transference of the electromagnetic energy produced by the heart occurs." In order to understand yourself and how to succeed in marriage, you have to go back to those emotions you absorbed in the SIB. "The mammalian nervous system depends for its neurophysiologic stability on a system of interactive coordination, wherein steadiness comes from synchronization with nearby attachment figures."

Nietzsche agrees. "The child is far from being buried in the man, as Nietzsche thinks. On the contrary, it rules him absolutely."

The third and final concept: the friction you are experiencing in your life, especially in your relationship to your spouse, is the catalyst and siren call to go back to the silence, back to the SIB, in order to undo the impact these inherited emotions are having on you. Our parents' and grandparents' aches and joys, all that they left unsaid, all that our parents left undone and incomplete, and every unexpressed and unfulfilled desire and emotion lingers in us creates every challenge in your relationship. I knew, four years into my new life in suburbia, that it was time to take these tools, and go get a masters in social work in order to create a foundation and platform to begin helping others go back in time.

All of our journeys begin at the kitchen table of childhood. Through years of therapy and my own intense methods of self-exploration, I have uncovered the hidden hopes, aspirations, heartbreaks, regrets, failures and longings buried deep within my bloodline. You have them too. It's the movie that runs silently in the reel of that DNA you carry around. It's the primal urge that randomly seems to break out of your subconscious mind once in a while like a wild bull, sabotaging your career or friendship or marriage. It's also that glorious beast that forces you to take risks and live deeply.

Waking Up Marriage: Finding Truth Inside Your Partnership is the culmination of over twenty years of research into the mysterious process of human development. Like the boy who sat at the kitchen table back in 1986, it is the consequence of a heart leaning in. My mission is to partner with you in slowing down so that you can go inside to listen to the childhood memories, fears and joys inside your welled-up heart. Once you hear those, you can then carry them back into your adult life and partnership. That is where and how your fully released adult life, love, partnership, and marriage begin.

Bill O'Herron 2019

CHAPTER 1
THE GREAT UNCONSCIOUS

"Everything that irritates us about others can lead us to an understanding of ourselves."

— Carl Jung

"All of humanity's problems stem from man's inability to sit quietly in a room alone."

— Blaise Pascal

Stove Top Betty

1979 was the last year General Motors made and sold ovens. Who knew that the same company made Pontiacs and electric stoves? There she was, though, that big metal box sitting tired but stout on our linoleum floor in the sixties ranch house my wife and I bought in the late 1990s.

We called that old oven GM Betty. She may have been a Kennedy-era relic, but she commanded a presence in our kitchen. Everything we did, whether chasing toddlers or debating holiday plans with the in-laws, was reflected on her dull gray belly.

She had plenty of electric horsepower left too, right up to the day our Home Depot renovation saw her being wheeled out. In those first few years of our marriage, GM Betty's coils never failed. She fired up hundreds of late-night formula bottles and held pots of spicy soups on her chipped grates.

Imagine if old Betty could speak, if all the appliances

in kitchens and family rooms could speak, with all the emotions flying and hurt feelings within all the relationships. She could have kept a marriage counselor busy for months. Those uncomfortable Sunday mornings, when my wife had been up earlier than me again, when the kitchen's sunlight, unfed kids, and dirty dishes exacerbated the tension from the previous night's fight. I had pissed her off with another flippant comment in front of friends, but did not know the extent of the damage until I got the morning elbows and stiff shoulder.

GM Betty became a symbol of those early years of my marriage. Everything was raw and new. I was thirty-three years old and had never permanently resided with a one-year-old, a dog, minivan, or someone of the opposite sex who did not share my DNA. Twenty-two years later, it is comical to consider what I thought I knew about love, myself, life, marriage, parenting, and adulthood. Maturity-wise, I was a high schooler.

Betty is a demarcation. She represents the end of marital innocence and the headwater entrance to deeper and much stormier currents. What happened in front of her indelibly changed my perspective, opinion, and ability to understand and embrace a mature marriage.

Teenager Inside

I had unfortunately mastered the ability to make adolescent comments about my wife and marriage when there were willing, friendly listeners and alcohol on hand. It seems so easy for me, for most men, to revert to our inner sixteen-year-old and puerile need for attention. The cheap, high school-like laughs we seek end up costing more than we think, though.

We jest about our spouse's driving record or the laundry, seemingly innocuous stuff. It is a sport to us, getting laughs like some standup comic by sharing personal data about our marriage that our spouse rightfully considers classified. This relatively innocent action, sharing more than we should, unaware of the impact of our words, is just part of the great adult unconscious that we inhabit. What does that mean? It means our adult attention lingers endlessly, precariously in thoughts, concepts, and beliefs, like a raft atop of the unfathomable sea and ancient feeling kingdom stirring below. "Ninety-five percent of our lives are lived unconsciously," says Dr. Robert Lipton in *Biology of Belief*. Entering marriage, especially in its early years, is an entrance into the timeless arena and halls of this great unconscious.

I had no idea of the puerile insecurity still living powerfully in me, the need that wanted others to embrace me. I could not imagine my words could hurt my wife's feelings back then, or that they poked her sense of self. It was just entertainment to the sixteen-year-old in me. How could I have known her sensibility, since I was clueless of my own?

I began to realize the real work of marriage was not between us and our spouses. It is in us and our deep-seated emotions. We are married to our old emotions. Our spouse is just a supporting cast member in a play that we must choose to enact.

Marriage is a relationship with self. Back in the kitchen with my wife in those early years, on the morning after a night out, it was like trying to kiss her while she was getting a basketball rebound. Her elbows were flying and hips were checking while my regrets were building because I had hurt her feelings.

These uncomfortable exchanges happened so many times that I started calling that spot in front of Betty the "paint" and the "three-second zone." I got "boxed out" of so many conciliatory hugs and apologies that I learned to tread lightly in front of Betty, especially when both she and my wife were grilling something hot.

As marriage unfolds, you wonder how all the emotion-infused debates and disagreements get started. The feelings and reactions and words get so big and intense over issues seemingly so small. What you will see, though, is that there is a whole other world, a literal kingdom of experiences and feelings breathing inside of you and your partner, just below the surface of interaction.

This topic about what rests quietly, mysteriously, inexorably, and so often unconsciously inside us all is what motivated me to write this book. When I started using my reactions to my marriage as the fuel to sit quietly longer, to do more therapy, my intuition and feelings showed me answers to every question I had. What did I want in my life? Why did I hate this and love that? Why did my wife and kids respond these ways?

I have been fascinated and obsessed with how many old emotions, sensibilities, longings, joys, and desires we all carry unsuspectingly into our relationships. I am in awe of both who we are and who we think we are when we cross the marital threshold. I am even more amazed at what is demanded as we move forward.

This is what I have been doing and teaching for the

last twenty-three years, to go back inside our heart. Until you sit alone and linger in your old feelings, everything else is an illusion, jibber-jabber, psychobabble, and therapeutic wind that is wasting your money. Just sit. Just sit quietly alone with your eyes closed and back straight and listen to your heart.

Why? Why sit? Many resist the notion that just sitting will help. Some mightily disagree. I guarantee that these skeptics have either tried and it was uncomfortable, boring, or considered time wasted, or they are simply nervous about unwanted feelings and memories arising. I understand and had that same perspective. Your marriage, though, is asking for all of you, all your resources, capabilities, and abilities to perceive, grow, and learn.

The rational mind, the one being used to read these words, is not enough. It has limited scope and depth. No offense to that side of the brain, but it alone is not capable of handling marriage. As Robert Monroe says in *Far Journey*, if we use only our rational faculties, then we are "only partially successful using an incorrect standard of measurement." It is beyond the rational and logical where we must take ourselves, and it is only by sitting quietly that we can grasp and access the resources, perspectives, and guidance to understand marriage. Eric Jaffe, in his article "Meditate on It," describes the power of sitting. He says it "relaxes the heart and strengthens the mind's ability to connect symbols and meaning."

Lee Sannella, MD spent a lifetime studying meditation. In his book *The Kundalini Experience,* he summarizes succinctly how and why meditation is the only method to address the psychological, emotional, and physiological stressors of marriage. "It reduces the noise level and changes the functioning of the nervous system's ability to handle stress so that it becomes more efficient, creating deeper possibility."

"When we are rational, using abstractions, we cannot take all features into account."
—Fritjof Capra

In the next few chapters I will show you the simplest ways to do this, to sit alone. This is where those "deeper possibilities" lie, in an old, timeless neighborhood and locale I call The Space in Between (SIB). This is where your marriage began, long ago. In here are the unabridged knowledge, facts, and certainties that your friends, parents, colleagues and innocent therapists will never provide or comprehend. In this SIB, there is a wisdom and "reality that lies...beyond the cogitations of the rationalizing mind, only grasped by intuition."

You are going to learn the roots of why you react the way you do in your marriage and in every relationship in your life. You will see that the battle you are waging with your spouse is you shadow boxing with your unresolved, unprocessed, and unexamined deep-seated emotions that are creating your maddening reactions.

It looks and smells like it's your spouse's or mom's fault, but it always comes back to you. Sorry about that. Everything that is challenging and hard and upsetting in your marriage is merely a reflection of what you are carrying in your right brain.

Marriage: The Great and Difficult Story

Running a marathon while getting a root canal is child's play compared to marriage. I believe that developing a mature, supportive, and loving adult relationship with your partner is the most difficult thing you will ever do. Why do so many fail at this, and why is it such a challenge? How can something that begins so reasonably, comfortably, passionately, and innocently become so unruly?

The teachings here will shine a light on both why relationships are so difficult, and why there is nothing more important than working on them. An eighty-year *Harvard* study recently stated, "The only thing that matters in life are your relationships." Therapists like me who have been living, breathing, laughing, crying, meditating, counseling, and studying relationships for over twenty years realize the same thing Valliant says in the study: "Finding a way of coping with life that does not push love away" is all that really matters in life. It is the key to health, happiness, and finding meaning in life, period.

Working on your marriage is important. Really important. Why? Because "a supportive relationship is the Number 1 predictive factor in having most positive outcomes in life." It is the healthiest thing you can do.

The work and commitment that you put into your relationship is the work of your life. I am going to show that this work will positively change the lives of your grandkids' grandkids. That is how big it is. It is time for you to pursue a relational life.

Marriage is Calling You. Simmer In It.

This is a book about how our relationships are asking and calling us to cross the gap between our powerful adult sensibilities that are impelled by logic and reason — and our even more dominant and ineluctable emotions stored in the ten-year-old children inside of us.

After twenty-three years of marriage, 7,000 hours of sitting quietly in meditation, fourteen years as a practicing therapist, and paying for five different marriage counselors myself, I know how marriages work, why they fail, and what it takes to succeed in them. You must carry your anger and frustration-filled reactions away from your spouse and into your cave, into your therapist's office, and to the chair where you sit alone. Your reactions store old wounds and misgivings. Your spouse just woke them up. If you are brave enough to own these reactions, your marriage will grow. If not, it will wither or languish at best.

The stories here have passed through my wife's scrutiny. When she read the pages of this book, she loved the vignettes about those crossroad moments, especially when she threw the plate at my head. Every marriage has four or five critical battles that help you to either turn inward to self-assess, or leave dents too big to undo. I am hunting for those moments with and for you.

If you are not willing to take the time and muster fortitude and courage to simmer in the feeling-experiences that arise in you in response to marital friction, you and marriage will not work. You will be a fifty percenter. Half of all marriages fail. Moreover, if you are not willing to sit quietly by yourself and allow your feelings to slowly rise up into your belly, heart, neck and forehead, over and over again, then this book is not for you.

One of Western civilization's greatest minds agrees that sitting alone will alter your life. Blaise Pascal, who in 1642 was not only one of the first inventors of the calculator, but who also has a law, theorem, and coefficient named after him, was adamant about why humans struggled and how to address our challenges. His advice and solution are unequivocal. They form the basis of this book and my life's work. He said, "All of humanity's problems stem from man's inability to sit quietly in a room alone."

Relationships fail, according to less conscious observers, for reasons like trust, money, infidelity, and irreconcilability. Those are excuses, though— labels for an unwillingness to sit alone to know the roots of why you are so uncomfortable and unhappy. Your unhappiness is much older than your marriage. Lack of money and trust are symptoms, not reasons.

When you boil it down, there is one universal, ever-present, overriding reason why a marriage fails: you have not done any work on yourself. If you fail to know yourself, you have no clue what you are bringing to the altar of marriage. Even if you do not want to be in this relationship, it is worth doing this work. Like Pascal says, it will change everything. The work has nothing to do with the other person. It certainly looks and smells and tastes like the other, but it is you.

Relatus and Your Cave

Do you actually know what the word "relationship" means? Here we are, immersed every minute of the day engaging, interacting, aching, laughing and crying in and through all these exchanges with friends, family members, colleagues and strangers, in relationships with all of them, and we do not know what the word actually means. Until death do us part, and yet you probably never asked the question of what a relationship means or does.

Marriage is a verb. The word relationship comes from Latin *relatus*, which means "to carry or bring back." Your deep-seated feeling-reactions, born in childhood and absorbed bio-electrically from your parents and theirs, all buried in your midbrain and heart, get kicked up and dislodged in the natural heat of marriage. Every day, living within the same walls with our spouse, currents of anguish and joy alight. We care about the other and our marriage, which means there is anger. A comment your spouse made about you is really a flashlight being pointed at a hurt inside your belly, a wound from comments your mom, dad, or town bully made when you were ten.

This is where marriage becomes a verb. Relatus means you take this awakened feeling of hurt today, at the altar and kitchen of your marriage, and bring it to your cave and simmer in it. Where is it from? What is this old hurt telling me of my current sense of self, my insecurities around money, self-image, or abilities to relate to others in general? Go find a quiet place, sit in your closet or bedroom, or outside by yourself. Then go to your therapist, find a good one. Both therapy and sitting alone are your cave.

Joseph Campbell said, "The cave your fear to enter holds the treasure you seek." Let's enter together.

Close your eyes with your back straight right now, please, while sitting in a chair, both feet firmly on the ground. We like to say, "Keep you back straight but soft, your shoulders square but relaxed." Lightly stomp your feet on the floor a few times, just to remind you they are there.

This is it. This is the pole position. Anything else is fluff.

Here are the fundamentals of sitting, what I call Listening by Yourself (LBY):

- As you sit in this simple position, back straight and eyes closed, please now take your attention, take your closed eyes and lower their focus onto and into your heart and chest
- This is where all the action is
- Imagine right now that instead of using your head and brain to think your thoughts and ruminate on your plans, regrets and pangs of resentment, that you now do all this thinking inside your chest and heart
- In other words, imagine your brain is actually in your chest for the next few minutes
- So, here you are, just sitting quietly with your eyes closed. Well done. If you did just this for the next fifteen minutes, you would have done a lot
- But let's do a bit more

- Now that your brain is quietly sitting in your chest next to your heart, see and imagine that all your thoughts are rubbing against and being heard and felt by your heart. It is as if your thoughts are being poured and filtered by your heart
- Now imagine that each time you take a normal breath in through your nose, this inhaled air now travels into your chest, heart, and brain, filling them to capacity with air
- It is as if your heart and brain, bedfellows right now, are balloons and with each inhale they expand, and as you exhale through the mouth, they contract
- Keep inhaling into the nose slow and steadily, holding the breath at the top of the inhale, and then blow out the breath through the mouth upon exhalation. Long breath out like blowing out a candle, as long as possible
- You could count these breaths and do ten to fifteen, or not count them. Does not matter
- After a minute or two simply forget about your breath, let it go. You found it, now let it go
- Now, with the breath left behind, just keep sitting and do one more thing: Simply listen to your heart and the back of your neck
- Sounds weird I know, but simply keep listening to the front and back of your heart, and the front and back of your neck
- Imagine you took speakers from your car or computer and attached them to the front of your heart and back of your neck.

- This will help you listen better. Just listen for as long as you can

This is the oldest exercise known to man. No need to clear the mind, escape or avoid thoughts, chant, focus on breath or a mantra, become one, find or look for a divinity. Just listen and wait. Wait for what? Just keep going, you'll find out.

This is all there is to it. I wish it was more complicated. What you are doing is putting your adult attention into the warehouse of your original, child-world created emotions. This ancient exercise, the adult returning to the child, creates a profound bio-electromagnetic, neuro-chemical, psychological, and emotional shift in the body. This is how you leave the great unconscious, the active, rational, adult-thoughts world and enter the kingdom of your intuition and your deepest longings, regrets and joys.

These regrets and fears will eventually reveal themselves as much older uncomfortable experiences that existed long before your marriage, long before you knew your partner. Your parents are the key players at the base of these old joys and pockets of anger, but again are just players in your inner-life soliloquy. Insights and understanding will awaken from your sitting. You will intuit the ancientness of these feelings and know that your partner's behavior is the catalyst for all this stuff you thought was everyone else's.

After you sit, you carry this wisdom about yourself back to your wife, boss, and children. Relatus is at work. Carry back a more uncovered and self-revealed you. Your thirty-year-old feelings of sadness about your father's indifference and your stepmother's insensitivity, buried in your stomach, can now counsel your adult, rational perspective.

You start to take ownership of your anger, which allows you to bring a much more composed dialogue with your partner. Relatus is the action of marriage, you knowing yourself better and sharing these revealed parts with your spouse. So many of us are not willing to take all this action. Waves of sadness and glee of the ten-year-old inside, cascading from events that seem like someone else's life, arise. Twenty-two years into my own marriage, I now understand. Everything will change when you take this action.

"And where we had thought to slay another, we shall slay ourselves."

—Joseph Campbell

To Love is to Destroy

How can something so commonplace like a marriage, a thing that begins so reasonably, comfortably, passionately, and innocently, become so unruly and disruptive? What did we miss early on that could have prevented it from unraveling? Nothing. You had no way of knowing. That is one of the key points of this book. It is impossible to know.

The muscles of your marriage are supposed to break so that they can build back up. That is how we gain insight and emotional intelligence, uprooting everything that lives inside. The discourse of relating with another creates raw vulnerability that reveals all your latent, immature perceptions and reactions.

Novelist Cassandra Clare said in her book *City of Bones*, "To love is to destroy, and that to be loved is to be the one destroyed." Carl Jung agreed when he said, "Everything that irritates us about others can lead us to an understanding of ourselves." A relationship is the most beautiful destructive force in nature, not designed to be rational and sensible.

I have wished for an easier way to work on marriage besides opening myself up. But marriage, and the work we do on it, always comes back to self. "There's no coming to consciousness without pain," Jung said. And even if the priest or person who conducted your wedding told you that your marriage was designed to break you open and undo your sense of self, you would not have understood.

Through the exercise of marriage, our feelings are supposed to unravel, unfortunately often within the belittling and disagreeing stare of our partner. But at some point, we realize that our marriage will evolve because the dynamics and our feelings towards it will change. We will learn what it means to embrace, celebrate, and exercise the behaviors and the forces around us that create change and growth.

The secret to a successful, healthy relationship is not a secret. It is messy hard work. It is the understanding and accepting of every emotion that is unearthed in you in the friction of marriage, and then re-engaging (relating) with your spouse with a new perspective.

You and your marriage are in the universe, a basic fact. What we forget is that because we are things in the world, we and our marriage are subject to all the same forces that press against every other object in the universe, "both violent and creative, destructive and cooperative," Swimme writes in *The Universe Story*. We are going to learn about your spouse and the Second Law of Thermodynamics in the next few chapters. Just remember, though, the sinews of your marriage, like the universe, the weather, the birthing process, and old tree limbs, are supposed to break, be undone, to create anew into time.

The vessel called relationship seeks and is designed, just like all universal forces, to break each person down in order to teach them. All the painful reactions within you and your spouse are part of the path and process of being in union. Things break in order to grow. Swimme further explains that these challenges are just part of living, that "these obstacles, these boundaries, these limitations are essential for the journey of the universe itself." Everything must undergo this process.

How serious are you? It will not be easy. It is OK not to be ready, though, not to be serious. You can come back to the work later, in another lifetime or marriage. Not my recommendation, but I want to give you an out.

At some point, whether we believe it or not, this lifetime or another one, we will have to jump into the fire of our inner world. Why do so many marriages fail? It is because this leap is so difficult. So many would rather avoid it. Leaping in means owning everything that is yours in the relationship, everything that we have said, done, not done, forgot and are afraid to do.

All You Can Do is Your 50%

Every relationship is 50/50. Whether you want to or not, you must learn how to own all of your 50% of your marriage. You can ask your spouse to wake up to an old anger towards a parent, for instance, one that he or she just keeps throwing into the current discussions, but there is nothing more you can do. You can demand that your spouse do more, but the only thing you can truly work on is your 50%. That is why so many spouses are so pissed at each other, because they are focused on the other and taking stock of their reactions.

This is not easy; it demands a willingness to admit mistakes and misperceptions. It is so hard to say sorry. Owning all of our 50% is called maturing, and maturing is painful.

The great physicist Niels Bohr hints that the solution and answers to the challenges in our marriage are in the marriage. "Every great and deep difficulty bears in itself its own solution. It forces us to change our thinking in order to find it," he said. The only way I could change how my words and behavior at parties impacted my wife, using the above example, is to understand that my boyish insecurity about getting others to like me was alive and well. My inner fourteen-year-old was oblivious to how delicate the bonds of an adult relationship are. In my cave of long hours of sitting alone, I found him and have been a caretaker of sacred marital information since.

Changing your thinking and looking in a different direction, at yourself, holds the answers. That is what Bohr recommends and what good therapy will do. That is also what sitting alone will do.

Men need to learn what a relationship actually is and how it works. We all need to learn what is underneath the hood of our marriage. When we are ready, the relationship and all the friction and revelry become the teacher. A relationship is an endless series of events and exchanges that activate intense emotions, in turn inciting action and reactions that are seeking resolution.

DLA™ and Why We are Here

According to the great Hindu culture, we are here on Earth and come back during many lifetimes for three main reasons: consciousness, awareness, and bliss. The only reason we continue to come back and wend our way through this sticky, fatiguing, joyous, and often achy emotional human life is to fully understand everything that lives in our inner, non-physical world — our emotional, right-brain, intuitive, and desire-filled self — and to express it in the material world.

Would you believe me if I told you the meaning of life is to understand (gain awareness) and then bring everything stored in your right brain, your intuition, memories, reactions, perceptions, etc. into the physical world? That is called creating. In short, we are here to create. Drop the mic, that is it.

The reason so many people are lost is because there is only one singular way to know what your unique memories, experiences, feelings, longings and perceptions are trying to tell you about your life and what to do with them. The only way to learn is to listen to them, listen to your feelings, have your left, rational brain simmer in them by sitting quietly.

The key to creating your life, to completing it here on Earth, is to use your left brain's reasoning and organizing skills to make conscious and real on the physical plane everything that lives in your feeling- and desire-based world, the realm called your heart and right brain.

You must first soak your left, rational, adult attention in your right brain's feelings by sitting alone. Soak and simmer your rational mind with these sensations and images for many hours so that these two worlds integrate. That is emotional intelligence, that is waking up to self.

Oh, the sweet naiveté of our powerful intellect. This rational part of us, our executive function, has so much to learn about our marriage. It is part of the problem with our relationship until it learns more about its right half brethren. Our youngest part of the brain that rules our adult thoughts is the neocortex. As mammals and humans go, it is a couple of million years old, but in its exact and current size and state, only about 200,000 years old. It organizes and analyzes just needs to meet the feelings burrowed in our reptilian brain center that currently haunt and unnerve it.

Our right brain, often referred to as our limbic brain or system, behaves completely differently. It has not and never will build a computer or design a spaceship, even though it wants to. It needs the left brain to sort all that out.

A big part of this challenge, as we will see, is that the archeology and roots of all the behavior, thoughts, feelings, and reactions within your marriage are old, ancient actually, and almost incomprehensible to your rational mind. "Where the hell did that comment come from?" says that analytical part of our brain, the further it travels upstream into the heart of the marriage. What an escape, release, and sanctuary for our adult attention when we work on spreadsheets and scheduling our month, just fixing problems. We get to avoid the butterflies in the stomach, pangs of regret, and the soft winds of uncertainty and doubt that creep into our reactions.

Sam Keen in *Inward Bound: Exploring the Geography of Your Emotions* reminds us, "We can only choose whether we will feel, and not what we will feel." It is time to choose to feel. I am going to show you the way.

Consciousness is just a fancy word for knowing the original roots and historical life events that created every feeling you have, and why you react, love, hate, and want the things you do. Seeking consciousness and awareness is the act of waking up to every single inner child fear and joy that is driving your current life and behaviors. This in turn begets the ability to understand that everything that occurs in your marriage and life was created by you. Because of what you are putting out into the world, from your inner world's frustration, longing for dad's attention, and anger at mom's belittling, these experiences are coming back at you. The outer world is giving you what you are putting out.

"Our feelings began in our reptilian brain, millions of years ago."

—Emily A. Sterrett

Awareness is maturity. Eventually I will own every last drop of anger, sadness, and insecurity around being a man. If I get it this lifetime, I might be able to take a break from cycling back to Earth again, at least for a spell. This is the power of what the Hindus are teaching. Wake up to self, nothing more.

Marriage is the greatest mechanism for your waking up because it creates the most discomfort, the most dislodging of emotions. Run to the fire of marriage, I say, and stand in it. That is what I am selling. The fire is your current sadness whose root lives deep below, from never being hugged, held, or recognized enough when you were eight or ten years old. That old sadness is coming out today as hurt and anger towards your spouse and his comments.

Unfortunately, the maturity level of your marriage — the ability for the marriage to grow, expand, and eventually become the team and bond with the other that you want — is limited to the least mature of the two of you. Your marriage can only succeed and develop as far as the developmental age or dominant limbic age of you two.

I call this your Dominant Limbic Age (DLA), a measure of how aware you are of your childlike reactions. The limbic system is the tissues, glands, neurons, and hormones in the body-brain that regulate feelings, thoughts, and all behaviors. The bulk of all our current feelings and reactions formed before you were twelve years old. Many men, for instance, do not mature beyond the emotional awareness and capacity of a teenager. When I got married at thirty-two, developmentally I was about fourteen. My wife would kiddingly say age ten, especially when I was wrong but struggled to apologize. My DLA in the early years of marriage was fourteen. If I had not started doing something to wake me from this adolescent slumber, the maturity level of our marriage was doomed to be stuck at fourteen.

We all need to go back inside and discover what our DLA is, that root age and point in our life when our left and right brains stopped cooperating with each other, stopped dialoguing. This discovery routine will be outlined in the pages and chapters to come. For many men, we begin shutting down our feelings in our teens, which in turn shuts down the capacity to understand why we react to women, for instance. I carried such ignorance, awe, and resentment towards the feminine energy for so long before I intuited that the fourteen-year-old inside of me was confused and angry, not the thirty-three-year-old me.

Because my DLA was fourteen, the psycho-emotional construct of my marriage and how I engaged my wife was never going to get beyond a high school dynamic. Not a great model for my daughters.

The Least Mature

Least mature means the person in a relationship who takes least responsibility, least ownership, and who is the least aware of how they respond to the world. You must be able to hate loudly in your world, relationship, and with your partner in order to love quietly and patiently. Men must grow up enough to learn to be comfortable when the feminine expresses her hate and frustrations during the war-like moments in marriage. Don't stand in the lava when the mountain erupts, let it flow. Don't take it personal, even though you lit the fire. Point your bow into the lashing wave, not against. The feminine needs to express. Men cower from and rebel from this hate. The longings from the past haunt an afternoon debate about money or holiday plans. Add in fatigue from sleepless nights with children, and a battle ensues.

The cheap laughs men get, using marital content as a punch line, leave their emotional residue as well. Maybe she calls you a jerk or you call her a bitch or just think those words, and tiny dents are created in each other's experience of the marriage. David Deida writes in *The Way of the Superior Man*, "The feminine always seems chaotic and complicated from the perspective of the masculine...Nobody will press your buttons or reflect your asshole to you better than your woman."

Regardless if you are both correct or accurate with your comments, the actions and words create feeling responses in the other. That is the basic dynamic of relating. When I am careless and flippant, small dents arise in my wife's experience of trust in me and my ability to know and hold the sacred boundaries of the relationship.

In the early years, I did not know that I was generating that response in her. We do not know until we feel and know our own hurt and joy. We do not know the feelings, longings, and frustrations in our spouse that we unconsciously jab and poke at with our words because we do not understand the emotions that live inside ourselves.

Married to Self, Shadow Boxing

Marriage is a relationship with self. Back in the kitchen with my wife in those early years, on the morning after a night out with friends, it was like trying to kiss her while she was getting a basketball rebound.

As the marriage unfolds, you wonder how all the emotion-infused debates and disagreements got started. The feelings and reactions and words get so big and intense over issues that seem small. What you are going to see, though, is that there is a whole other world, a literal kingdom of experiences and feelings breathing inside of you and your partner, just below the surface of interaction in every kitchen and every other room.

Studying Self in Arena of Marriage

I have spent the last twenty-three years studying, watching, and counseling men and women through relationships. I have danced, cried, laughed, and been burned at the stake of my marriage, have had a successful private counseling practice, and have gathered insights that I believe will change your perception of how to relate. Carl Jung reminds us that "The meeting of two personalities is like the contact of two chemical substances: if there is any reaction, both are transformed."

My wife and I have argued and uncovered truths with five different marriage counselors over our twenty-three years. We have laughed and cried with three teenage daughters, two sets of in-laws, four dogs, sixty foster dogs inside four houses in two countries, through my nine jobs, three totaled cars and fourteen years of graduate school loan payments. If I had a dollar for every time my wife asked for the big D, a divorce, all my debt would be gone. Carl Jung reminds us that "there's no coming to consciousness without pain.

But my marriage flourishes. It has been intense. We have survived and found a camaraderie because I realized early on that not only was I the problem and the solution, but much more importantly, the friction of marriage was kicking up an ancient well of imbedded emotions living just below my thoughts.

Marriage Full of Kitchen

"Stand in the fire of my own feelings" became my motto. It became my life's mission, especially after an exchange with my wife in the shadow of GM Betty.

So often our most intense marital arguments occur in the middle of the kitchen. Maybe the laws of the hearth are different than those of other rooms. Perhaps it is the food, one of our basic mammalian needs, that throws everything off. I am not sure this makes sense, but I have seen dogs and kids bathing in the same kitchen sink that hours before held a soaking, day-old oatmeal pot. The sacred marital altar is within the kitchen walls.

In-laws are excellent at burning toast and then mindlessly stuffing clean forks in the napkin drawer. Boyfriends' advances are continually rebuffed the next morning in front of the coffee machine, and teenagers and husbands continually glance at over-stuffed garbage bins but never take them out. Glasses and cups break, dogs urinate, and knives slice fingers all in the reflection of smeared counter tops and refrigerator doors. It is like the high seas of yore in kitchens everywhere, without the scurvy.

As the father of three teenage daughters, I have seen

pouting, shirts ripped, and morale battered all for the last piece of French toast. It seems logic and reason need not apply when it comes to this hallowed ground of bread, butter, and broken hearts and glasses. How do these rational discussions so quickly devolve, and why are they always about the same three or four topics? John Gottman says in *Seven Principles of Making Marriage Work* that research supports this cycling of relational disputes, with 69% of couples fighting over the exact same topic every time they battle.

It is impossible to know what is going to unfold over time in either of you as the relationship travels further in time and into each other's hearts, taking on more and more, heading upstream. The energies, awareness, and behavior involved in getting into a relationship are completely different than those used to sustain a relationship. What happens in year one of your marriage is nothing like what happens in year eight.

On the brighter side, kitchen hugs are the best, especially when you come home and get to share great news immediately. So often your partner is in there. You got a raise, or your mother-in-law decided to cancel her trip in the spring. Those congratulatory kisses seem even sweeter when they are in front of the steaming, overstuffed dishwasher. So many of the pleasures and battles of relationships start, end, or are transported over these cluttered countertops.

I am fixated on the kitchen because it is where the idea and theme of this book emerged. When my wife punctuated one of our early marital discussions with a plate thrown at my head, demanding that I call the divorce lawyer in London, poor GM Betty caught some cheap Chinese plate porcelain in her grill. Betty was big but not very quick. To this day my wife remembers the fight but not the throw. I remember the throw but am unsure sure how I ducked. Keanu Reeves in his final scene of the *Matrix* had nothing on me that morning as I avoided that plate.

Right here is where it all begins, where all the work on relationship starts. Stand in the fire of your marriage. You are being called to celebrate and dance and cry and laugh in and through everything that occurs between you and your partner. Duck, yes, but do not run from the plates. They do not need to hit you for you to feel them, but you need to stand in the fire of the feelings that arise in response to every emotion, every plate that flies, throughout the unfolding story of your marriage. The work of relationship is in you, catalyzed by the other.

The energy, the hate, longings, and love that caused my wife to release that plate had been simmering and boiling years. Turns out that her relationship with me, and mine with her, started when we were eight years old. Crazy, right? Those feelings in her at that moment had been brewing for twenty-six years. I had known her for two.

Feelings Started Decades Ago

How can that be? It makes no sense. If I told you that the story of that plate at my head in Nineties suburbia started in 1970 at a kitchen table 2,600 miles away, would you close this book?

In the following chapters I am going to take you even further upstream, further in time before 1970 to where and when all our marriage stories began. In *A General Theory of Love*, the authors Thomas Lewis, Fari Amini, and Richard Lannon write that "early emotional experiences knit long lasting patterns into the very fabric of brains neural networks." The experiences behind the emotions that incited my wife's Roger Clemens-like throw occurred decades earlier.

This probably does not make sense, but it will. If you learn to sit quietly and do therapy, you will change generations to come, because the nature and reality of an emotion is stored as an electronic charge within the body of your midbrain and heart. These electromagnetic particles are swirling electrical currents, as measured by an electroencephalogram. They dusted and filled the seemingly empty space of your kitchen, your Frosted Flakes, and your grandparents' hallways during the seventies. The electricity of your emotions and those of your ancestors are consuming your kids. That is why knowing, accepting, and altering the curvature of your anger and doubt will travel down generations, changing the lives of great grandkids you might never meet. But those youngsters will smile because of the inner work you do.

Kitchen Table Massacre

Maybe my wife, with her sacrificial plate release on that fateful evening, was not ready to settle into the suburban life and let go of the city environment we had recently left. Maybe she did not love me, or love where she was at that moment in time, saddled with a newborn, a husband, a dented, five-year-old minivan, and lousy local

Chinese food. I am sure I had made some callous, presumptuous comment that put a finishing touch on her deep-seated frustration.

All the questions and subsequent answers to why she threw the plate and the emotions that led to that action are important. Those questions are where all of her own psycho-emotional growth and understanding begins. But for me, for the partner on the other side of the allegorical plate, I need to stand in the fire of *my* emotions and reactions and experience in those moments, not hers.

On that night when that plate flew, while dining with my wife and two young daughters, my perception of the reality of marriage changed forever. I would never look at a relationship the same way. During that meal at the chipped wooden table that had survived two basement floods, my quest began to learn and understand how a marriage works and succeeds. In front of Betty as my wife erupted in reaction to how I was correcting my daughter's table manners, my experience of and respect for marriage, and how I responded and worked at being a husband, changed forever.

I felt like the physicists Planck and Einstein when they were probing the elusive atom. Einstein expressed his awe at the mystery of how matter and the universe behave when he said, "All my attempts to adapt the theoretical foundation of physics to this new knowledge failed. It was as if the ground had been pulled out with no firm foundation." He went on to say, "Whenever the essential nature of things is analyzed by the intellect, it must seem absurd or paradoxical."

In that moment twenty years ago, and in the couples counseling that followed, I saw why relationships fail. I could see, like Planck, that when your rational mind watches how you and your spouse behave vehemently to each other, it does not add up. "When we are rational, using abstractions, we cannot take all features into account," said Fritjof Capra in *The Tao of Physics*. "We have to elect a few. We construct a map of reality which is linear." To the logical part of us, the math of marriage is off.

"A kind of sub war between left and right brainers has been going on for centuries. The right brain has not changed for thousands of years. It has not evolved," writes Robert Monroe, in *Ultimate Journey*. It is like two different dimensions side by side, never speaking to each other except maybe when dreaming.

Post-Plate Couples Counseling: Where it all Began

Within a week of that great porcelain launch, we went to counseling. Within fifteen-minutes of the start of our session, my wife expressed the feelings that incited her reaction at the table that night. As she was describing her frustration toward me while I was correcting my daughter's table manners, my wife started to close her eyes. As she sat on the couch, talking through her heart about her anger, her shoulders were relaxing and opening, so that suddenly there was what I call a hole in her neck for her head and thoughts to drop into. Her rational, adult attention softened and entered into her feelings via that hole.

As if returning into a dreamscape, she slowed her words as the counselor and I just watched and listened.

There was a hush. She held the space silently, and I remember hearing the desk clock hum. Almost startled, she opened her eyes and said, "He used to come to the table a little drunk. He was so grouchy, telling me what I should be doing in gymnastics. I hated that; I was nine years old for God's sake. What an asshole!"

My autocratic tone with our daughter that night awoke the stored anger and frustration with her father's behavior thirty years earlier. It was the exact same setting. She was almost the same age as our oldest. Eureka! My presence, actions, and especially my reactions, the ones I imbibed and learned unconsciously from my home, woke up her nine-year-old's hurt. That is how and why our marriage to each other started when we were both in fourth grade.

Every single unruly reaction in marriage has roots that go far back to who and how our parents and grandparents were and felt. This is why it is impossible to know if your marriage will work and what will emerge. It is impossible to comprehend because we both did not know the reactionary sets living in us. Only in the discourse of your relationship and the replaying in therapy do these old, forgotten, and somehow displaced parts of us show up.

This initial session set off a series of tectonic breaks and openings in our marriage. No fairy tale stuff, just us getting much better at watching what was lurking emotionally inside ourselves when we started to collide and the debates fired up. As life started showing up, as in-laws judged our choices of furniture and friends bought bigger houses, we tried to feel the pits in our own stomachs about our ancient regrets before lashing out at each other.

Does this sound dramatic? Am I bating you to read a few more pages because the magic pill of marital joy is there? One image of a kitchen table long ago, and everything just changes like that? If you have the courage to stay with it, to keep going back to this deep well of the inner life, then yes, your life will become your own personal "greatest story ever told."

"Truth is no match for emotions."

—Einstein

My First Therapy Session

A year and a half before I got married, pre-plate launch, I skeptically and begrudgingly scheduled time with a therapist. I was single and living in London. It went something like this:

After twenty minutes of her questions and my answers, Dr. Moore sat up, took her glasses off in a classic therapeutic if not autocratic pose, and asked, "Have you ever seen that Harrison Ford movie, the one where he's standing on the edge of a cliff leaning out, looking into the abyss?"

"*Raiders of the Lost Ark*, one of those... yes."

She took a long, well-timed clinical pause. "Well, that is where you are right now. In the third movie he ends up stepping into the abyss and when he does, something appears, catching him, a beam of light. That is where you are right now with these bigger life questions you're asking."

Nothing like a casual, Tuesday afternoon chat about

the abyss and my personal void. Sounded like my love life at the time.

If I knew in that moment what was about to unfold over the coming weeks and months, as I sat in that overpriced psychologist's office in Chelsea, weighed down by a gray and gnawing wistfulness and discontent, I think I would have frozen time and walked out.

It was not the words in my conversation; it was the lumps of feelings stirring. This was the first time in my adult life that I had slowed down enough to just sit and try talking about my life. It was the first time that I had tried putting words to the dull ache: a kind of billowy sadness, not too heavy, that had followed me for years, underneath my affableness, the pleasantries, and the buoyant, often boyish exuberance. I had run out of room in my life, though, the one understood and crafted by my rational brain, the one that quells memories, tries to still the ache in the knees, shoulders, and belly with work, sex, drink or exercise.

Surprised by Empty

Writing these words now, twenty-two years later, it is easy to feel my way back into that chair in front of her desk. That thirty-one-year-old me had a heavy heart. It seemed like it was about to spill. It was not heavy or broken from anything I could touch or explain.

I was living a young man's life coded with material ease, working hard during the day but fluid with travel, dinners, ski trips, and general first world facility. It was my next ex-girlfriend, after the one with the visa issues, who had urged me to go see a therapist. "You are insecure and defensive, and still tied to your mother," was one of her most poignant refrains. How hard did I resist that one?

"No, I'm not. You're insecure," was one of my favorite replies. Pretty original and mature, right? Little boys do not like being critiqued or told the truth, especially by the feminine. It makes me, I mean them, feel small. So often they just want to show mom, the feminine, how good and powerful they are, to be that hero-to-the-death boy-man, and to assert their independence from their need for mom's approval. I guess I ended up believing her. I was insecure, even though I was not really sure what that meant. But there I was in that chair within weeks after she dropped me like a hot rock.

It was quiet when Dr. Moore took notes. I guess she was expecting me to come back. My shoulders were heavy as I slumped in the chair, cradled in that stately Victorian-era office, surrounded by those rows of wood-paneled bookshelves. Like in the movies, the office had the dusty, weathered green and burgundy hardcovers. It was like she had put the dust back on them to make me feel even more forlorn and distant from all that was familiar, established, secure, and historically right.

The office had three walls lined with those books, those great accounts of deaths and even bigger rebirths, staring down at us. I was just a thirty-something kid from New Jersey, a part of me thinking, *How the @#%! did I get here?*

Been Here Before

I heard an echo as she spoke, a hollowness that I had felt back in third grade. I had moved across town in the middle of that year, and my new school had bigger class sizes, so the atmosphere was less friendly and more chaotic. I would stare out the window, sad, as if my heart had no home. Not feeling a part of anything or anyone, it felt like a dreamscape sitting in that classroom.

A tear or two would fall while gazing through those cathedral-like windows, wishing I was somewhere else, someone else, the mailman or a lady walking the dog. Heck, I wanted to be the dog. If I could just get lost in or become part of someone else's life right then, I would not feel as lonely. My heart bubbled to slip into some better time and place.

That was in third grade, and I felt the same way in Dr. Moore's office. I just wanted to feel less empty. It is a bit cliché these days, the story of the finance guy losing his vim for the game, not caring about winning and making money, then quitting and seeking to make things better somewhere else. But I did not feel like a cliché. I felt small after many years of feeling pretty big in my dry-cleaned suits and polished shoes.

How could I know what was coming as I took this first step in slowing down long enough to allow the vague sensations of longing and unease to fully emerge and release? Slowing down and listening, I realized months later, is where it begins. Tolerating, no, celebrating bodily discomfort is not a popular sport. We all suck at it. But your life and marriage are asking you to do this, now.

None of us give our bodies ample time to speak up, to share the wisdom and knowledge about what we are really want, love, hate, and care about. That hazy, dreamlike, third grade sensation-experience of being separate and lost in my little world did not go away, it just went to sleep.

It was ready to speak up again.

Our heart beats with memories and desires that live outside of the linear, beginning-to-end timeframe of our cogitating, analyzing cortex. The matrix of my inner life at thirty-one, with its malaise and emotional withdrawal, must have stirred up the sediment of my third-grade memories and sensibilities.

Maybe I should have just ignored the call, the pangs. I am sure they would have gone away, right? How are your pangs doing, the ones that are calling you every day? What if you sat down in a chair right now and just let those aches up? It would be easy to name and feel them. There would be some tears. That is what we are about to do.

Counseling Session with John and Amy

A similar moment to when my wife and I went to our first counseling session happened years later when I was counseling John and Amy. Amy, according to John, had this built up rage towards him that he could not understand. She loved John, they loved each other and their two boys, but she admitted that at times she wanted to throttle him. She could not figure it out.

They were both on the couch as she started recounting how angry she was a few weeks before during Thanksgiving at John's parents' house. She was sharing more details of the event, her eyes softened. John and I said nothing. They both leaned back on the couch. More silence. Then Amy looked down at her feet and said, "You know that horse was much stronger than me... I couldn't stay on her. I was scared." She paused again.

She opened her eyes, glaring fiercely at me and said,

"My dad, what a jerk, had no right making me stay on that horse. What the hell was he thinking?"

She had never addressed this issue with her dad, his insistence that she ride the strongest horses when she was young. He wanted to toughen her up. But she was ten, and back then she felt like she was letting him down. Her adult self could now frame and voice the illogic, but as a child it was the fear-disappointment combo.

Now, twenty-eight years later, John's actions were waking up that fear and disappointment, but it had been alchemized further into sadness and rage that was sleeping quietly in her limbic, emotional body. She had forgotten that those historical dad moments had occurred. She might have never known how deep that echo of "dad is disappointed in me", was buried, entombed in that defeated and empty heart of a woman denied access to her father's full love.

A woman's primary need is a fullness of love initially from the father or primary male growing up. For the masculine, it is more an acceptance from his mother that allows him the confidence to the release himself into the world. What her dad was or was not able to express built the foundation of how much she then needed, and so sought unconsciously from John.

Unfortunately, Amy's deep-seated sense of failure and incompleteness at her parents' kitchen table was dormant for those years until she got married. John unknowingly woke up her wounds. Watch how the loop of this open wound never shuts, never completes itself until the inner work begins:

- Amy carries around this sense of unworthiness

in her father's eyes.

- Her father has been dead for ten years, so there was never a resolution, a chance for them to at least share their respective experiences of those moments.

- This unworthiness always incited the drive to prove herself, always trying to show the world — which to her is always her father — that she could ride any horse, succeed in business, even though it never fulfilled her.

- When she entered the arena of marriage, the desire to be held and respected and adored by dad is living quietly in her belly and heart. She begins building the family nest, kids arrive, her instincts and creativity are magical. She feels a sense of fullness with the new house, great curtains, some new friends, and the Home Depot kitchen just works well.

- All is quiet and good on the outside. John comments one day, one spouse to another, two adults in relationship, that she is spending a bit too much money and recommends preparing a little less food every evening because they end up throwing it out.

- Here is where the old sadness of disappointment and incompleteness turns to rage. Amy, like all of us, has a soft, child's heart that does not feel completely full and unconsciously wants to feel whole. In every child heart is a longing for the parents to fill it with wholehearted attention, appreciation, and unconditional approval. This is what human mammals seek and ache for.

For the daughter, much of that ache is for the dad's love, which comes in gazes and hugs of approval and acknowledgment. If the daughter does not receive enough of these, unconsciously there lives a sense of disappointment, an echo of, "I must not have been good enough, but I will keep trying."

Amy received some affection from her dad, but not enough to satisfy her child heart. That is normal. When her husband, the main masculine force in her life and the embodiment-replacement of fathering energy, questions her, that chunk of self-doubt and hurt alights. It is subtle. He makes a seemingly innocuous comment, and the longing in her turns into shock, an emotion that releases itself as outright rage. It is the sadness-anger paradigm.

Everything she never said to dad, every feeling of hurt and all the times she wanted to ask for his attention but never could, turned into hate for dad, as well as anger at herself for never asking and receiving.

Marriage is the Best Way to Wake You Up

Here is the beautiful thing. If Amy had never married, those unconscious scars that form the foundation of how she reacts toher husband would most likely never have surfaced. They would have continued to gnaw away at her sense of self and the relational bond. Each time John would question her choice of wallpaper color or the state of her messy closet, it would set off this "dad is disappointed" button.

Notice how the work for Amy is not around John. John is a character who opens the scar of "letting dad down." This is so pervasive in relationships, a relatively innocuous comment by your partner lights up an unconscious self-dent. My unconscious anger towards my wife, that has nothing to do with her, builds up a callus of resentment, confusion, and disgust in her. The space between us, the psycho-emotional, bio-magnetic space that holds us, gets wider and heavier. And this is where our kids play, live and breathe, in this space. A light, ill wind through this space of marriage ends up thickening so much that many relationships never recover. Time to change it.

After Endless Hours of Sitting, What I Learned

My wife had major surgery on her foot years back, and during the worst of it, I had to continue working and commuting. I was out of town for weeks, leaving her to fend for her foot, three dogs and three girls. Suburbia never stops arriving. It was one of the toughest spells of our marriage.

One night, as she was laid out on the couch exhausted, with the IV drip in her arm, I sat down next to her. My heart was sad for where we were, that I could not help her more. I leaned over and said, "Sweetie, you and me 'till the end, all the way, you're my life, nothing else matters." I remember that moment, but two years later she was recounting the vignette to a friend. She said that in that moment, lying on the couch and hearing those feeling-words from me, unwound so much of her discomfort. Something bigger than us, a union and team of two could and would somehow hold and carry her downstream.

The more I sat and meditated throughout our marriage, the more my thoughts cracked in half. I realized that her feminine beauty, the organizing and overwhelming force that ridiculed and cut my boyish reactions, was the ancient mothering, teaching, and embracing energy men unknowingly seek. She had a belief in the masculine that was still trying to emerge in me, that fully released itself in the boy-man sharing of vulnerability during that night when she was on the couch. The belief released a love from her that she did not know was there. My spilled heart catalyzed her essential feminine love and trust. Our marriage changed that night on that couch.

"To take the risk of loving, we must become vulnerable enough to test the radical proposition that knowledge of another and self-revelation will ultimately increase rather than decrease love. It is an awe-ful risk."

—Sam Keen

The Power of the Feminine

It took eleven years of marriage, well into my mid-forties, to really sense and feel this kind of bond. I was banging away at the material world, often staring out my Manhattan office window, wondering where the years would lead. Gnashing and dialing phones, wallowing away as my heart held its breath until that evening's sit. The sitting opened everything up. My heart had been rendered, wrenched, opened and seasoned with the sweetness of my wife-princess, a woman who knew me, who knew my deep boyish faults and the warrior shaman I often became.

Women create the circle space. Men live in it, move through it, and go out into the world filled with what women put into that circle, whether men want to believe that or not.

All around us, the malaise of others' eroding relationships, couples weighed down by the heavy and steady resentment, were like icebergs crashing and crumbling, never fitting, never able to move together. We kept doing the work, though, and I kept sitting.

Waking Up to the Real Dance of Opposites

This is the portrait of our lives in a universe that is governed by opposites. Ying-yang, light-dark, proton-neutron, profit-loss, and more. The Second Law of Thermodynamics is all about two opposing things interacting until their differences get evened out. Hungarian biochemist Albert Szent-Györgyi said, "To regulate something always requires two opposite factors." The world of feelings, sensations, and hunches that are not exact or logical mist up and introduce themselves to us, to those sitting alone for long hours.

I see so many business and finance men and women believing so much in the logic of numbers and spreadsheets that move through their work. But their memories are just waiting for the right time to come out. The friction of marriage releases them. Marriage is two people moving in a confined space together, naturally and ineluctably following the same principles as all other things: colliding, breaking, dying to the big moments, then being recreated.

Imagine this. There is only one thing, one thing in the entire universe that you can control: how you feel. You cannot control your boss's insecurity, your mother's disagreeableness, or your husband's short temper. The only experience that you have any domain over is the endless stream of feelings and emotions living, breathing, and circulating inside your body. And it is the one place we spend the least amount of time focusing on. Feelings are the only tool we need for waking up.

Anatomy of Why Relationships Fail

Patterns of discontent travel down generations. The lives of our grandparents are repeating in us, stuck in the bones of your soul. The world of my ancestors is for me to learn and understand. "Go into your grief," said Carl Jung, "for there, your soul will grow."

You were a good student, went to a good school. You have had a couple well-paying jobs since college, took your time to meet the right person, get married, bought the house, moved to the suburbs, had kids. I am right there with you. But a relationship is nothing that you have ever encountered. It is the hardest thing you will ever do, ever.

At parties, the easy and common question pops up, "How are you doing?" There is often a subtle pause. We all know that despite the words "things are good" coming out of our mouths, if you follow those vowels further down the throat to the heart, that is not always the case.

When I am asked, "What can I do to feel more content? I have tried a few things, like getting more exercise," the answer I have is simple, and I pose it in a question: "Have you ever just sat quietly, back straight, in a chair or on a cushion?" The discussion either ends there or it alights curiosity.

We crossed the marital threshold slightly deaf, dumb, and blind to the emotional rigors it would demand. Many of us have a natural, inexperienced and unseasoned perspective about friction. We also have a normal lack of understanding, and a rational, almost innocent and puerile fear and uncertainty around what self-reflection, spirituality, maturity, growth, and self-awareness really are and how they can change our lives. The state of our marriage, then, is a reflection of this fear and uncertainty.

How deep are our unconscious drives and obstacles? Some of us will not get to what we want in this lifetime. Others will get shards of their desire. But for so many of us, we do not even know what we desire and that is the hardest road to travel. We do not even know what we want. And the arguments and friction of marriage end up killing us. So we shut it down, shop closed, call the lawyer and say, "I cannot take this anymore." Divorce 1, Self-Awareness 0.

I get it. Trust me, I do. We push it away, shut ourselves down, and go back to our ice cream, chips, and *Friends* re-runs. More than a few of my NFL Sunday afternoons have been undone by the emotional weight of serious kitchen battles. I have plenty of battle fatigue. Potato chips and reruns sound awesome right now.

But when you boil down the fancy physicists' wording of this critical Second Law of Thermodynamics, it states that two opposing things will continue to interact until their differences get evened out. You came into your relationship an emotional teenager and will leave it a teenager as well if you do not allow this friction to wake you up. You are just putting off the inevitable, your inability to own up to everything that is yours in the war of relationship.

Listening to and sharing these feelings is extremely tough medicine, kind of like gulping a jar of aspirin. The bitterness is almost unbearable, but man do the muscles of your marriage feel better over time. There is a new kind of love and companionship.

Being in a relationship is supposed to get lonely. The teenager in you is still alive and trying to figure out his way through life.

"And where we had thought to slay another, we shall slay ourselves," Joseph Campbell said. "Where we had thought to travel outwards, we shall come to the center of our own existence."

Time to wake up.

Chapter 2
The Space in Between

"Once connected, objects affect one another forever no matter where they are."

—Bell's Theorem

Seems Like it is Them, Not Us

When your mother-in-law somehow, again, invites herself up to spend the weekend, those hollow lumps of anger and resentment wash through your stomach when you hang up the phone. You wonder, "How can she be so oblivious to what I want?"

By the way, who invented the concept of and nomenclature "in-laws"? It needs to change because the word law implies some statutory obligation to like, obey, and otherwise enjoy their time. I suggest calling them "volunteer-a-laws," anything that intonates that all interaction with them, holidays or not, is not mandatory.

Why don't other people understand how I feel? When a boyfriend forgets to call because he is running late but had been asked to, that shoulder-pinching gasp of frustration consumes you. How can he be so disrespectful? Insane, you think. If he just took a minute to think of someone other than himself.

One of the classics for men is when our wives throw us one of those demeaning, "resting bitch face unleashed" glances after some comment we make at a party. When I get one of those, half my body blanches. It is like a brief, psycho-emotional bloodletting. It must be a character-building event for me. I should have a lot of character by now.

These uncomfortable, gut-denting moments are the miraculous, unavoidable, incredibly challenging, and dare I say, daily occurrences along the marriage continuum. All normal. Two people spending an inordinate amount of time together in one space is going to create lots of friction. The agitation and friction in marriage is in abundance.

It seems obvious too that all these daily, uncomfortable and disquieting emotions we experience are recent. It feels like they started a couple of years into the marriage. More likely, the intensity of the outer and inner marital turmoil kicked in when the in-laws got more involved or after the birth of the kids. The disconnect just seemed to arrive more frequently. Clearly, our spouse, father-in-law, or parents are creating our anger, frustration and uneasy sense of vulnerability, right?

Your Marriage Started in Fourth Grade

Actually, all these sensations predate your marriage. Every emotion and response you have in your marriage started way before you ever met your spouse. I tell my counseling clients, "Your marriage started when you were in fourth grade."

On paper and to your logic-seeking adult mind, you are wed to your partner. But really, you are married to the silent, thundering inner kingdom of indelible, deeply rooted feelings and response patterns that you carried across the marital threshold. The relationship you have to your inborn reactions is driving every single interaction with your spouse. Your marriage certificate has your partner's name on it and you are staring at him as your blood boils. But the actual science, the bio-magnetic, cellular, neuronal, and psychological reality of your marriage lives inside of you. Your emotions, stored as very small, spinning electrons, woven as neurochemical loops inside your heart and mid-brain, are what you are bound to. Your spouse is just a firebrand poking at the tapestry of your feeling-studded cells. He or she is not the problem. You are looking under the wrong couch. If your relationship sucks and you are not happy, it is because too little time has been spent returning to the feeling-studded world of your youth, the one you witnessed, inherited and absorbed from your parents and family.

This original place, your physical childhood home and the ravine full of experiences and reactions that you unknowingly soaked in, the SIB. Every question about why your marriage is or is not giving you what you want and expected, can be answered once you learn how to travel back to this space.

What is the Space in Between?

SIB is the place where you grew up, in between your mother and father or whoever the primary maternal and paternal figures were. This locale was much more than a physical location with messy kitchen tables, TV reruns, and old photos on the mantle. This SIB, like the teeming and fiery atmosphere present at the Big Bang moment that stored every single element in today's world, is where you were formed. Everything that you are — as well as everything that you are not familiar with or have forgotten about yourself, family, parents and ancestors — was formed in the SIB. It is the physiological, psychological, electromagnetic, and biochemical headwater of every action and reaction that courses through you now.

Who our parents or caretakers were, how they felt about themselves, and every flutter of discontent, anger, and joy they ever had are stored in us today. Bell's Theorem confirms this, stating "once connected, objects affect one another forever no matter where they are." Our connection to our parents, to this space of our origin, impacts us for the rest of our lives. It was the place, field and time through which the current of our parents' and ancestors' lives coursed. Through the cluttered and dusty hallways of childhood, their lives were transferred into you. Their loves, longings, joys, and losses became yours via the silent, simple, and yet explosive presence of electrons. It is where all the key moments and events occurred which formed your sensibilities and desires.

What Really Happened in this Space?

Just close your eyes right now, put your right hand on your stomach and take five slow, deep breaths. Focus all your attention on your heart and stomach, as if your brain, nose, and mouth were sitting in your heart-chest cavity. Just breathe normally and slowly into your chest.

Take another forty-five seconds for a few more breaths, eyes closed. Pay attention to gravity, really focus on the weight of your body in your chair or couch right now. Now, slowly imagine that you are sitting at your kitchen table when you were in fourth grade. Keep focusing your attention on your heart and stomach. Imagine being within those four walls right now, whether it was the kitchen, dining room, or porch.

This is the *Kitchen Table Meditation*. I use it all the time in my counseling practice.

Kitchen Table Meditation

As you sit there at your young age, notice what is on the walls, the colors of the floor and chairs. Pay attention to details. Notice what you are feeling, listen with all those parts of your body: stomach, heart, neck and top of head. Notice, I did not say the front of your head. Listen with the back of the neck and top of the noggin. What do you sense, what do you sense others are feeling? What is the mood and temperature? What do you think your mom is feeling right then? Is she happy or sad? Do not worry if you do not know.

Are there any photos or paintings on the wall? As I do this now, I can see my kitchen table and my family around it on Elm Street in 1974. An episode of *M.A.S.H.* is about to begin. I have done this mediation one hundred times. The chairs are metal, the carpet is red and black, and the refrigerator is brown.

Stay in this place. Relax yourself more by continuing to breathe slower and deeper, paying attention to whether your stomach expands out when you inhale and contracts inward when you exhale. That is the way it is supposed to work, belly out like the sitting Buddha statues when you inhale, belly squeezed back towards the spine on the exhale.

The longer you stay in this place of low physical tension, just sitting in and with your heart in the kitchen of your youth, and allow it to fill your senses like a lingering dream that you are drawing back into, the more you begin the process of introducing your rational adult, quick-to-react mind with your younger, more susceptible and receptive one. This is how we enter our past. It will not always be a smooth entry. There is plenty from our youth that we would rather forget. But to know why we feel, love and hate all that we do now, we must start right here.

The electricity and chemistry of this place, of this emotion-saturated landscape that you grew up in between your parents, follows the exact same constructs of electromagnetic motion within all objects everywhere in the universe.

Einstein, the Great Marital Counselor

You probably know this next basic fact, but did not realize that becoming familiar with it again was going to change your marriage, but here it goes. Everything in the universe, you, the computer, this desk, your neighbor's barking dog, every object everywhere are all tightly packed electrons spinning around at about 1,300 miles per second, at different frequencies and patterns. Einstein, the great one himself, reminds us in *Relativity* that electrons are "the leading player in the universe and intimately involved with light, matter, the law of nature and our lives." He goes on to say, "All matter will absorb all the energy impinging on it in the form of electromagnetic waves."

Allen Schore furthers these basic truths about what was happening and what you were experiencing while eating your Froot Loops at home growing up. In *Affect*

Regulation and the Origin of the Self he states, "Electrons are responsible for absorbing vital energy-informational particles of different spectrum from the surrounding environment and for releasing energy-informational particles from a human body."

What this means is that you and I were these curious, dirty jeaned, pajama clad, and sometimes well-behaved packets of young electrons completely and inexorably immersed by the electronic actions and conditions of the world our parents formed. Where the plot really thickens, though, is when we realize that it is not just what we saw and felt, tasted, and reacted to that animated our bodies and minds. There was a much quieter and much more intense world of experiences that we never saw or recognized. This was the world of our parents' experiences, their interrupted dreams, loves and aches that lingered every day, every minute, stored too in those tiny neuromagnetic bundles in their hearts and bellies. Why stop there? Guess where their emotions came from? Their parents, right. On and on this goes, back upstream in time.

If you think your grumpy grandfather and the Depression Era woes that dented his dreams have nothing to do with why your marriage today feels derailed, then you should probably keep reading. This is not psychobabble or scientific bluster. Our homes were a pulsating research laboratory of bonding and colliding electrons. During the first ten years of your life, your nervous system acted "as an antenna which is tuned to and responds to the electromagnetic fields produced by the heart of other individuals," says Rollin McCraty in *The Heart Has Its Own 'Brain' and Consciousness*. Your heart was silently tuned to your parents'. It was like a TV channel you never knew was on.

Nothing Rational about the Child's World

It is also important to remember that in those early years, from birth to age ten, a child's body, physiology, and psycho-emotional makeup are much different than an adult's. A child is truly a biochemical sponge. Its brain and body are galloping and coursing with new cells. Ninety percent of all brain growth occurs in the first five years of our life. That is a lot in a short amount of time.

A child's body also has proportionally more surface area than an adult's, as well as thinner skin, higher respiratory rates, much less mature blood-brain barriers, and a more enhanced central nervous system receptivity. The young brain is also fully immersed in the expressions and activity of just the lower brains, the reptilian and limbic mid-brain areas, which means children are almost purely emotional. The third brain area — the frontal cortex, which is the thinking, organizing, and rationalizing part that guides our daily adult life now — has not even begun its eventual reign. This part does not begin to develop until we reach age ten to twelve, and it will still be another twenty-five years until this rationalizing bit will be fully formed.

Watch an eight-year-old try to sort, sift, organize, and rationalize his unruly feelings when his buddy grabs a sandwich from his plate. There is no deliberation or self-reflection on what an impassioned reaction might mean for his career or social standing. His left brain and executive functions are in seed form, under the soil, so there is no lifeguard to manage what he releases, or what is coming at him in the form of moods, temperament, and the effects of his parents.

You get the picture. We are pure emotion when growing up, and these emotions all get stored. Clearly, this landscape of our youth is a place biologically designed for us to do almost nothing but feel, listen to, soak in, survive, and consume.

Close your eyes again for a moment, and go right back to that kitchen table place you were in earlier, but now incorporate the image and sensation of how physiologically and psychologically open and porous your body and heart were. Watch and feel not only what you could see in front of you, but also what was in the air, inside the feelings and within the gestures of your parents and family members. Feel this place.

Those early years are amazingly rich, as we biophysically merge and collide with our parents and their hearts. Like the weather sculping old mountain cliffs and the incessant winds carving and permanently twisting those trees at the top of the mountain, the events and actions of our childhood shape the entire fabric of our body's system, especially the neural part. This neural or nerve piece of the body is the highway through which all those electrons are traveling, to and from the heart, solar plexus, and brain.

"When people touch or are in proximity, a transference of the electromagnetic energy produced by the heart occurs."
—Rollins McCraty

A Whole Life Lived Before Your Rational One Began

Most importantly is that all of this activity, all of what you soaked up was pre-conscious, way below and before your rationalizing facilities were even created. Think of your adult attention and thoughts right now as the limbs and leaves of a tree, above ground and poking into the sunlight. These are your thoughts, active, obvious, and mostly knowable, as you sit at your desk at work, drive your car, call a friend, finish a spreadsheet, think about college invoices, or just check your phone.

Now think of the root system that soaks up all the water and nutrients deep below the soil, feeding those above-ground limbs. These meandering, porous shoots are your childhood experiences and unconscious reactions blending, seeking, exchanging and merging inside your heart and stomach, underneath the form and fabric of the seen and knowable. From this hidden stratum is the source of your entire adult life, thoughts, and reactions. Two very different worlds, grown from the same tree.

There were no logic seeking or organizing brain parts formed yet, early on, that could consciously resist all that parent world stuff around you. Therefore, the passive nervous and heart-limbic system of the child is filled with the sensations of all those around him. Grumpy grandfather's experiences, never known or seen by you, were nonetheless transferred into you.

Absorption of Our Marital Challenges

It is an amazing story, your story of how you ended up,

again, staring at the TV and eating another crumpled bag of potato chips at 12:30 a.m. I have been there plenty of times, languishing in my personal suburban and marital malaise. I am angry or exhausted, or just do not want to be in the same room as my wife.

Or, you are stuck drying dishes while staring into the chaos of your house and developing a bitterness towards your partner. The frustration seemed to emerge from nowhere but is now everywhere. Marital discontent is like that weed in the middle of your driveway — no idea how it got there, and no matter how many times you clip it, the thing just keeps coming back. To find the root, we must dig in that soil, back to the origin, the very origin of our growth.

A mother's deep and quiet remorse about her father's indifference and absence is transferred into her son's and daughter's hearts during those early years. The "heart's electromagnetic field acts as a carrier wave for information...plays an important role in communicating physiological, psychological, and social information between individuals," says *Science of the Heart* from the Heartmath Institute. What I call that remorse-electron current flows from the mom into the spongy, receptor heart cells of the children. Over the years, the subtle, pungent, and unconscious carrier waves of mom's discontent silently mist her children's world.

This is how the emotional, electromagnetic pre-disposition, in this case an unconscious wanting and needing attention that never arrived, becomes the child's. But this is not a tale of woe, it is an ancient one of return and recapture. We are going to find the truth so that we separate what was theirs from what was ours.

The child does not know this soft, latent, and eventually chronic self-doubt that began in the sandbox has found a home in him. It is years later, as this youth enters the adult world of relating, that the emotions are stirred and poked when this subtle yet overriding anxiousness appears. He wonders how there can be a childlike longing in this adult behavior.

Why does that child seem to be drawn to less emotionally mature and available partners, ones that leave him wan and empty? We now know that it is doubt and insecurity that were breathed into his young heart, stuck in the neurons across his mid-brain and heart, feelings that never allow him to stop questioning his worth and value. He never feels good enough in his current life because of this inherited ache.

This is the long generational reach of behavior and reactions carried by our neurons and electrons. A parent's unconscious feelings become the vibrational template of the kids, which in turn, draws experiences into this next generation's lives that repeat all that was incomplete in their parents.

Tang, Unconscious

Maybe your mom browbeat your dad every morning, while you stirred your Tang before school. You were thinking your guileless, fifth grade thoughts about recess, baseball practice, and Christmas gifts to come. The sound waves of your mother jabbing your dad's self-esteem and the bio-magnetic indent they left in your dad's belly and heart traveled in currents that registered and imbedded them- selves throughout your nervous system. It was your mom's anger, your dad's decaying self-worth, and whatever com-bination of subtle reaction-feelings you had. Witnessing this behavior when you were young does not seem relevant today to your thirty-seven-year-old self.

That cereal bowl is long gone and your parents are divorced or in Florida. Who cares? But it is those electro-magnetic eddies within your body that you release at your partner when she questions your focus at work and how you dismissively answer her questions. In neuro-biological terms, any smallness or self-doubt-infused feelings were born back then. Molika Ashford writes in *How Are Memories Stored in the Brain?* "Memories are stored pattern of links between nerve cells in the brain." The way to release the feelings and the information they hold is to go find those memories in your kitchen meditation.

If your dad was overly bossy and domineering, picking away at everyone's foibles, there is likely now a dynamic, unconscious imprint and residue that has you more sensitive and defensive about any overbearing behavior. Fast forward to when you crossed the marital threshold — you had an allergy towards browbeating, a sensitivity and reaction pattern to this behavior resting below the surface. You were not conscious of it, but your partner's behavior triggers these sleeping patterns and forgotten memories.

Your adult perspective does not want to believe that by going back to those early moments you will unravel the mystery of your current disappointment and frustration with your spouse. It must be the other person. That is what your over-caffeinated, stimulated, and slightly exhausted rational mind is saying.

Relearn the Emotional Language of Youth

You are not a "single entity of a single mind: a human is built of several parts, all of which compete to steer the ship of state," Dr. Ezequiel Morsella wrote in *Behavioral and Brain Sciences*. The emotions formed and gathered from the collective pool of experiences in your childhood home, now resting inside your mid-brain, speak a language different than the one we use as adults to operate our day. In fact, within your mid-brain there is a bundle of nerves called the Reticular Activating System that serves as the link and acts as a gatekeeper that allows only a certain amount of sensory information to enter the upper neocortex, the home of our rational self.

A confluence of opposing old and new brain currents, youth-infused vs. adult logic-seeking, unfolds inside the RAS. It connects the lower brainstem to our cortex. It filters the body's sensory information, managing "all the signals from the external world and internal environment, and then determines what will enter our adult, prefrontal cortex," says Richard Davidson, Ph.D. in *Physiology of Consciousness*. This is where boy meets man.

The word "reticular" means net in Latin. This net, a bundle of nerves, is the barrier, the middle linebacker tissue desperately trying to protect your adult perspective from those Tang-stirring memories—those barely re-collected feelings that a part of you knows were not super happy ones. Your logical self wants a simple world that works easily, without those frivolous, silly emotions. But all those heavier stored sensations hold a wisdom, trying to tell you something. They are not just shards of broken promises and regrets to be discarded, but living packets of energy that contain guidance and direction about who you really are and what you want.

This is what Joseph Campbell means when he says, "You must give up the life you planned in order to have the life that is waiting for you." The life he is talking about lives in these stored feeling experiences. Electromagnetically, our analytical, adult neocortex is preventing this life from arriving since it is actually designed to shut down the feeling messages traveling up the midbrain. In *The Kundalini Experience,* Lee Sannella writes, "Our egoic body-mind is by tendency recoiling from everything... avoiding relationship." Your inner world is trying to have a relationship with you. Without it, you and your marriage cannot be fully revealed and realized.

"Like beaches erode and give way to the tides, let yourself be undone by your own emotions. Pain will give way to relief. This is what the storm is for, this is how you understand, this is where your life begins."

—Bill O'Herron

This is Where the Work Is

Our work together — your work, your goal if you want your marriage to thrive — is to move that linebacker away, to introduce your adult self to the language of those earliest emotions. That is the basic theme of all real inner work, to turn from yourself as an adult and return to emotions of your inner child.

We do not know how vast and important the SIB was and is, or why we need to go back to it. Marriages fail because they ignore the call from this world. Everything that enrages you about your relationship is a feeling formed during childhood. Nietzsche agrees. "The child is far from being buried in the man," he says. "On the contrary, it rules him absolutely."

Your marriage is a simple physics formula: the moments when your spouse is debating and confronting you, there is a bio-physiological reaction in our body's emotional network, which includes heart, stomach, and limbic midbrain. Within seconds of the debate beginning, and due to the zeal and electricity of emotions flaring in you, a current of old memories and reaction patterns erupts from that midbrain center. Your adult logic never saw it coming, never knew the patterns were there.

These sensations of vulnerability, caring, loving, and anguish, stirred in you during these relational debates, form a radiating wall of bio-electric impulses that bypass the brain's analytical center. The latent frequency of electrons from the midbrain are too strong, blowing past the RAS net, setting off actions, reactions, and words in us like a rogue wave. We are carried away, swept away by youth-infused feelings. You start calling your partner names and using sharp words. We spit our reactions like an eight-year-old, giving voice to our youngest, rawest, and least understood parts.

Right here is the starting point of the work on our marriage. Eventually, our partner's actions and feelings can and will be addressed, but it is our feelings and reactions that are ruling the course of the marriage. Remember, feelings are real, authentic, and riddled with all the ancient wisdom of your life. Nothing else in your life actually matters more than the getting your adult attention to allow these feelings to come up and speak to us. Robert Monroe asserts this when he says in *Far Journey*, "Emotion is the key to and driving force underlying every thought and action in human existence." It is hard to argue with him, a man who spent over forty years studying, experiencing, and researching human awareness.

Attention Turned Inward Will Change Your Kids' Lives

Turning our emotional attention back to the world of our childhood, that elemental place where the lives of our parents unwound, begins the exercise of emotional maturation. Maturation is your left and right brain, your entire self, fully accepting everything that you are and everything in your life. It is knowing that you created everything that you experience, from the frustrated parent or boss to the angry wife. It is knowing that you cannot control or change anyone else, only be alive to your reactions to these characters in your life 24/7.

Turning inward is the work, and because of the power of this transference of electrons, this handing down emotions through generations in the SIB, ensures that the work you do today on self and marriage, will change who your grandkids' grandkids become. Our emotional maturation will alter generations to come.

Are Emotions Filled with Electrons Too?

It is amazing that our invisible feelings, memories, thoughts, and beliefs are all filled with electrons as well.

They are physical things. They are sensed experiences that created a momentary yet strong interruption of the neuropeptide balance in the cells of our heart, belly, and brain, says Bruce Lipton in *Biology of Belief*. Each new thought-feeling gets stored as a new, specific, and imbedded electron pattern within the body's neurons.

For example, a feeling and memory are created in the body when an event occurs, such as mom walking out the door in a huff when you were young. A normal sensation of sadness is then sparked within our young, mammalian heart.

Our evolutionary, unconscious need as a mammal is to bond when young, for survival and health affirms Krause J, Ruxton G.D. in *Living in Groups*. This event, her walking out, sets off a neural, sensory cue in those ancient, limbic brain neurons under our curly locks. There are need to bond cells built-in to the ancient mid-brain of young humans. With mom walking out, that electromagnetic need wave, that mammalian desire to be held and nurtured, is interrupted. With that basic need going unmet, a sadness-longing impulse is generated which is the converse of desire. A 2018 paper from *Front Psychiatry*, "Vagus Nerve as Modulator of the Brain-Gut Axis in Psychiatric and Inflammatory Disorders," describes the ineluctable physicalizing of a seemingly non-physical experience like sadness. The experience of that boy's sadness interrupts his steady electromagnetic state with a feeling-impulse of "sad," which is then sent through the body's vagus nerve that stimulates the stomach and heart, leaving a neuron lump in the belly and a newly formed groove in the child's neural, mid-brain patterns.

That groove is semi-permanent, soaked with longing.

The only way to uproot and mend this groove is to introduce this longing to the adult self for processing, understanding, and eventual acceptance.

Source Moment

Watch a puppy when its mom walks away. Same thing. All mammalian nervous systems interact neuro-chemically the same way, wired to bond and attach. From this moment a new electrical frequency is set in motion. Our early childhood was all about frequency. This new neuro-magnet set now has an original image and context tied to and surrounding it: mom, door, loss, and so forth. This historical event becomes the elementary root and source of an unconscious sadness moment.

Roberta Flack's song "First Time Ever I Saw Your Face" is a trigger for one of my life's sad-anger moments. I was at summer camp during sixth grade summer and a bunk-mate played that song on his shoebox tape recorder very day during post-lunch rest. I was unhappy that first week of camp, boyishly longing to be somewhere else. To this day, any time that song comes on the bio-magnetic current of my heart-attention turns toward a longing for something familiar and easy.

Just like all rivers have a precise source for their currents, humans too have source events. "Everything a person is and everything he knows resides in the tangled thicket of his intertwined neurons" asserts the authors in the groundbreaking book *A General Theory of Love*. Roberta Flack has no idea her song is woven into my tangled thicket.

The reason these source moments are so powerful is

because they are stories wrapped in physical, emotional, psychological, biological, and electromagnetic material. They are whole-body, not just thoughts like our adult mind often believes. To children they form an inner, neural mythology that keeps running below the surface of our adult lives.

Linear Versus Emotional Time

Dr. Bruce D. Perry says, "It is the experiences of early childhood that create the foundational organization of neural systems that will be used for a lifetime." These events, even when young, are long gone in historical, linear time. But in emotional, electron time, they are still humming, and become further charged by emotional losses as we enter adolescence and early adulthood.

So yesterday your husband forgot to take out the garbage. This sparked in you a frustration that your request was not honored. Your sense of not being heard and respected — coupled with his adolescent distracted-ness, impatience, and inability to understand how in-complete promises undo trust — rekindled feelings and thoughts of your childhood and an often-inebriated dad.

Even though your husband needed to own his word, his contract of "I will take out the garbage," and there is a lot of work for him to still do on himself, your anger had nothing to do with the garbage. The garbage run, or lack thereof, is a point in linear time, but your hurt is part of a long thread in emotional time.

Your Grandmother Jumped into Your Marriage

Neuron radiation means that all our kin, from all those dusty black and white photos at your grandparents' house, sent their lives and loves down the years to us via those alternating, neural currents in their limbic bodies. My wonderfully talented grandmother held a strong remorse electron current from the Forties. Today it does not matter why she did for the purpose of my inner work. I just need to know where the some of this source was so that I can recognize and separate what was hers and what was really mine.

Her remorse simmered. It was a quiet trepidation throughout her life to extend herself into the world. She was creative and desirous of doing more, but could never undo those painful dents, that shadow of incompleteness and fear born years earlier.

It was not always overt when we visited her, but there was a longing draped around her hunched, distant gaze. When I went back into my SIB through hours of meditation and therapy, I felt such an ache and longing that it would bring me to my knees. At first, it had no name, place or time. Something just felt missing when I lingered in the silence of my feelings, which confused my adult attention because I had lived a pretty charmed life.

I liked my Seventies childhood. I played some baseball and soccer, kissed a few girls, drank a few Budweisers, and actually enjoyed doing homework. What the hell would I be longing for? The longer I sat and listened, though, by the time I reached my early thirties, the more I felt that my heart was soaked with something my rational self might never comprehend.

I had found a forlorn hurt, my grandmother's ache. I began to realize an inheritance that 23andMe would never comprehend. Twenty-three years ago, when I first started meditation, those first pangs of sadness awoke. What was different was that I did not long for things in some past, or regret what had not occurred, as she did. My desires were pointed to the future. I yearned to create into some tomorrow but felt hindered by the weight of a past. I had found a world, only discovered by sitting quietly, that would be my source for everything that was meaningful and real. It set me off on this search and my research. Only by going into my SIB could I ever understand this rich, powerful sadness that was sent down to me.

The hearts of our parents act like cell towers, sending out their joys and desires. The mythology and beliefs of our parents and ancestors were written and sung in the bio-magnetic frequency of their hearts and bodies. Their dreams were and are the language and coding of their DNA sequences, which formed and powered their genes, in turn becoming the foundations of ours.

Passing Down the Impatience

A man will naturally harbor anger and resentment towards his dad for all the years the man never was available, resenting all of his dad's surly, inattentive, and emotionally neglectful behavior. I have counseled many male clients who have this suburban family mythology. Maybe this man's dad drank, or traveled, or just did not know how to be a parent. This man's frustration for his dad will live quietly in the neuro-transmitting cells of his stomach and mid-brain for years. In his twenties and thirties, this latent frustration never gets loosened. He has his career, buddies, sports, casual girlfriends, and long stupor-filled nights in front of the TV.

His emotional state is never disturbed enough by love, loss, vulnerability, or the exasperation of caring beyond self to stir up any deep-seated emotions. This boy-man is the classic emblem of the modern, business male warrior.

And then he gets married. The intensity begins. The whirl, proximity, and passion of his wife's love and desires, the arrival of children, the sleepless nights, the discourse with in-laws and his wife's spending habits all crack open his heart and mind. His rational mind, that could always escape with his buddies to a bar, or just go off and read or watch TV, is confronted with lives of others now in his purview of care.

The disquiet and anger formed by his unmet desire for his father's affection — which he had never addressed and unwound, feelings that have rested for years as a dull, nameless ache — are awakened. They emerge in different eddies of his marriage, sometimes as frustration when his wife is unavailable due to the basic household and parental demands. Or when the kids cry.

These reaction patterns in him, echoes of his father's neglect, arrive in all the basic flavors. Underneath most of them is a sadness and a longing, but they come out as the opposite, disparaging remarks to his wife or possibly sardonic criticism of his kids. This is why marriage is such a wonderful challenge. We do not know what we will find in ourselves as the marriage unfolds, until life shows up.

Loss Becomes Hurt, Becomes Anger

Five years ago, I was counseling Laurie, a forty-one-year-old mother of two. She was riddled with an incessant frustration towards her husband and a deep anxiousness about losing money and their family's place in the community. Even though her family's current financial status was secure, she could not stop worrying.

Laurie said she was always criticizing, questioning, and demeaning others as well. These small bites of sarcasm, she said, would interrupt her conversations with friends and family. It was like a faint voice, an echo, pinching her ear, cutting at her thoughts and sense of self. She said she always felt unsure and less than all her friends, but instead of trying to be more accommodating to their views, she said she was always judging. What was more disturbing to her was that she started to notice her teenaged daughter doing the same thing with her high school friends.

This is a universal experience. When any person is not feeling whole and creative — and unable to fully open up to others, especially those we care about — we end up judging others. If a woman, in particular, does not feel full in her giving and receiving of love, if she holds back her need to give, then she cuts off this stream of creative generosity. When this flow is stunted in ourselves, then automatically and unconsciously we seek to cut it off in others. Whatever we do inside unconsciously to ourselves, we end up throwing out and up at others.

That is what Laurie was doing to her friends. So was her daughter, which was damaging her relationships with her girlfriends in high school. Her daughter was making innocuous but snide comments about her friends. Friendly fire, she thought. But she would come home in tears because her closer friends were avoiding her, clipping her out of their chats and parties.

Laurie's husband walked on eggshells as well, careful not to set her off. As I asked her more about her background and childhood, she started to share stories about her mom being an intelligent yet sarcastic force in her life. It was never an easy conversation with her mother. Her mom always commented on everything, her choice of curtains, the kids' clothes, and even how she toasted the bread.

During one pivotal session, as I had her close her eyes, breathe deeply, and recount some of her earlier years, Laurie began sharing vignettes about her grandmother who had passed away ten years earlier. With a hypnotic-like tone to her voice, like she was talking from a dream, she said her grandmother had been a talented singer and painter way back in the Twenties. But during WWII her husband was sent off to Europe, leaving her with their four young kids.

That husband, Laurie's grandfather, came back a decorated veteran — but her grandmother never recovered from the fear, anxiety, dread, and sense of impending and imminent loss that consumed her during his absence.

During Laurie's childhood, she spent long hours at her grandparents' house. There was a sweetness, she said, to her grandmother. She appreciated and delighted in talking about the arts, her garden, the unique shades of each season, and the daily visits of the birds. But underneath and behind these endearing observations was a seething frustration and anger. No one, no politician, friend, family member or newscaster could escape her vitriol. She cut everything down, especially her husband. It was at times like the onslaught of German tanks all over again for her grandfather, facing the relentless, derisive commentary coming from his wife.

An Ancient Tale of the Unlived Life

Can you see where all of this is going, as we expound on the SIB, absorbing emotions, and source moments? Think about the relative ease and comfort that Laurie's grandmother experienced as a mother of four. She had a beautiful home and doting, successful husband. And then the war and life broke this for her. From that singular moment, her husband walking out the door, her fear and anxiety became unconscious anger and rage. Her ability to sense and recognize joy and possibility died during those war years, waiting for a serviceman to arrive with a flag at her door and news of her husband's death.

That flag never came, nor did her belief, trust, or faith in abundance ever return, even though her husband and family were safe. That sadness and unreleased grip of loss and melancholy became the familiar center around which she circled, a vortex that then engendered an emotional disposition of unending sarcasm and gently meted rage. This vortex had stormed and been released into her daughter, her granddaughter Laurie, and finally even Laurie's daughter. Four generations were being impacted.

Carl Jung tells us how deep and strong the current of our ancestors' lives is, the one we are born on and swim in, and how important it is to at least recognize the correlation between our parents' lives and our current issues and challenges. He states, "Nothing has a stronger influence psychologically on their environment and especially on their children than the unlived life of the parent."

Dr. Jacques Benveniste says, "Life depends on signals exchanged among molecules." The science of frequency transference tells us we inherited much more than hair color, height and our grandfather's last name. Laurie inherited the current of her grandmother's temperament and disposition, and it is from these currents that the spirit of her emotional life began. This is where the work lies for her and her marriage.

Laurie Will Find a Cross

Loss and recovery are the death/rebirth experience, the foundation of every religion and culture. The ability to walk our rational adult self back into old memories, to kill our self-conscious and analytical fear of these old, painful, tear-infused sensations is all Laurie's grandmother had to do. It is what all of us have to do.

The figure of person nailed to a cross, whether we want to believe it or not, is a symbol for the psychological and psycho-emotional exercise of Laurie's grandmother dying from an abject fear that she would be left alone with four young children when her husband was killed in war.

That is the way home and the theme of this book. What will it take to get you to climb up on that cross, to quiet your left brain long enough to feel the inherited myth of your longings and fears, so that you can release the energy these longings store? That is death-rebirth, to engage the fear that kills the resistance to it. That is the story of life, nature, and the universe.

The disquiet and longing of Laurie's grandmother, which divided her own marriage for so many years, will be the unconscious backdrop to Laurie's marital challenges until she understands and harnesses these deposited, emotional currents. Wherever we are not feeling complete in life, marriage or work, that unsettledness inexorably informs our reactions. Therefore, Laurie will turn towards the death-rebirth process herself, since her grandmother could not or did not know how. Laurie's heart is unconsciously asking, her discomfort calling.

This is her life's inflection point. She will do the loss-recovery work that was not done, and she will alter the flow of her ancestral river banks. The following generations will not have to be flooded with the kind of heavier currents that have filled her. Without loss you cannot create space for opportunity to expand into. I know, much easier said than done. Undoing the unconscious repeating of unlived lives is your homework.

Stop Reading Others' Stories, Find Your Own Myth

The myth of each of our families, the story and actual lives of our ancestors lives still, right now, in each of us. Where you are not feeling complete — the angst and frustration, the relationships coming undone — rise up because the moments that undid your grandparents and their parents are undoing you.

My job as a teacher, coach, counselor, father, husband,

friend, son and brother is to push others to go back inside to find those moments, stay in them for as long as possible in order to release the truths stored in the feelings and perceptions. We all emerged from the balm and storms of the electromagnetic environment of home, a dialect of timeless images, thoughts, sensations, smells, and flashes of memory composed and now stored in our heart, stomach, and limbic right brain. It is in these that the treasure of our life and marriage are stored.

Laurie was exhausted from the weight of her frustration, so she was willing to do whatever it took to get relief. Both the universe and I love it when another soul is willing to jump in. Let's see how she did.

CHAPTER 3
R.O.A.R., BACK UP RIVER

"A perception changes the physical, emotional, and psychological fabric of the human via the science of electrons in the body."

— Jane Roberts

Belly Up to Your Feelings

By our fifth counseling session, as Laurie shared more stories about the hours she spent with her grandmother as a kid, she began to feel a discomfort and nausea in her stomach and chest. We know where that nausea comes from. The unlived life and the frustration-anger that soaked her grandmother's heart and put a derogatory sting into her words left their imprint on Laurie, via the electron currents from her mom's belly and heart.

As science tells us in *The Heart Has Its Own 'Brain' and Consciousness*, Laurie's "nervous system acts as an 'antenna' which is tuned to and responds to the electromagnetic fields produced by the heart of other individuals." In Chapter 7 we will delve further into the how much our stomach knows, senses, stores, and controls our moods and motivations. Gut feelings are electric, real, and central to dislodging old feelings. Our gut is the warehouse of all our desire and fear, the home of all the why's of our life: why we love, hate, and want the things we do.

Laurie's mom was a carrier of her grandmother's sadness-anger enzymes and neurons, across the inner stomach, heart, and midbrain kingdom. She unconsciously reinforced and maintained them through her judging, criticizing, and distrust in life and love. Frustration, like hair and eye color, became an inherited trait.

Christopher Bache, PhD reminds us in *Lifecycles* of how Laurie's and her mother's behavior unconsciously emerged from the imprint of behaviors and sensibilities that moved through the grandmother. Bache states that who we are, how we act, and what we believe today are "not independent in time but part of a casual chain with roots deep in your inner history."

As Laurie sat on my couch and talked about the hours she spent in her grandmother's kitchen, as well as the orneriness of her mother's disposition over the years, I could see her hands clench and shoulders tense and pinch inward. "Roots deep" echoed in me. I asked her how much she wanted to undo some of this tension and find out how to begin addressing why she and her marriage were struggling. She said, "I don't know. It's painful. It's like being swept away by a current. All I end up doing is fighting with my husband." I took that as a green light. It was time to take the trail back to her SIB.

Introducing Your Rational to the Irrational

This therapeutic work she was about to do follows an old, universally known path. I have spent the last twenty-three years chasing, plunging, and calling into this perplexing inner world of emotions, abandoning the familiar and knowable almost daily to try to get at the truths about myself. That is not a sales pitch, just a fact. I have been studying, experiencing, and counseling clients through the basic format of self-undoing and awareness because it gave me information and relieving joy that I found nowhere else.

Along with the yoga, astrology, breath-body work, acupuncture, hypnosis, medications, psychotherapy, journaling, past-life therapy, and eye movement desensitization and reprocessing that I have done, I have also spent countless hours working with Native American and Druid medicine men and women in Connecticut, Arizona, California, New Mexico, Pennsylvania, Peru, and England. There are few modalities of self-exploration that I have not either tried or studied. I confess, as a self-awareness addict, that I have lots of issues, especially around the exorcising of these issues.

Remarkably, the format and template of the work with the body-stored memories and emotions that the old cultures like the Native Americans use is familiar. It is very similar to the therapeutic and curative modalities and framework used today to address PTSD. Both use the same roadmap and process.

Over the last seventy-five years, the US government has done exhaustive research on PTSD. In response to the countless soldiers that returned from WWI, WWII, and the Korean War, the U.S. Department of Veterans Affairs turned its attention to the persistence and severity of the post-war, psychological symptoms that so many soldiers suffered. How serious is this emotional anguish these veterans face upon their return to a more civilized home environment? According to Veterans Affairs, from the September 2019 post on their website www.stripes.com seventeen soldiers a day commit suicide.

The foundation of the therapeutic approach used by

counselors and clinicians to address this stress in veterans adheres to the same principles and techniques I use with clients. Both approaches seek to guide clients back inside their body — to meet the moments that created specific emotional imprints or dents, to express these feelings, and then offer these feeling-experiences up to one's rational self and sensibilities.

Road to Acceptance

Once our adult attention has been re-introduced to the experience and the ensuing grief, pain, or any other affect that was initially too overwhelming for the child or soldier to understand or process, the most important part of this recollecting-of-self journey begins: acceptance. Nothing moves a person forward more powerfully than a full physiological, emotional, and perceptual acceptance of whatever happened and all the collateral impact from that event.

Acceptance is the elixir and the vital tool for human growth and change. But it is often a much longer and elusive inner experience to truly find and capture. Too often the adult, logical mind thinks and says it has accepted something from its history — but the limbic body, especially the intelligent heart and stomach, have not fully let go. The great Carl Jung said, "We cannot change anything until we accept it. Condemnation does not liberate, it oppresses."

True cathartic, life altering acceptance is achieved only when both the left and right brains together accept. The logic-consumed rational, adult brain and the intuitive, feeling-infused child-heart must both experience and agree that whatever occurred in the past has now been comfortably integrated into the full storyline of one's life.

Acceptance is a returning to feeling whole, at home, and safe. As Gohl Sasson describes in his article "All About Sadness" www.cosmicnavigator.com; sadness around a specific event or experience, for example, "finally leads you back home, finally passes away, burns in the warm hearth. When you find your home, when you get a moment of oneness...Sadness only passes when you finally manage to experience a moment of connectedness."

Laurie's ongoing reactions to her husband, to being married, and in her life in general were generating such powerful feelings of frustration and anger. It was time to begin her trek. I was going to start helping her acknowledge these feelings, registering and identifying where in the body they are stored, and then start bringing these archived feeling-experiences up to wallow and simmer in them.

As you recall, this is the motion of relationship, the relatus from Chapter 1. It is the upstream course back into non-linear, non-logical time to those core, original events: getting bullied at school, getting dropped like a hot rock by your eighth-grade girlfriend, or a just a really grumpy relative. From this inner locale, you begin the process of understanding the context of why, all the whys of a grandmother's behavior or broken high school hearts.

Laurie would begin to understand that the unresolved pain and deep sense of incompleteness in the matriarchal figures in her life were still lodged inside. Once she opened to this, she could make sense of it and accept her inheritance. John Bradshaw says in *Homecoming: Reclaiming and Championing Your Inner Child,* "When the emotion accompanying a traumatic experience is blocked, the mind cannot evaluate or integrate the experience. When the emotional energy blocks the resolution of trauma, the mind becomes diminished in its ability to function." Laurie became exhausted by this quiet drip of trauma that she experienced through proximity to her mother and grandmother. But she would have the power to break this thread.

Inner Child Meets the Adult, Girl Meets Woman

So many of us struggle in our lives and marriages. So often we try to make changes, try to find the motivation to be more productive, less anxious, more positive and have more energy to complete all that we desire. But we seem to end up in the same dispositional place over and over. We lose hope and pull the plug, which normally leads to divorce.

The home of human motivation, consciousness, self-actualization, and change is in the middle of the brain, in our mid-brain's RAS region. It is where the left and right brain signals meet. It is where the stream of all our emotional impulses travel up to seek release, resolution, and understanding. It houses and creates our consciousness and awareness. Everything that we are doing, thinking, perceiving, and wondering about emerges and emanates from this centralized brain zone. In *Physiology of Consciousness*, Richard Davidson says, "This is where the underlying capabilities of our rational functioning are drawn from."

In fact, the roots of all our thoughts and beliefs grew

from the very soil of our RAS, fed by the experiences, sensations and emotions of our youth. Allan Schore writes in *The Science of the Art of Psychotherapy*, "Nature appears to have built our abstract and rational apparatus not just on top of that of biological affect regulation but also from it and with it." And therein is the rub. This mid-brain region, which is intimately connected to our heart and stomach, is a sacred place, your personal Holy Grail database, that you re-enter and explore now. If you wait, you are just going to continue to be unconscious, confused, and reactive.

Nighttime in the Switching Yard

Why is this RAS so important? Think of your old, childhood fears and joys, that were stuffed inside and left behind as your left brain formed, excitedly traveling on a train every day since childhood up from your belly and heart on their way to your sensible, analytical brain district. It is the neuron express. Not a long journey for these scared and giddy feeling-memories to travel. But when they reach your RAS they want to keep going, to "meet" your adult self and perspective. They want to meet any adult energy so that they can be recognized and honored. "What fun" your old emotions think.

But your busy, slightly agitated attention is not really up for it, not exactly comfortable allowing this heavy cargo to unload. So, at this mid-brain switching yard, your rational attention pulls a switch to divert and cut off these sensations from going any further.

Ezequiel Morsella writes in *Behavioral and Brain Sciences* that our brain is being bombarded by such an endless cascade of "old brain signals that it gates or blocks most of this sensory data. Only a small trickle of information is permitted into the prefrontal cortex." This is the physiological and biological basis for the divided self, this war between our thinking and feeling self. Our thinking self is scared of our feeling self.

When Laurie's frustration with her husband fired too strongly, the data processing center in her RAS shut down. New information does not get delivered to her conscious building brain, keeping her stuck.

We are so naturally and easily lulled into believing that our logic-seeking, analytical self should always be driving, that it knows best. But we are missing the whole other half of our life by avoiding this inner world. Robert Monroe in *Ultimate Journey* says, "Our left brain, conscious mind cannot categorize love, friendship...and resists 'anything that interrupts' its cognitive processing." Our adult perceptions get annoyed by the excitability of our unruly feelings. The emotions of our spouse upset us. And when we are confronted on our behavior by our partner, for actions and reactions that we "thought" made sense, the ones born in the SIB, we are upset by such questioning and then react in our historically set manner, again and again.

In this gap between our adult and youth-based experiences, physicalized in our RAS, is the arena of opportunity. It is where the meeting of these two worlds will occur, where all our issues live, where all our marital challenges start and continue. This is where boy meets man, girl meets woman.

Motivation Killer

This colliding, repulsing, and high static confluence in our mid-brain is the biological basis of how motivation is squelched, according to Spencer Rathus in *Psychology: Concepts and Connections*. Our analytical self cannot integrate the charges from below. So much emotion-based static overwhelms our higher brain's ability to organize, so it literally spins aimlessly above this fray. It is electromagnetically intimidated, overwhelmed, and literally repulsed by the old brain impulses. So, nothing new gets done, nothing gets resolved inside. We say we want to work on ourselves and our marriage. We recite our affirmations and get out our notebook to begin figuring it all out. And then, it all stalls.

The RAS is the bridge to our evolution, maturation, and ability to complete our lives. We have to physically counteract this pushing away of our feelings by our adult mind. The only way to do this is to relax and slow down the frequency of our brain waves. Induced relaxation of our higher brain will ignite child-like trepidations and joys, normally dormant and released only unconsciously in flash points of marital debates or drunken tears. Memories of fourth grade will seep up. Our heart will warm with joy for a childhood pet dog, soften from a long-stored sadness for a deceased grandparent. Or butterflies of discomfort arise from memories of being picked on by a fourth-grade bully. That is the point, to let it all up.

When the brain wave frequencies of our neocortex neurons are actively and consciously slowed down, magic happens. When we close our eyes and breathe deeply into the solar plexus, Morsella says in *Behavioral and Brain*

Sciences, "Neuro-transmitting hormones are released into the blood that begin to synchronize the lower and higher brain centers." This is where the magic begins. Our rational mind will not speak with our whimsical lower brain unless it is resting.

"The cave you fear to enter holds the treasure you seek."
—Joseph Campbell

"Hurry up. Where? Up the river?"

Every time I am doing this work with counseling clients like Laurie, leaving the shores of our tidy, rationalizing self and visiting the land of the child inside and all our strong, unruly, and sometimes fearful feelings from childhood, I think of Joseph Conrad's classic book *Heart of Darkness.* It is a story about traveling up river, into the remote African jungle. The movie *Apocalypse Now* was based on this tale, which is an allegory of returning to these more primitive, raw, unruly emotional parts of self.

In one scene, the central character Marlow finds a note as he is traveling up the Congo River. He's searching for Kurtz, an ivory trader who has turned away from civilization, abandoned the psychological confines of the ordered world to live with the natives. They are to bring him back to civilization. As Marlow and his crew feel the thick, untamed jungle close in on them, they find a note on the shore with words scribbled on it. "'Hurry up.' 'Where?' 'Up the river?' 'Approach cautiously.'"

This was my favorite book in high school for reasons I better understand now. My teenage self felt that the adult world did not get it, was somehow missing some of the wonder, elation, and creative mystery in daily life. The platitudes and mundane notes of suburban life so often seemed one dimensional and restrained, while my inner world felt rich, tribal, and intriguing.

The adults from my childhood were raised during the Great Depression, so it makes sense why my generation often experienced a divide or disconnect from them. Their gift to us was a profound sense of possibility and wonder which were simply less available to them.

This conflict and confusion drew me to books with themes like Conrad's. It also drew me to eventually working in the field of counseling, trying to help others bridge this yawning divide between the sensibilities and perceptions of adult consciousness and the deep well and fervor of childhood sentiments. It is an ancient divide, the timeworn riddle and mystery of being human. It is also the simple and wonderful reality and challenge of our lives, the cosmic plan, to begin the journey of understanding that these two powerful parts of us exist and need to be reconciled. Yes, "approach cautiously."

You might see the word cautiously and recoil a bit. I have seen the nervous eyes and shoulders of my counseling clients when we begin to talk about their past, about doing this work to unwind their memories, to travel back upstream. No need to fear, though. Your adult perspective will be introduced to feelings it thought were long gone and become guarded and wary. But remember, these feelings are invisible; they cannot hurt. The initial contact with Kurtz, your feelings, might be uncomfortable. There might be tears. But like any exercise, it becomes easier.

The world-renowned author and teacher Joseph

Campbell spent his entire career studying the topic of what Laurie was going to do as she relaxed and focused on her heart. This therapeutic practice and ritual, initiated by deep breathing, is the exact same one that all civilizations across history have used.

In *Primitive Mythology*, Campbell calls it releasing oneself "from the local system of illusions and put in touch with the mysteries of the psyche itself, which leads to wisdom concerning both soul and its world, and thereby performing the necessary function for society of moving it from stability and sterility in the old toward new reaches and new depths of realization."

Begin, Eyes Closed

"If you do not mind, Laurie, please close your eyes," I said as she sat on the couch in my Connecticut counseling office. Just like during *Sesame Street* or *The Electric Company* from childhood, I would like you, the reader, to follow the bouncing, therapeutic ball of relaxation and self-awareness, as if you are Laurie.

"With your eyes closed, let your body feel heavier as you sit there, paying attention to the weight of your body being held by the cushions and legs of the couch," I said. "Now, as you sit and feel and pay attention to your body and hear my voice, sense and tell me what is the strongest feeling you have right now?"

"Anger," she said. "Can I have more than one?"

"Of course, what else?"

"Frustration with the anger, which then brings this wave of anxiety," she explained.

"Perfect, now where in your body is this wave?"

"I've never thought about where. I feel this tension in my heart, my chest, and like a thumping in my rib cage. I also kind of have this nausea at the top of my stomach. Probably why I end up eating something every time my husband and I argue."

The horses were on the track. She was now at her starting gate. The feelings of anger and frustration, in the middle of her body, are the set points. This is where we will enter her inner world. From here I will go through the process and account of what occurred with Laurie that afternoon.

She had identified the places in the body where her strongest emotions were bubbling and stirring. The next step is for her, for you, to deepen the quieting of your rational, organizing brain so that the body can begin voicing itself fully. The only way to do this is through deep breaths.

Spiritus

The word spirituality comes from Latin *spiritus*, which means to breathe. When you breathe deeply into the solar plexus, it begins to stimulate the body's neuro-electric network, basically switching off the fight or flight button and turning on the safety-relax switch. To get spiritual, which just means to get real with yourself and to stop allowing your adult brain's fixation with reason and distractions that push away old feelings, you have to breathe into the stomach.

I walked Laurie through my fundamental breathing exercise.

1. As you sit with your back straight, eyes still comfortably closed, put your left hand on your stomach.

2. Pay attention to your hand on your stomach, feeling the warmth of your palm around and on top of your belly button.

3. Now, take a long, slow breath into your nose, and as this air enters your nose, guide it down your neck and spine like you are swallowing watering down the back of your spine.

    Keep directing it down through the back of your lungs, heart, past your solar plexus at the bottom of your rib cage, and into the middle of your stomach, where your hand rests.

4. As you are inhaling this air into your stomach, push your belly button out, noticing your hand being pushed into the middle of the room as your belly expands out.

5. Do not worry about your six-pack abs or svelte tummy somehow being compromised as you push your stomach muscles out. We will look for and find your svelteness later.

6. As you reach the end of this inhale, hold it for a count of 5, 4, 3, 2, 1. This wakes up the solar plexus, slows and steadies your heart rate.

7. Now, exhale all that air slowly out of the stomach. Push it back up and out your mouth while making a sound on the exhale. The sound is like "ahhhhhhhh."

8. As you are exhaling, use your hand to gently push your belly button back toward your spine. Feel, exaggerate, and keep pushing your stomach inward, squeezing those muscles inward, past where they were when we started, really trying to get your belly button to touch the back of your spine.

9. Exhale all that air for a count of 5, 4, 3, 2, 1.

10. Now, just sit there and notice your body, thoughts, shoulders, and arms. Sense a weightiness as your attention is slightly less jumpy, more willing to be in the body and to notice itself in the body.

Notice if your arms, chest, heart, and back of the neck feel heavier and actually more tethered to your thoughts — as opposed to your body being some foreign mass that your thoughts never really pay attention to.

Repeat steps 1-10 five times. Note: the most important part is to get the stomach to expand out on the inhale, and actively squeeze and contract back in on the exhale.

Heart Yoga, Feel the Stretch

The science inside the belly breathing is as powerful as the positive impact it has on you. When you inhale into your stomach and gently stretch those muscles out, the largest bundle of nerves in the entire body is activated. This switchboard of nerves, called your solar plexus or "a mesh of sun," is what scientists call the second brain. It is where vital neuro-transmissions of information are sent to and received from the rest of the body. One of its primary tasks is monitoring and regulating the heart's activity.

The first thing that happens when the solar plexus is awakened is it signals to the heart that it is safe to slow itself down. Deep stomach breathing resets the body's nerve control system called the autonomic nervous system (ANS) that regulates your heart rate, digestion, body temperature, respiratory rate, sexual arousal, and more. Pretty much everything that your body is doing without your awareness is managed by your ANS.

The love and longing stored in your heart, the anger in your liver, worry in your spleen, sorrow in your lungs, and all that fear in your kidney that you are not conscious of and that are silently and restlessly stewing and prodding your conscious attention, all are jolted from their slumber as your ANS stirs. How? The light friction and tension of the muscle tissues stretching activates the electrical current in the nerves inside your heart, mid-brain, cortex, and lungs, which it turn lowers and eases the pressure on the heart's electrical current. Dr. Dharma Khalsa says in *Meditation as Medicine* that as soon as the heart gets this electrical indicator from your ANS, it does not have to be on high-beat alert and bear all the burden from all that unconscious worry, fear, and sorrow weighing down the body's "power lines." It activates a signal for relaxation-inducing hormones like melatonin, serotonin, and epinephrine to be released.

Buddha-belly breathing sets off a party for your heart, like taking your shoes off after a long day or a five-mile walk, plopping down on the couch, and bodily sighing in relief from gravity and time. We can buy a jar of melatonin right now for $9, or take antidepressant medicine like Zoloft, Lexapro, or Prozac that increase the body's serotonin levels. The global market for antidepressants will be nearly $17 billion in 2020. I have used these drugs. They help slow down the psychological and emotional strain of self-loathing, fear of loss, and sense of disconnection from the world that the child spirit in us accumulates. But breathing deeply will take you all the way into your body, into the actual cells that hold your fear and sadness so that you can understand and convert these firings into growth action. That is the courageous task at hand.

"The ability to symbolize feelings and put them into words provides a powerful tool for emotion regulation."
— Carrol Izard

Kitchen Table World

Laurie did well. After five of these long, slow breaths she began to sink back into the couch. Her shoulders, arms, and neck loosened and softened. She said her arms felt heavy, like there were thirty-pound weights on them. Bingo!

Knowing that there was a source moment, or a series of similar moments in her past that created this imbedded anger-anxiety in her, I asked her to imagine being at her kitchen table when she was in fourth grade. She easily went there and described the cluttered countertops, the white and yellow curtains lining the windows, and the musty smell of coffee and burnt toast. I liked that she threw in the aromas. Since the cells in our nose are connected directly to our brain's limbic-memory center, I knew she was in a heightened state of relaxation.

I asked her to imagine her family was there in the kitchen with her at one of their evening meals. It was easy to tell that her awareness had drifted into that room long gone physically, but still animated in her emotional time. In her case it was Scranton, PA in the early Eighties, and she was now there at the kitchen table with her two brothers and parents.

"Now, if you can, tell me what you are feeling right now as you watch and sense your parents' interaction," I said. "Imagine, though, that you're talking with your heart, not your head. Use words formed and spelled by your heart and stomach, not your head." I was trying to ease her back into the fourth-grade body which sees and speaks to the world in an impression-reaction language. "What does your gut sense your mom is feeling? What is she doing? Listen to your heart as you sit there. Ask your heart what mom's heart is feeling towards your dad. What is he doing right now? How is he feeling?"

It is about simmering, waiting for the feeling-effects from original childhood moments which were infused into Laurie's fourth grade body, to begin being introduced to her adult self and attention. Her rational self has been too busy doing and avoiding to hear what those sensations can teach her.

Keep Your Adult Attention Quiet for As Long as Possible

I reminded her that her adult, rationalizing judgement was going to try to interject its perspective and conclusions. It might rationalize these childhood-born sentiments that come up. It might poke defensive claims like "mom's childhood was hard," or "it is not easy having three kids," or "our neighbors in the early Eighties always seemed to have more money, so it was not easy." Even though those insights and adult-constructed conclusions might be historically accurate, we were looking for her fourth grader's unabridged experience.

She spent over twenty-five minutes in this deep, SIB place when she was in fourth grade. I helped to move her forward in memory-time to eighth grade when her parents split up, and then further into tenth grade when she started dating her first boyfriend. The most poignant moment came when her stomach helped her to remember when her mom erupted at the kitchen table one evening, yelling at her dad because he had not finished painting the dining room. She stormed out, knocking a plate full of food onto the floor.

Laurie, talking slowly and deliberately, as if floating but grounded in this dream place, said her body convulsed when her mom left the house. Her chest and upper belly felt sick in that moment, back in fourth grade as well as right there in my office. She realized that was the first moment of pure overwhelm in her life. It was a fear that her mom might not come back, a sadness for her dad's weakened state, and the first irreparable dent in her sense of emotional safety. It was also the moment when one generation passes down its psycho-emotional disposition to the next one. Her mom's sadness-anxiety current had now pulled Laurie in, like a swelled river pulling smaller tributaries into its torrent, forcing all the lesser streams to go its way.

The last few minutes of her visit back in emotional time found her in eighth grade. She said she was standing in her bedroom looking out her window as her dad got in his car and drove off with the last of his boxes from the house. "That's when they split up," she said as another tear dripped. She said that is when her fear-anxiety really swelled. "I did not know if I would see him again, mom was so pissed. Mom felt the world owed her a better deal, better life. She got so bitter after that."

Re-Entry

When she said, "owed her a better deal," I knew that Laurie had found one of the biggest, obstructive rocks in her life-garden. She had verbalized the heaviest, electro-magnetic charge within her mom, that unwieldy, relentless resentment-regret-anger triangle. It is a life and growth killer, probably the stickiest and most difficult emotional dent to set free. I was not sure if she realized, though, that this resentment-anger vortex smoldering in her mom was the one gnawing at her and killing her marriage and most of her relationships.

So many times over the last five or six years she snapped at her husband: "How could he not see how I felt when he went off to work and I was stuck with the kids?" She had admitted in earlier counseling sessions that her husband was an attentive and thoughtful person and a conscientious and loving spouse and father. He had more work to do on himself, but she said her anxiety and resentment never let him off the hook.

When they would be getting ready to go out to dinner, she would hate and criticize him for how she looked and how she could never lose the weight. It was his fault. She so resented that he would not affirm or contribute to her negative commentary when she was nattering about her friends or people they knew. Laurie thought that was disrespectful of him to not agree with her judging of others. That floored her. She would end up muttering "asshole" under her breath after some of these exchanges.

She also regretted that they did not have as much money as some of their friends. Off to the islands for the holidays friends would go, sharing their plans at one of those Saturday evening parties. Meanwhile, she would burn with regret, glaring at her husband for not giving her "a better deal," a better life.

"How do you feel, Laurie?" She leaned back into the couch and opened her eyes. She was re-entering the room. She gazed out the half-opened window, sun almost gone from the horizon. A couple of birds chirping on a tree limb scraping the building and the faint acceleration of commuters heading home were the only sounds we heard.

When you leave rational time through deep breaths and enter the world of our instinctual, primitive, intuitive, and feeling-based body and brain parts, it takes time to reenter the hard and fast present. The body and brain need to adjust back into linear time, like coming back from a dream. There is normally a melancholy and wistfulness too, upon reentry, like something familiar and familial has been released. Even if it is an ancient resentment that we have re-experienced and reconciled, there is a wistfulness, even an initial sadness, to let it go because it has been such a big part of our lives.

Sounds and sights that you never paid attention to now are heard anew. I knew how she felt. I have traveled back into emotional, ancestral, and childhood-history hundreds of times. For Laurie, it was a debilitating anxiousness that was her connection to her mom. The little girl in her never wanted her mom to leave or let her struggle alone. So, like all kids, she took on her mom's emotions as a childhood expression of love, respect, and sharing of the burden.

Interrupt the Old Loops of Emotion

"Have I become my mom?" she wondered. "Is it really all my crap, like, that I felt and buried all this fear and regret, and the world around me is just like reminding me of this stuff?" I waited, just holding as her adult perceptions caught up and listened to what her feelings were telling her.

If we wait long enough, the answers come and we get to the big whys, but waiting takes patience, courage, and a willingness to trust and befriend old pains and sorrows. They are in us to guide us though. "The cave you fear to enter holds the treasure you seek," Joseph Campbell said.

By leaving the shore of thoughts and following her feelings of anxiety-fear back in time, upriver, the previously unconscious or forgotten memory of mom hating dad woke up. No analysis, just re-experiencing it. Do not waste the universe's time thinking about your regret; feel and find its roots.

Once she identified the feelings as we started this process, and located where in the body they were, we stilled her attention and directed it into that current of overwhelming emotions that she imbibed from her mom. By bringing her adult cognitions into that early Eighties kitchen table memory, her forty-one-year-old self recognized the historical context of what and why she felt what she does every day. She interrupted what was previously unconscious by welcoming her left brain to her child-self right brain. As a fourth grader, she could not separate her emotional world from her parents'. Her executive brain functions were still in diapers. But now she can. It is like her forty-one-year-old self reached her hand into the stream of anger and regret, pouring from her mom through the electrons of that kitchen, and pulled her drowning fourth-grade self out.

The power to understand these whys and release the hold these emotions have comes from the ability that your logical perspective has to draw meaning and context to these illogical, impassioned experiences. Your left brain, which has been trying to keep these old emotions from interrupting daily life, ironically now becomes the arbiter, moderator, and mechanism for resolution. The limiting and imprecise understanding of our personal history that our left brain starts out with becomes flooded with the context, bodily sensations, and emotion-studded memories it does not realize live below.

This dialogue between our two halves changes everything. It is the lottery jackpot of all human development and consciousness raising. Laurie can now begin the journey of separating the feeling world that is authentically and originally hers, from that of her parents and grandparents. If she had not done this, that child energy in her would just continue to drift lost, anxious, and empty, leaving her present self in the same state.

But now she can recognize more objectively the storyline of her family myth: the overwrought woman, raised by a wonderful yet demanding and draining mother who married a man that she could not or would not love. Laurie is a continuation of the myth, but now with a new awareness of some of its fallacies and deep, unconscious instabilities. Instead of being consumed by the shadows of this story, she now can create and infuse new possibilities into the current of her inherited family tale. She was willing to look inside to try to save herself, her marriage, and her kids. She wanted to figure out how to love them without the aches. As John Bradshaw says in *Homecoming: Reclaiming and Championing Your Inner Child*, "We must risk being vulnerable if we are going to be intimate."

New Perception Changes Everything: Solution to Marriage

As we revisit the tumult of our space in between, we become more like those football coaches with binoculars in the coach's box. They get to see the whole field, not just the ground level play. It is a whole different perspective. The good news is that Laurie does not have to fully agree with or actually forgive all those involved in her family mythology. Forgiveness is great, it is good to have it, but it is not a prerequisite for releasing old patterns or undoing the hold that our emotional past has on us and our marriage.

This work will inevitably create a new, adult

perspective on our childhood perceptions. It will create an update to our embedded software as we bring a parent's perspective to our inner world. Laurie will now be the parent to the fourth grader. Jane Roberts writes in *Seth Speaks*, "A perception changes the physical, emotional, and psychological fabric of the human via the science of electrons in the body." When we relax and open old memory-feelings up, the ones that were stored as biochemical firings, it creates a physical response within the brain's housing. Candice Pert says in *Molecules of Emotions*, "Physical mechanisms produce our experience of the world."

Just by allowing ourselves to relive and re-experience the moment and sensations, we literally, physically loosen and shift the frequency of that electron loop. That original twenty-five-year-old event that left a big, tire track-like neuronal groove in her midbrain can and will be physiologically changed. The reliving and feeling back that Laurie did, and the questions and probing of her heart, will move her to continuing to better understand why her world unfolded like it did, and why she reacts the ways she does in her adult life. Thomas Berger says, "Asking questions is the source of all knowledge."

"The key to living your full capacity is to have your left and right brain in simultaneous and synchronous action."
— Robert Monroe

Integration

Your goal in life is to complete it fully, and your marriage and all your relationships are essential pieces of your life purpose.

Together, they can make sense of the past so we can begin applying this wisdom back into our life, into our marital actions and reactions. That is what Laurie was beginning to do. As we did more sessions, she shared that she was able to more clearly recognize and watch her reactions. When her husband compassionately talked about making sure they stayed within their monthly budget, or that he had to spend a few more hours at work away from the family, she could feel that ancient hurt and regret start to swell. She could sense it, but was now much better at not succumbing fully to it. She was able to let that ache of vulnerability arise, own it, but not set off a brush fire.

Carrol Izard in *Emotion Theory and Research* summarizes perfectly what occurs when the child within meets and is guided by our adult self: "The ability to symbolize feelings and put them into words provides a powerful tool for emotion regulation, influencing emotion-cognition relations, and developing high-level social skills." All knowledge of self begins and ends with the coalescing of opposing forces within us.

I Call it ROAR

As mentioned at the beginning of the chapter, for over seventy-five years the U.S. Department of Veterans Affairs has been studying and working with veterans who have "soldier's heart," "shell shock," and "combat fatigue," which today are all commonly referred to as PTSD. One of the core therapeutic techniques for helping soldiers to address, relieve and holistically process the agonizing stress of trauma is the exact technique that I used with Laurie and all my clients. I call it ROAR: relax, open, accept, and relate.

It ties in with John Bradshaw's work of re-parenting, where we bring our present, adult-self back into our inner child work. Over the following sessions with Laurie, as we went back in time again to revisit her fourth and eighth grade self, I had her visualizing her forty-one-year-old self actually sitting at the table with fourth grade self, as her mom steamed with anger. The forty-one-year-old held her hand, went outside and walked in the garden and played on the playground with her. It deepens the electro-magnetic, neuron connection between the heart of the living child inside and active thinking, adult self.

ROAR is the basis of all the work I do, work that we all need to do.

1. Relax: As Laurie did, slow deep breaths set off a cascade of physiological relaxation responses in the body. It is the ticket back into your inner kingdom, the realms of fears and joys that are driving every action and reaction.

2. Open: Here is the crossing of the Rubicon. This is where and when you take your most uncomfortable feelings and let them lead you back into your family myth, back in time to the place and people that elicited these original feelings. You can start with our Kitchen Table Meditation, or just back to the playground, car, or whatever place most readily allows these feelings to come up.

PTSD works calls this part flooding or Prolonged Exposure. Whatever it is called, it is about heading upriver and wallowing in the scenes and experiences of discomfort.

3. <u>Acceptance</u>: This is the granddaddy of them all, the big A. It is discussed at length above. At some point, like Laurie did, through this therapeutic unraveling of our inherited emotional dents and imperfections stored in our neurons, we fully accept who and what we are.

Despite all that was unlived and incomplete in our ancestors, like the fear in Laurie's marrow that lived as subtle but a profound whispering trepidation of impending failure, we have to own, celebrate, and viscerally come to terms with our dispositional life. There is no changing the course of our life and marriage unless we are accepting the myth, history, and characters that brought us here.

An Native American elder told me twenty-one years ago, after a day of fasting and then a night sleeping alone out on a butte in north central New Mexico, "Remember Bill, until you realize that you chose your grandparents' grandparents, you will never come to terms with your life and mission." That is a big bite of acceptance, the perspective that we actually choose our life circumstances, carried by our relatives, since their psycho-emotional framework and life circumstances will bring us the most growth and awareness.

4. <u>Relate</u>: Relate and return, which means integrating the new perceptions and emotional openings and placing them into the fabric and storyline of our life. For Laurie, it meant realizing that the traumatic feelings of anger and disrespect that her mom had led her to finding and marrying a person who was mature and grounded, someone who was willing to support and embrace her foibles. By viscerally accepting our inherited past, we see how the pieces fit.

For me, after plunging into and cracking my inner world open years ago, and recognizing the lumps of incomplete lives across my ancestral lines, I integrated and celebrated this new consciousness by starting a journey to learn how to teach others how to R.O.A.R.

My grandfather was a surgeon, my paternal grandmother ran the Red Cross of Western Massachusetts. I, therefore, by doing the inner work, sought to place myself into the long continuum of my family's mythology of working in the curative trade.

It is time to ROAR your way back into your marriage and life. There will be tears of regret and uncomfortable bodily sensations. But the elixir of accepting our lives has no equal.

Exodus 3:14 says, "I am who I am." Look past the author, the place, and the era of these words and into the spirit of it. Sit quietly for as long as you can, ROAR, listen to your heart ache and open with its truth, and at some point, you will not just know what these words mean — you will feel your heart soften and tear up with its acceptance of them.

CHAPTER 4
A DANCE WITH FRICTION

"Friction is a positive force precisely because it's only when we're in opposition to something that we learn how to move forward."

— Hugo Macdonald

Consumed by Thoughts

We get so consumed, lost, clouded, and distracted by the whirl of our day. Endless thoughts and sensations poke and beckon for our attention. We are continually thinking about and replaying a client's patronizing comment or soaking in the thought-candy rush of news and sports headlines on the phone. Or we are lightly stressing about the pending visit of our girlfriend's mother.

Our adult attention, tucked away in our neocortex and secluded from our instincts, worries about the kids' undone homework. It is being stuffed with the distracting rattle of radio news about more tariffs, reliving the thought-stress that the dishwasher is still broken, summer travel plans are still un-booked, and our husband's inpatient grumpiness that needs to be addressed. All of these shards enter and exit the frontal cortex, "the orchestrator, linking things together for a final output" mentions Robert Knight on the site www.sciencealert.com.

Fifty thousand thoughts course through your brain every day. This is why I believe your brain, your heart, marriage, wife, husband, and overall wellbeing would all like you to slow down more and take more moments to think something else, anything else, or really un-think so you remember something else. Real remembering is the secret, and it involves accessing a different location and current in the body.

Thoughts Seem Random, But Soaked with History

It is crucial to realize that these fifty-thousand daily thoughts, cognitions, and judgements racing across the movie screen behind your eyes and underneath your forehead are neuro-electric charges, welled up, skimmed and collected from different parts of the body. The brain behind your forehead, your neocortex, is merely a collection station, not the source for these cognitions.

As you read the words *movie screen* in the sentence above, for example, you might recall an actual movie or experience at the theatre. I think of seeing *Jaws* in 1975 and using my raised knees and bin of popcorn to block the scary scenes. Just the idea of watching a film can generate a gush of warmth and enthusiasm for an escape into another world for two hours.

Thoughts of excitement, fear, and escape are automatically tethered to the word "movie." You hear your phone ding as you are reading this and thought sensations of curiosity and anticipation dart into your forebrain. It is your girlfriend saying she cannot make dinner, your boss bugging you, or a friend who has a question and needs your attention. All these cognitions, inspired by that one chime of that overpriced phone, have deep roots within the emotional and psychological memory experience of your life. Every thought throughout your day started somewhere else, from another time and place.

"The brain interprets signals from the senses and creates images in the brain that are the individual's perception of reality," AR Biad says in *Debugging Human DNA*. Each thought emerges like a leaf of a tree. You and your body, the tree, are a composition of all your experiences that are stored electro-magnetically. As you see or hear or smell something, your brain neurons receive this information, instantaneously draw up stored memories linked to these physical sensations, and then throw a thought impulse against your neocortex. These thoughts are, therefore, soaked in your perceptions and expectations.

Choking on Thoughts

"Thought itself is a system that simultaneously takes place in the brain, the body and the environment around us," we read from a 2013 issue of *Discover*. "In fact, we fundamentally perceive the world in terms of our ability to act on our environment."

This is why many of us believe that our thoughts own us, that we cannot seem to escape their incessant drip. They often do own us. That is why it is so important to begin the process of untying ourselves from these idea-beliefs that have been created without conscious knowledge of how, where, or when they were formed.

The thought of writing a book or being an author, residing with me for so many years, fanned a sting of incompleteness and inadequacy that was often paralyzing.

It was not a conscious response. The very words "book" or "writing" would blanch my body like a gut punch, and quickly unwind my sense of meaning and self-worth. I could be in a great mood, and the friendly question would arise: "How is the book going?"

That was all it took. The next thirty minutes I would have to silently drag myself out from those wet wool-like ideations of all my unfinished work in life and that memory vortex of incompleteness. Even a sensation of uneasiness would alight from third grade and a one-page paper about a cat that I struggled to finish. It was like a horizon I could never reach, one which created a subtle ache. I would still be conversing and casually engaging people in the room or office, but my stomach and heart were in a dirge of regrets.

My ears heard "book," which sent a neuron signal to my stomach and heart which stirred ancient sensations of frustrations and worry. It was like a red dashboard warning light that read "less than, less than." The thought of all that was still unwritten sent an electric body charge soaked in the experience-memory and perceptions of undone and unlived.

Your Heart and Stomach Getting in the Game, Big Time

The story of our mighty, unwieldy, deeply rooted, and so often involuntary thoughts, as mentioned above, start way below the brain. Our heart and stomach are really the key actors in our thought dramas. Before we learn how to address our thoughts and perceptions about ourselves, our marriage, and all the challenges, joys, chaos, and friction contained in relationships, we need to know the history of a thought. From there we will get to know how this history clouds and hinders our ability to confront the friction challenges in marriage.

That chiming of your phone, or the word "book" to me, these vibratory sounds, trigger the auditory nerves in the brain to send a signal down to the heart and belly. Once the heart and belly get this signal, they then send signals back up into the brain. But these signals are now soaked with neuron coding from past experiences that reinforce whatever feeling triggered them.

That is the rub, why it is so hard to change our thoughts and mindset. They are caught in this brain-body loop. Our stomach and heart, which are connected to our mid-brain, store all our memories and life experiences within their own set of neuron cells. They, like our mid-brain, are biochemical warehouses of our life, holding the encyclopedia of all our collected sensations. So the signals that they send back up are bigger and louder because they are saturated with old emotional, reactionary content housed in the stomach. The heart also has its own intelligence. Paul Pearsall says in *The Heart's Code*, "The heart's nervous system contains around 40,000 neurons similar to those found in the brain proper. Its elaborate circuitry enables it to act independently of the cranial brain to learn, remember, and even feel and sense."

Did someone say three brains? Crazy, right? The stomach actually has its own nervous system that functions like our brain. Sandra Blakeslee writes in *Complex and Hidden Brain in Gut Makes Stomachaches and Butterflies*, "The gut's brain is a network of neurons, neurotransmitters and proteins that zap messages between cells like those found in the brain proper and a complex circuitry that enables it to act independently, learn, remember." Just when we thought we had one brain, which is unwieldy enough, along comes the realization that our other one packs a bigger punch.

Dr. Michael Gershon, a professor of biology at Columbia-Presbyterian Medical Center in New York, tells us more about the wonder, magic, mystery, and sheer intelligence of our belly, that part of me that I endlessly fill with guacamole and potato chips. He explains that "nearly every substance that helps run and control the brain has turned up in the gut, including serotonin, dopamine, and benzodiazepines." It is like a rave party in our stomach, a fiery, impassioned, histrionic symphony of our feelings that has its own hours and life, separate and alien to our rational self.

Get Under the Hood of Your Thoughts

That auditory signal trigged by the word "book," that sparked an ideation of incompleteness, left my ear and brain and went charging down into my stomach-heart. In turn, this thought found a matching electrical and neuron charge of incompleteness already in my heart and belly. It is like our brain center is the post office, and our heart-stomach region is a huge neighborhood of houses. Different, specific packages are coded and sent to the specific houses that match that zone. Fritjof Capra writes in *The Web of Life*, "Scientists have observed that the central nervous system which connects sensory organs with the brain, is enriched with neuropeptide receptors that filter sensory perceptions." In other words, all our perceptions and thoughts are colored by emotion."

Each part of the body — in this case my stomach — has tiny antennae that sense and filter each unique signal they receive. Emotions are tied into these chemical charges. Each thought can influence and alter the tone, hues, and texture of the signals that get released back up to our consciousness-forming, rational brain parts. The website *The Human Memory* reports that memories exist not in a single place, but are scattered in a network of neuronal connections. It becomes a loop. This is how the thought of "book" becomes a growing emotional experience of incompleteness.

The region of my stomach that stores the currents and sensations of loss, fear, and procrastination was awakened. Probably much of my overeating comes from trying to quell the static of these unconsciously stored cells. That gut punch C-grade from my junior high school English class, the one which has been living and breathing its own life in my gut since Jimmy Carter was in office, begins to bellow. Those bellowing feeling-neurons then ascend to my forward brain where faint images, not immediately perceivable to my adult brain, are sketched of grueling, 4 a.m. typewriter sessions in college, scrambling to finish a ten-page essay. It becomes a silent torrent of reactions, all started by that single word.

This is why we have to get underneath, though, and beyond our brain constructs in order to understand the roots of our perceptions, beliefs, and true sense of self.

Adult Brain Needs to Get on Board

When that flush of discontent and incompleteness stings

my body, it feels like a piece of myself has been cut off from the present, adrift in sensations of vague and heavy uneasiness. In turn, the things and people around me, for a few minutes, seem foreign and distant, until this wave of electromagnetic discomfort weakens and washes over. Like the tide, they will come back, just as readily and mightily.

Like the rainwater coursing out of my roof's gutters, carving grooves into my lawn that set up all new storm water to follow that same path, our emotions actually form neuron grooves as well.

This firing of neurons, laced with discontent, "engraves new circuits in the brain so that we become more prepared to recognize situations" that create the same feelings, writes John Bradshaw in his seminal book *Homecoming: Reclaiming and Championing Your Inner Child*. He adds that the bio-physiology of our neocortex, in all its supposed wisdom, functions to "overcome memories and suppress the past, while the energy of the original trauma remains like an electrical storm throughout the biological system."

How is that working, this suppression stuff? Not well. The more I felt incomplete, the higher the propensity for this to continue.

Everything that is unconscious, all that crap of incompleteness in me, would just keep spinning around if I left it up to my rational self to sort it out. Only through the process of opening, releasing, and understanding this old and current discontent can I move myself and marital discourse forward. Only through real, sustained, conscious relaxation of our adult brain, via sitting alone and therapy, can we still this electrical storm.

"A man who has not passed through the inferno of his passions has never overcome them."

— Carl Jung

Thoughts Create Themselves

Our stomach and heart memory systems are so powerful. A single sight or sound can and will unravel the psychology of a day or lifetime. A counseling client recently told me he feared he was going to get fired from his job. He went on to say that his boss does most of his communication via text.

During our counseling session, he was trying to keep his attention away from his phone, but struggled to do so. At one point the phone dinged twice, but both were just messages from friends. There were so many bubbles of apprehension drifting up from his heart-belly, as his rational attention leapt forward in time, wondering how to confront the challenges of paying bills and college tuition if his job was lost. He recounted, as well, memories of moving neighborhoods when he was young, when his dad lost his job, and the sense of sadness and weakened emotional anchors.

Back and forth his thoughts swung, wistful for the things not done at his current job, fearful for what the weeks would look like trudging through the new job journey.

95 Percent of the Time, No Hands on the Wheel

All old experiences, good or bad, have left their neuron

coated dents. But as we are moving through our day, we have no idea how, where, or why our thoughts arise. In fact, science has shown that "most of our decisions, actions, emotions and behavior depend on the 95 percent of brain activity that is beyond our conscious awareness. The unconscious mind operates at forty million bits of data per second, whereas the conscious mind processes at only forty bits per second" says Robert Lipton in *Biology of Belief.*

That unconscious part, what some call subconscious, is not some mysterious black and white world painted by Freud and his Oedipus-like characters. That unconscious part is the world of our life experiences that are stored in our limbic body network, a part that our rational mind does not know is there. Our higher brain just needs to be reintroduced to these memories. Nothing more.

Our head does not know our heart. The higher brain center of my fifty-four-year-old self needs to go back inside and recollect, re-experience, and get the information and lesson that each event holds, as Laurie did in Chapter 3. The challenge is that our rational self is scared, rightfully, and overwhelmed by the might and bite of these emotionally charged and stored sensations.

For me, for such a long time, instead of showing up in front of the computer to write, I continually choked on my expectations around an historical struggle with finishing. Just the thought of writing and the fear it created in my gut, was rooted somewhere in my body like a knot or clog in my internal lawn's sprinkler system. "Until you make the unconscious conscious," Carl Jung said, "it will direct your life and you will call it fate."

Pharmacy in your Stomach and the Suburban Malaise

Scientists have found nearly every substance that helps run and control the brain has turned up in the gut, including serotonin, dopamine, and benzodiazepines. Think and chew on that psychotropic nugget for a minute. The very chemicals and amino acids that alter the electric currents within our highly attuned, rocket science formula-solving neocortex — and form the ingredient base for anti-anxiety drugs like Valium, Xanax, and Ativan — are all living and swimming inside the stomach. They are just waiting to be activated, stuck in our clutched, unattended to, and unreleased stomach muscle cells.

That is right — instead of heading over to CVS to get your next dose of stuff for whatever-ails-you pills, doing deep breathing from Chapter 3 will help you change, understand, and embrace your thoughts and beliefs. I have made my share of CVS runs, just to be clear. Without the intelligence of your heart and stomach, you are living and thinking into your life with only half of your resources.

How many breaths do we need to do in order to catalyze the experience of feeling our thoughts so that we know their roots? If you keep sitting and breathing in the silence, which often takes a willingness and courage you may have never mustered before, you will find out. Our body, via our solar plexus, has a reboot button. If you trust the breath, it will let you know how long it takes to wake up.

We are fighting and holding back all that we feel. When we sit alone in our meditation, an old sadness for a childhood dog might come up. Or we might feel a general, dull ache of monotony, malaise, or sense of missing something during the nine hours of our daily job. This urban and suburban existence, without the soft intelligence of our unconscious memories, will keep us longing for something and someone else in our life. I call it Suburban Malaise.

This malaise is part of the reason why your marriage is in shambles — you believe someone else will fill that void. Our longings for more might be deep, or just shallow desires to feel less anxious and worried about the kids, the bank account, and our general ability to live healthy as time unwinds. Maybe it is a recurring frustration with a spouse and the rutted patterns of interactions with him. Whatever it is, we do a heck of a lot of things to avoid feeling.

That suppressing leads us to try to escape the aches. We do a lot of dulling. Staring at our phones is now the most popular way of dulling the world inside of us that is dying to come out. It is killing us to come out.

Our unprocessed and unexpressed feelings do not leave or take a vacation when we have managed to push them away from our rationalizing. The world of our feelings never sleeps. Feelings are living their lives in the silent but animated world of stomach and heart neurons. "Forget us," your feelings are saying, "at your own peril." Our head brain unwittingly receives these electric ill winds and currents and adapts them into the language it knows: the left brain, logic-seeking dialect.

Obsessed with Survival

The left brain is obsessed with survival. It is linear and

reactive, and does not like strong, unruly, uncontrollable sensations. It gets overwhelmed and will therefore take those sensations of physical discomfort and anxious nausea and throw a quick image up into your conscious mind encoded with discomfort. A thought about losing your job will pop up, or someone close to you being hurt, or you will have an overcharged, discomfort-laden reaction to a headline of a terrorist attack or weather tragedy. In other words, what you are thinking is really your feelings, just in a language that your rational, material, physical self understands.

It is time to reverse this course, to do some unthinking and more feeling. It will not be easy. You need to alter the current of thoughts and feelings about yourself, your marriage, your partner, and your life, and these very slight shifts are going to open up new perspectives.

Our thoughts are not only amplified images and recurring echoes of what we have felt or are afraid we will feel, but almost as importantly, they are the result of who we believe we are and our expectations about our ability to actually act and have an impact on our environment. In other words, our thoughts cloud how we perceive and experience the world, and not the other way around. They often hinder and halt our movement forward because they chain us to a self-perception that just seems so real, but might not be.

Our View of that Hill Matters

To demonstrate how our self-perception and thoughts impose themselves in our view of things, researchers in their study "Jack Needs Jill to Get Up the Hill", published in *UVA Magazine,* took a group of volunteers to a hill for an experiment. Each volunteer was given a certain set of circumstances as they were about to climb. Before they started, though, they were asked to estimate the steepness. They learned that how each volunteer assessed the steepness of the hill was different, depending on the resources they had to prepare for the climb as well as their existing life circumstances.

Those given a heavy backpack felt the hill was steep. Those standing next to a good friend felt more relaxed, in turn feeling supported in a relationship and seeing the hill as hardly steep at all.

The volunteers' thoughts about the hill, therefore, had very little to do with the actual hill and everything to do with what was transpiring in their inner world: their comfort with their immediate relationships, the "weight" of their sense of self, as well as their personal history and experience with embracing and taking on physical endeavors in general. Research showed that even though our rational mind is talented at measuring, calculating and figuring the physical world out — and carefully analyzing what it believes is reality — it actually experiences and appraises each moment based on the emotions behind it. Our rational mind so wants to know the truth about that hill, but it will never get to the correct steepness calculation until it understands and releases the intelligence stored in the feelings.

Why spend so much time discussing the gap between what our thinking and rational-self experiences and perceives versus the mysterious, unthinking emotions imposing their will on our adult life? Because these powerful, often unwieldy emotions are dictating the movements, reactions, tone, and outcome of all our relationships. Dr. Emily Sterrett perfectly summarizes in *The Science Behind Emotional Intelligence* how these old, stored, and slumbering emotions, once awakened by the natural, impassioned discourse of marriage, send us down a reactionary path that we seem to have no control over: "We are often oblivious to how it is that basic feelings states 'own' how we think (or don't) as we operate on automatic pilot."

Dr. Bruce Lipton concurs, reminding us of how ineffective our rational, executive faculties are at creating more awareness, maturity, understanding, and healthy perspectives in our life and marriage in the face of these unrevealed and unexamined feelings bubbling below. In *Biology of Beliefs*, he says, "The truth is that you are not controlling your life, because your subconscious mind supersedes all conscious control. So when you are trying to heal from a conscious level — citing affirmations and telling yourself you're healthy — there may be an invisible subconscious program that's sabotaging you." Our logical self cannot do this life on its own, it needs help.

Sounds dire, this "superseding of control" of our sensibly constructed adult life to these unknowable childhood fears and longings. Downright unfair and, well, illogical. No wonder so many marriages fail. Who can blame those folks? It is not their fault, right? That is what Lipton is inferring, right?

Your Marriage and its Friction are the Work

Wrong. This just in, hope is everywhere. Your marriage, and all the emotional friction it generates in you, is the instrument, altar, and arena that will release you from the grip your feeling-experiences have on you. The friction you are experiencing with your spouse — the anger, the frustration with his boyish insecurity — are all catalysts and siren calls to do the work on yourself. Your spouse might change, grow up, and learn to perceive your needs and sensitivities, or he might not. Or she might not. But you cannot change your spouse's actions and reactions. Since you cannot change them, use them. Use your reactions to your spouse as the reflection pools for your intuiting of the joy, sadness, regrets, and longings that are breathing inside.

The agitation and resistance you have for the other are there to expose you to you. Without marriage, its irritations, and the vulnerabilities it incites, those unconscious pains, regrets and joys in you would never be fully roiled and dislodged. Without the late night, fatigue-infused debate about who will feed your eleven-month-old and take out the dog, or the intrusive mother-in-law to wake up your insecurities, the opportunity for maturity is less. Maturing is bringing these old reactions up and owning them.

In the endless battleground of love and joy within all the friction of the field of marriage, man and woman become who they are each supposed to be. The exercise and work of marriage is the place for you to reach your full potential.

The upsetting comments your girlfriend hurls at you is the universe's message that you still have not confronted anger and self-esteem issues fomented in the SIB when you were eight years old. "You will have to face the basic discomfort and dissatisfaction that is the hidden texture of your life," Deida writes in *The Way of the Superior Man*.

We know that all the aches and shame living deep in the well of the midbrain and heart are slumbering. You need these to be shaken. Invite the chance to be challenged, exposed, and betrayed in order to find release and resurrection.

"These obstacles, these boundaries, these limitations are essential for the journey of the universe and you itself."

— Brian Swimme

Friction, Oh Friction

Friction and resistance are two of the most significant phenomena of the physical world. Enrico's Fermi's Second Law of Thermodynamics states that there is a natural tendency for the energy in all things to move and progress towards increasing disorder, moving into a state of what scientists call entropy. Entropy is when an object has used all its own fuel in its continual and natural opposition and resistance to the objects it encounters. As it resists, its original form dissipates and changes, therefore entering into a more disordered state.

If a hot and cold object interact, for example, eventually the hot cools and the cold warms up. The two equalize their energy over time and this natural state of distributed energy will be maintained. Everything that exists is under the spell of this Second Law of Thermodynamics, including your marriage.

The Big Law

The minister or friend who wed you should have read, as part of the marital vows, the definition of this Second Law. No escaping this friction stuff. It needs to be discussed and embraced and more seriously reckoned with.

All life emerged and exists because opposites collide. Albert Szent-Györgyi says, "To regulate something always requires two opposite factors." It is not like this science was on your mind, though, when you were choosing the venue of your wedding, but the Second Law was certainly following you around and down the aisle. It eventually, quietly tip toed its way into the holiday and vacation plans with the in-laws and long discussions about household finances.

Resistance is built into the map of relationships so that we crack open. Because we care, because we want our marriage to work, we inexorably pour ourselves into our marriage. There is nothing more frustrating than a stuck marriage.

That is why the emotional friction in a marriage is so intense. All the disagreements. The disappointment you feel when your boyfriend or husband is unable to listen, to really hear what happened to you and not just what happened. You are not looking for the fix, just the quiet and open heart of another so that you can relate, share, and unravel.

Think of all the static and resistance: Your husband challenging your choice of wall paper, kids throwing up at night, insufferable neighbors judging your lawn (or your insecurity about judging it) and then parking in your driveway, your mother-in-law's critiquing of the curtains.

This friction and the discomfort of arguing is one of the top five reasons why marriages fail. In *The Seven Principles for Making Marriage Work,* John Gottman discovered that "69 percent of marital arguments are perpetual and are about the same few topics, while 96 percent of the time you can predict how a conversation will end within the first three minutes." Think of that. Two thirds of the time, married couples debate the same three or four topics.

Gottman is right as well. It is easy to tell how a marital discussion is going to end just by how the first few sentences are received. All we need to know from this research is that you are fighting the math if you hope and wish conflict away, if you hole yourself up in the tired and timeworn mistruths that marriage is about love and flowers and smoothing over the potholes. Flowers and love are important, but without understanding your entropy — what is being opened, shifted, and seeking its release from your feeling-reactions — the resistance is going to shut you down.

The hit parade of major topics my wife and I have battled over are my driving habits, in-laws, approaches to disciplining the kids, spending habits, and household clutter.

Friction creates energy, space, growth and movement. It was only when I stopped hesitating to bring up the difficult topics with my wife, which I knew were going to start the inevitable argument, that our relationship got real.

Use the painful topics to raise up the lament. Joseph Paul Forgas writes that "Studies have shown that sadness is beneficial to us in ways that actually enhance our wellbeing. When we are sad, we can remember details more accurately, have better judgement, and have more motivation than when we are happy."

You Entered as Isolated Systems

There you and your spouse are, intimately entangled in this natural and ineluctable state of unfolding energy exchange and consumption. You each entered marriage as isolated systems, each with a certain level of maturity, understanding of the dynamics of relationships, and each with deep personal histories and plenty of unexpressed and unconscious desires and reaction patterns. As the marriage unfolds, you continually confront each other's stuff, and via this ongoing exchange you release all the stored emotions.

You likely challenge your husband to pay more attention when discussions get deeper, or you question and test your wife's real need for that sixth pair of sneakers. In-laws, kids, neighbors, friends, bosses, your inner child that you had no idea was so insecure and needy, and the mortgage company all seep into your marital orbit, adding more fuel to the endless motion.

Across the friction of marital discourse, the beautiful disorder — and the opportunity to forge new awareness and insights as your energy — gets chipped away. You become less contained and isolated by your old perceptions, self-concept, and interpretations of your partner's actions. The Second Law infers that you two opposing things will continue to interact until all of each of you has been fully released.

Stand in the Fire

We have to keep moving all our individual energy, parts, inner experiences, longings, and unconscious reactions into this friction arena. The evolution of our marriage, as well as the opportunity for each to fulfill individual potential, demands we embrace, celebrate, and exercise behaviors and forces that unearth and release everything we have. Friction is the catalyst, not the impediment. Stay with it.

Stand in the thermodynamic fire of your wife's or girlfriend's displeasure with your lack of responsibility for the domestic chores or your flippant comments about your wife's driving or cooking.

During the early years of my marriage, the Second Law showed me the little boy still living in me, the one still looking for mothering attention and favor. My wife commented one day, "That is your responsibility. You don't need my approval." My heart sunk. I had just finished painting a bedroom wall or trimming the hedges, or some other ordinary and expected domestic exercise. Meanwhile, she was scrambling around with three young kids in tow, twenty-four hours a day with no timeouts, offseason, or holidays.

My level of emotional maturity was borderline high school. I was still learning and experiencing the exhaustive responsibility of being a husband and father, so my boyish heart was reaching for her recognition, the emblem of the doting mother. Her comment was the friction on my heart, which helped me to go further inside and dredge up and recognize the needs and desires of that ten-year-old boy's sensibilities. The thirty-eight-year-old me had to be the one to recognize and honor the big and small accomplishments of all my activities.

By sitting and meditating for hours I felt that ten-year-old's longings to be seen and heard by mature adults. The little boy had natural, unexpressed tears of loneliness, exuberance, and longings to just ride his bike with his dog. He felt nervous and sad and joyous. He did not know exactly how all of this life stuff was going to work, how the adult world really worked, but in union with the thirty-eight-year-old, he seemed relatively okay that over time it would.

The ten-year-old was physically gone, all grown up-ish, but his need for attention was still vital and normal and necessary. The discourse with my wife opened all this potential for awareness. I was harnessing the friction of her words, not fighting them.

Leave Nothing Inside

Marriages fail because one or both people lose the desire to continue releasing themselves into the vessel of the marriage. If you both continue to open — continue to take the anger and frustration stirred up in you by your partner and use strong emotions as catalysts to do therapy, or to sit quietly and listen to what your anger is telling you — then the marriage reaches its full potential. Whatever is left inside and not released into the marriage becomes the impediment to your life's full expression.

In the *Divorce Mediation Project*, 80 percent of divorced men and woman say their marriage broke because they gradually grew apart and lost a sense of closeness, did not feel loved and appreciated. If we do not find the roots of our own anger, frustration, joys and longings, then we cannot understand and be available to our spouse and his anger and joys. We cannot appreciate the other without appreciation for self. That is when the closeness breaks. Be with your own anger in order to get its lesson.

Dance with it, Please

It seems counterintuitive to turn toward this fire and discomfort. But it is our thoughts about the friction, discontent and chaos, and the resultant ache and desire to avoid it that are killing the physical and non-physical spirit of our marriage.

Our marriage ends up looking and feeling like that hill in the experiment. The marriage and the hill are not the issue. It is our belief that since our prior actions to make changes or address issues in the marriage have not worked, then any new advances will also not work. So we stop trying. The weight of our perspectives makes that darn hill and marriage too steep.

Take what your spouse throws at you, though, as if it were a poem, scripture, a new language, or even music. All of these, especially a new language, must be heard and read over and over. Only then can the sensations, wisdom, coding, and classification of the information and message be found, used, understood, and then enjoyed. Absorb with your powerful, conscious, wounded heart. Do not defend with your unwilling brain.

Do the work, commit and invest time, sit quietly and do some therapy, and let your emotional patterns arise and be made conscious. When we avoid the friction of our marriage, we leave pieces of our life unlived, unremembered, and unexplored. "People will do anything, no matter how absurd, to avoid facing their own soul," Carl Jung said. "Who looks outside, dreams; who looks inside, awakes."

Work Your Way into and Through Uneasiness

In my life, marriage, and especially in my counseling practice, I seek to open myself and others up to the beauty, sorrow, and pain of our feelings. Go for a run right now or lift some weights. Do something that stretches and pushes you. Then, immediately after this physical exertion, sit alone. The stimulated endorphins make the sit deeper.

Feel your eight-year-old self and maybe a tear arises. Why? Because in these bodily feeling-experiences lives an intuition. It is a language within sensations that reveals to your rational self the silent truths about why your father and grandfather were unhappy and what you can learn from their lives.

In the body is a silent library of timeless wisdom about you, resting underneath and inside these sensation-feelings. It is another world, just on the other side, trying to surface. It is easy to get to if your dogmatic, skeptical adult brain will let you.

Pay Attention to Something Else for Five Minutes

Close your eyes right now as you sit in your chair. Keep your back straight:

- Put your attention fully on your stomach for 10 seconds, or as long as it takes to actually imagine being inside your stomach as it rises and falls with breath.

- Now put your attention on the front and back of your heart.

- Think and feel how many emotions have traveled through this muscle, how much grief and happiness have been warehoused here over the last thirty-two years, or however old you are.

- A First Century Chinese encyclopedia has identified seven primary emotions in the *Book of Rites*: Joy, anger, sadness, fear, love, disliking, and liking. Imagine how many tiny electrons of these seven have visited your heart. Just open up to this image.

- Now put all your attention on the front and back of your neck, for at least 10-15 seconds.

- Now put all your attention on the middle of your forehead, as you lift your eyeballs up about an inch above your eyebrows, smack in the middle of your forehead. Eyes are still closed.

- Linger and put all your attention right there in what the Hindus call your third eye, for 20-30 seconds, listening to the back and front of your forehead.

- Now, put all your attention onto the top of your head for 30 seconds, listening to this part of your body now.

- Finally, take another 30 seconds and listen to all five parts of the body we just traveled through: stomach, heart, neck, forehead and top of head. See and feel into all of these places.

- Just 30 more seconds: listen as if your body had something to tell you, something to share, recommend, laugh or cry about. It might not right now, but you will never know unless you listen.

This exercise will draw you out of your normal, linear perceptions. It will demand your attention on things that are probably uncomfortable, the endless tug of an inherited self-doubt or possibly self-loathing. The author Jane Roberts talks in *Seth Speaks* about this quiet place when we consciously and actively relax ourselves. She says that you may "become aware of some of the other streams of consciousness... hear words, see images that appear out of context with your own thoughts." Do not get hung up on things like consciousness or any new age hogwash that might come up. Just be in your chair and give me a few more minutes of your time in this locale.

The great thinker and author Eckhart Tolle says that being still like this, "looking and listening activates the non-conceptual intelligence within you. The mind becomes still. A portal is opening up." Trust that you can find this non-conceptual place. Jump into it. It might take a little bit of trust, though, a pinch of faith that sitting there right now will actually help with something. It will, and it might even scare you.

The author Ray Bradbury beckons us in *Fahrenheit 451*, almost teases us to stop fixating on everything that is easy, familiar, and soft: "We are increasingly detached from ourselves, others, and so much of life. The dangerous consequences of our quest for the easy life...cram them full of non-combustible data, chock them so damned full of 'facts' they feel stuffed...they'll feel they're thinking."

With cars these days you barely have to show up: automatic doors and seats, climate control and automatic drive adjustment. Do not get me wrong, safety is essential. But they reflect how we are all looking in the wrong direction, avoiding the aches and simple frictions that make us stronger, more awake.

Got Friction? How About Some Chaos with Your Marriage?

Brian Swimme, one of the greatest minds in the field of cosmology, talks elegantly about the original moment in time when the universe began in his book *The Universe Story*. In every corner of the cosmos was a fiery explosion. After a while as the chaos simmered to slightly less chaos, particles like "protons and neutrons joined and gave way to building blocks of what was more like today's cosmos with hydrogen and helium."

Billions of years later, smart guys with white coats in laps conceptualized these events and framed truths and laws that now govern you and your marriage. You would never imagine as you sit in traffic, with your coffee continually about to crest your mug's rim as you stop and start, that these laws and tendencies were driving your behavior. The probability of you tolerating your husband's grumpy immaturity or your wife's inpatient anxiousness is intimately correlated to these original forces beyond time.

In *The Universe Story,* the universe, like marriage, "is both violent and creative, destructive and cooperative," and like the painful reactions fomented in you, "these obstacles, these boundaries, these limitations are essential for the journey of the universe and you itself." There is a cost to achieving real lasting love: the energy you consume to feel and lean into everything not easy.

Everything, every current member of the cosmos above, below and to your side right now, is going through and experiencing the exact same thing that you are. You, me, the cat, your marriage, the mosquito hankering for my arm outside the window, the stars, fish, and trees — all are just packets of atoms flying around.

Everything is an electron-filled signaling device sending and absorbing bio-electric stuff. Everything is also heading in some direction, going somewhere, becoming something. Everything is in a continual state of becoming more, evolving, just like your marriage. We need the friction, the breaking, the sense of our egoic self being destroyed so that you can feel something richer inside. This in turn allows you to intuit something deeper in your union with your spouse.

Everything Else is in it with Us

The acorn is on its way to being a tree, conspiring with

itself, the soil, sun, and a bit of water to stay alive just long enough to crack open. In *The Universe Story* it is the "third tendency in all things towards fulfillment of their inner nature...in biology this is referred to as the epigenetic pathway folded into a particular ontogeny."

All the roughly thirty trillion cells in the body also all came from the same explosive place and moment a very long time ago. We are in relationship to everything because we all come from the exact same home, same exact spot, all sharing and breathing the same bio-electric magnetic stuff and all instinctually brooding on and wanting the same thing. To finish up, to complete.

The notion that everything is in the same boat has a bit of misery-likes-company aspect to it. In counseling work, especially group therapy, this sense of being similar to others is one of the most powerful tools. It is called *normalizing*. When people share their stories with others, they feel less abnormal. They recognize themselves and their issues within others. It helps lighten the senses of overwhelming, loneliness, and the frustration of going it alone. Lean into the intensity of the journeys of all living things on the planet, like a seed or a bird huddled in a storm, so that you take more time to appreciate and accept the discomforts you experience in your marriage.

Three Questions

When my wife threw that plate at my head in front of GM Betty nineteen years ago, it was my first experience with unbridled, emotional disorder in a relationship. Because I had already started cracking open my sensibilities through the practice of meditation, I had a vague sense of what she was going through.

My wife was trying to express thirty years of frustration. I knew I was on her list of culprits, those who had resisted and impeded her in some way. More importantly, beyond this moment of her blinding anger, I embraced my role in her life and our partnership unfolding, and how my inner world was going to be positively impacted. I saw and welcomed friction, chaos, anger, hate, sorrow and regret as natural and universal companions to an intense love that my wife and I were going to encounter.

A few years later, I started asking questions about what was important to me. These three came up:

1. Did I really dance with all the friction in my life?

2. Was I brave enough to stand in the fire of my reactions so I could understand what I absorbed and inherited from childhood, and why I act the way I do?

3. Did I really own my stuff, my boyish reactions, learn from them and carry this wisdom back to those I loved?

CHAPTER 5
THE EIGHT RELATIONSHIPS OF MARRIAGE

Charmed Life, Some Missing Pieces

"Men are mules," thought Margaret O'Connell as she walked home from work in 1929. O'Connell was the grandmother of James, my forty-three-year-old counseling client. She died in 1972 when James was five, but her life and the events and people in it were still breathing in him. He remembered her line about the mules.

James was struggling at work and was becoming increasingly frustrated and confused with his marriage. It was his reactions to his wife that troubled him the most. It was also her recent behavior, especially her mean-spirited outbursts towards him and their two children.

By our third counseling session, we started moving the conversation away from the current characters and events that were creating his discomfort, instead focusing on the sensations and flashes coming up in him around these topics. The events and people in our life-story are not the issue. It is how we feel about ourselves in reaction to them.

He began to realize that most of his stress about his job and marriage came from an undercurrent of anxiousness about money, a gnawing sense of unease and lack. He said it felt like somehow, just around the corner, something adverse was going to happen involving loss.

It was a latent, quiet aching lack of abundance which arose mostly when thinking of the success of friends and colleagues, or whenever his wife wistfully regretted not having something that her friends had. "There are times when I wonder how I am going to keep this ship rolling," he said, "this whole suburban Home Inc. thing. Never ending bills, private school, f-ing cell phones that cost $350 a month, all of it."

"Where in your body do you feel this ache?" I had him shut his eyes, do a few deep breaths, and then go back into a recent scene where he and his wife were overreacting to each other.

"I don't know where, probably my stomach, like a lump. My heart flutters too, like it is worried about something that I don't even know," he explained. He was hot on the trail, his life the best show in town, the only channel to watch and follow. As he relaxed and unfolded his body more, he started talking about his parents. There was a sense and anxiousness around loss when growing up. "I've never really lost much, always been pretty successful," he explained, "but it's like a shadow of discomfort. Probably why I liked to smoke, maybe trying to kill that angst."

He mentioned his wife's intuition was probably picking up his fear as well, which made her unconsciously uncomfortable. Woman take care of the nest, and if they sense a weakening in the masculine or even a small threat to their circle, their nurture-survival enzymes can animate a bio-genetic spirit of fear and frustration that alchemizes to anger. That anger can be a catalyst to waking the masculine up. At first the boy in the man kicks back and fights it, not seeing through it. That is a heavy bite of friction for the suburban dad, but it is the best medicine.

Archeology of an Emotion

The steady, uncomfortable current of scarcity that James felt in his stomach and chest became the locale where we focused our attention. Over two more sessions, and in his listening by himself at home, he began to sense a bodily unease around lack much older than he thought. We talked at length about his parents' lives, but more importantly and poignantly we talked about his grandparents.

What he was about to recognize was that there was a singular, historical moment that created a deep, emotional fracture in his relatives. This event some eighty years ago, and all the ensuing emotional reactions, flowed down bio-magnetically into his kitchen, into him, and into his marriage. Like in archeology, James was going to discover an ancient, original catalyst for his reactions towards his marriage. By finding and understanding it, he will be able to uproot and unwind its deleterious impact.

Did all of our parents and relatives, through the electro-magnetic storage and releasing of emotions, unsuspectingly bestow their lives across our kitchen tables and holiday meals? After all, early emotional experiences knit patterns into a brain's neural networks.

Marriage is Eight Relationships All at Once

I believe this knitting holds the answers. Each of us have deeply ingrained response habits, triggers, patterns, and behaviors from what we witnessed, inherited, experienced, and bio-magnetically imbibed from four vital, core, and universal relationship patterns from our youth.

I believe there are four distinct relationship patterns

knitted and living inside of me that create all my marital reactions to my wife. I call these inherited, relational patterns archetypes. These four archetypes are our relationship with and experience with other men, other women, marriage, and self.

Carl Jung, one of the first to study human archetypes, said in *The Structure and Dynamics of the Psyche,* these learned and ingrained psychological and emotional response patterns are "primordial images, fundamental units of the human mind."

Living inside of all of us are these basic reactions to men and the masculine force, women and the feminine, how we latently understand and behave in a relationship, and finally how we conceive of and perceive ourselves.

I have carried all four of these automatic reaction patterns into my marriage. My wife unwittingly brought her four as well. Marriage is the confluence of these four patterns, therefore eight relationships at once.

Who knew marriage was an algebra equation? It is the arena for these eight unconsciously sourced relationships to be exposed, wrestled with, and reconciled. I tell my couples clients that their marriage is not a simple dyad, one person interacting with another over time. It is a system of currents. Family coming over for the holidays, for instance, kicks in one or two of these inner four archetypes in your husband, as he is lightly undermined or even belittled by his mother-in-law. Or the wife, not being asked by some friends to attend a neighborhood party, could feel that elementary school-aged sense of being left out. This old wounded perception of self, which influences how she parents, is one of four key archetypes.

These archetypes or energetic patterns are your

dominant, mostly unconscious and automatic response impulses and imprints. Each of these is being activated at different times.

Margaret J. Wheatley writes in *Beyond Einstein*, "everything in the universe only exists because it is in relationship to everything else...acquisition of knowledge of any kind occurs only with an energy transfer, storage of information, whether in a computer disk or in our brain". It is paramount that we examine how these four relational patterns get released into our marriage, imposing their unconscious will over our helpless logic.

Why is it so Difficult?

This is another reason why marriage is hard. You were a good student, went to a good school. You get it, have had a couple of well-paying jobs since college, took your time to meet the right person, got married, bought the house, moved to the suburbs, had kids.

But a relationship is nothing that you have ever encountered because your lower brain is storing these four, latent, ingrained patterns of responses that our rational self is so innocently unaware of. Our logic walks us through our day, but how we respond in each moment is determined by these ingrained patterns.

A relationship is a progression over and into time. It is bigger, though, than just the two of you in it. It is the vessel through which the next generation forms. The sustenance and force that carries the successful relationship forward is the belief that tomorrow is better, that I am better heading into posterity, and that my grandkids' grandkids are better off if I am supported, loved, and challenged by my spouse in this relationship.

Mice Brains, Long Memories

Science has explored and confirmed that we really are living remnants, newer branches jutting from an old tree of our relatives' lives. We are unique, will-infused, and powerfully independent branches, but projections nonetheless.

In a longitudinal study reported in *Nature Magazine*, "Fearful Memories Passed Down to Mouse Descendants," researchers quite cruelly shocked mice every time acetophenone, a scent often compared to almonds or cherries, was introduced to them. It became apparent over time that their offspring were deeply affected by this scent, reacting the same way even though they were born long after the experiment. "A third generation of mice — the 'grandchildren' — also inherited this reaction," the study reported, "as did mice conceived through *in vitro* fertilization with sperm from males sensitized to acetophenone."

The lower brains of these mice were building up neuron receptor proteins that were hyper-sensitive to this smell. It is like a callus or the constant rain runoff of my neighbor's gutter onto my side lawn. Conditioned neurons and rainwater both carve a rutted path, making a person and a lawn more susceptible to the same actions and reactions. The fix is in, as both nature and our brains are so obstinate in their proclivities and urges.

The complexity, power, and transformative nature of neurons are powerful. The sensitivity to that acetophenone is now inexorably ingrained in these next generation of mice because the parent mice's chemo-electrical connection sends signals across to the next generation. It is just like getting a better reception from certain channels, back when TVs had antennas. Parents created the station and program, and that specific signal they send is readily, unconsciously, and bio-magnetically received by those who come next.

Einstein alluded to the wonderful, mysterious, and animating mix of forces that we are. He wrote in his *Special Theory of Relativity* that "human beings are half biological, but the other half is energy."

Energy is an overused word, indefinite and too esoteric for those who want hard evidence why their marriage is not working. Energy just does not cut it for many, either as an explanation for their boyfriends' imbecility or for a wife's short temper. But in order to know what is driving behaviors, we need to use the same tool and resources that delivered these patterns. We need to put our adult attention in the physical stream of these old emotions and energy. This allows us to listen to them tell their story to our rational brain.

That is why a successful and mature marriage demands that we remember, reexamine, and relive old moments. When we know the root moment and can feel the charge, we can begin to biophysically, emotionally, and psychologically accept it. We then integrate the knowledge into the fabric of our life now, like Laurie did. If we can therapeutically and consciously re-feel, retell, and understand our ancestors' past — not just our own — instead of letting their lives unconsciously slumber and undermine our behaviors, we can become our ancestors. We can retain their gifts and strengths, but let their uncompleted charges go.

We'll honor our ancestors and change future generations by allowing the old stories to rise, releasing their electromagnetic ghosts and dents. Then, absorb the wisdom. Exorcising and intuiting this past invite true knowledge.

James's emotional life was about to change as he not only remembers his grandfather's story, but allows it to consciously pour through his heart, then mind. This is not theory or just thoughts. Your chance of being in a relationship that lasts is based on a willingness to create space inside so that your ancestors' experiences are not unconsciously repeated, but transformed into your present by intuitive awareness.

A Deep Discontent

Over a few more counseling sessions, James continued to pour his attention into his emotional and energetic response to money and his sense of self at work. He said there was a longing in him, a faint and insistent discontent and unease around his work life. His twenty-year marketing and management career had been successful. He understood and read people well. He had a good feel for when clients and prospects were open to his input and prodding and when to back off. He knew getting clients to buy was always an exercise and dance around trust, motivation, needs, desires, and timing, and he liked the psychology of this.

Although he liked what he did, he never loved it. He liked people, but there was a small hole in his heart and in his sense of self. There was a haunt of doubt and concern that some kind of misfortune was imminent and a regret for somehow being in a career that precluded him from contributing to the world and community. He always wanted to be a coach, "But try paying a mortgage and the water and grocery bills for hungry mouths in suburbia on a coach's take-home," he said.

He loved his wife, kids, friends, and family. From the outside he lived a charmed suburban life, filled with vacations, parties, and all the smiles and tears tied to kids' soccer games and movie nights, the disorderly family dinners, and bedtime reading sessions that a father could ever want. Besides the recent long moments of resentful banter with his wife, eating at their shared trust and camaraderie, he felt life was good. He even celebrated the fact that he drove a minivan. Clearly, he had drank the suburban Kool-Aid and was all in on his family world.

He quietly cheered at times, though, for the stock market to go down so that his overall sense of feeling less-than, compared to others, would lighten. He felt the stock market was the great collective conscience, a barometer of wellbeing, and if it could just creep down sometimes, he could feel richer due to others feeling slightly poorer.

Stocks down, his sense of self up. That was a psycho-emotional equation he knew was off. Looking for lack was, obviously, keeping away the very thing he wanted: abundance. A sensibility that cheers for scarcity likely emerged from an old place of loss and defeat. He was about to find out where this fear of loss came from, where the roots lived and breathed. It was going to blow him away.

"Cherokee women's close association with nature, as

mothers and producers, served as a basis of their power within the tribe."

— Theda Perdue

Our Spouse is the Spark

So often it was his wife's spending patterns that heightened his sensations of lack. She would come home with another living room lamp or more plastic toys that he knew his kids would quickly discard. Or she would overstock the refrigerator with food that ended up rotten, curled, and stiff. "How many new lamps do we need," he asked me, "how many heads of lettuce do you think I have thrown out in the last five years? It drives me crazy."

As we continued to seek out and focus on his bodily sensations of frustration, he knew the food and lamps were triggers. The spending actions of his wife were poking those lumps of loss in his stomach. He described it as nausea, subtle pangs of fear as he carried grocery bags into the kitchen. It was a sense of scarcity that bellowed from his gut and soaked his hips and legs. They felt hollow. It felt like running scared while standing still.

In *Molecules of Emotions*, Candace Pert writes, "Every change in the mental-emotional state causes a change in the body physiology." Our bodies are tied to some historical event that has been captured electrically and neuro-chemically within our mid-brain and stomach. It is stored as a fear-loss neuron signal.

The single event or a series of similar events are long gone, dusty and forgotten to our active, rational, and practical mind. Why is our rational brain not able to foresee or prevent such outbursts? Because when emotions run too strongly, our rational brain shuts down. The pesky amygdala, which is a cluster of neurons connecting the mid-brain to our left brain, prevents "new data from going into the prefrontal...kicking in the hypothalamus, where higher levels of noradrenaline are produced, in turn impairing the prefrontal cortex regulation," writes Patrik Vuilleumier in *How Brains Beware: Neural Mechanisms of Emotional Attention*.

In other words, James's old emotions around fear alight a physical response that bypasses and overwhelms his rational, forty-three-year-old brain and sensibilities. Something associated with the past "can bypass the brain's executive functions almost entirely as we find ourselves exploding or sweating in dread," says Dr. Sterrett in *The Science Behind Emotional Intelligence*. James' trepidation about his family's material and financial future then hit overwhelm, even though that adult-aged, rational piece of himself knew his reaction was excessive. Their bank statements did not merit this fear, but off he went. He would continue to confront her spending.

"I can imagine how this questioning of her ends," I said.

"Yeah, she gives me that look, the 'are you retarded' look."

To me, her reaction makes sense. I believe she continually feels overworked, underappreciated, and creatively stifled by all the basic demands of mothering. I can imagine the bouquet of belittlement and anger she hands back to James.

"Instead of complaining about money James, go make more," she often told him. "You have no idea how little I spend compared to other moms," she'd add. He said from that point the conversation often devolved into her recanting his unwise business decisions, the bosses he pissed off, and his general lack of adult commitment to his career.

Releasing Others, Turning In

His comments elevated her concern for the sturdiness of her nest and jolted the trust she wanted to bequeath him. He knew his wife had nothing to do with his reactions.

His glance at a single receipt from Macy's would trigger a marital brushfire. He would query her purchase, which then created a twinge of doubt in her about whether she needed that item. Her doubt became frustration about his lack of trust in her decisions. Suddenly, she would leverage her feminine, emotional memory, drawing from history and return fire with a wry and sarcastic comment. "Those jabs hurt," he said, "because she was right. I realized her doubt and fear about me, my ability to excel, were lingering inside. I guess they only come out when I lash at her."

She was calling up an adolescent immaturity and boyish need in James to be recognized by a matriarchal figure. It is one thing for the masculine to feel less than and small in isolation. It is a much heavier weight when the wife's misgivings are stacked on top.

At one point, with his shoulders slumped, emasculated with head in hand, he looked up and said, "Ya know, all I ever wanted was to be a f-king coach and teacher, maybe own a restaurant. It's like shadow boxing in a career waiting for something else to show up."

Marriage draws us to the edge of whether or not we are able to own everything that we feel. Your spouse will draw you to a feeling state where walking away makes the most sense, since he or she is hurting you. We push away the other because of the awakened feelings and aches from long ago. Oh, mighty friction!

But those are the inflection points. They are designed to push you back into your forgotten world of desires, love, and anger. James had no intention of giving up. He said there had to be more to this story. "It's like ghosts battling through my marriage," he said. He felt that long shadows and memories were creating these profound responses. He went from feeling like a forty-three-year-old adult to a fourteen-year-old kid right there in his kitchen. He said they seemed to be reenacting the debates they witnessed growing up, the ones their parents had.

Bingo! We had a winner.

Back Up Stream

James was willing to do the work to open himself up. Once again, Marlow's words from *Heart of Darkness* about the river bounced in the back of my skull. "Our family's lives must be drawn back up from the well of time," I thought.

When another person or client is willing to jump in, sit quietly for long periods, to grab an oar and canoe back up into her inner history, it is a celebration for me. When one of my counseling clients realizes that the friction of marriage is arousing his or her deep-seated and unconscious experiences, the world slows down, smiles, and becomes softer and smaller to me. It makes the hours of all my work worthwhile.

Even when only one person decides to wake up, seek greater awareness, and shift their bio-magnetic current, it positively impacts those around her. Chaos theory tells us this: "One flap of a seagull's wing would be enough to alter the course of the weather forever" say Edward Lorenz in *The Predictability of Hydrodynamic Flow*. The smallest actions or perturbations in someone's energy and sense of self can create huge alterations in the systems they interact with.

For me, talking to someone else about everything that is nonphysical and non-linear creates a camaraderie, a kinship. My life goal is to help others wake the inner hero who will find meaning within all the unleashed emotions, within the tears, joy, and certainties of knowing why and how our feeling world formed.

James, through our deep relaxation work, his hours of sitting, journaling, talking to his parents, and writing out his story and origins, began to realize that his wife, like all partners, is an echo, a mirror, the catalyst, and his chosen awakener of his four archetypes. Only by slowing down and going into your cave does this realization occur.

Four Universal Relationships Within Us

The banks of a river are ever in contact and communication with the water, continually shaped, reformed, and crafted from that incessant current. We are those riverbanks; the continuum of our life is the water. James is an accumulation of the streams of psycho-emotional experiences washed down from his family and his grandparents, layered with old moments that are stored in the heart, stomach, and limbic brain.

As Christopher Bache explains in *Lifecycles*, you are an "aggregation of life experiences stored in your limbic body. This moment now is not independent in time, but part of a casual chain rooted deep in your inner history." More specifically, we have unconsciously carried and dragged our archetypes into our marriages.

Carl Jung explains in *The Structure and Dynamics of the Psyche* that these patterns "are the living system of reactions and aptitudes that determine the individual's life in invisible ways." They are invisible until they manifest, often loudly as surprising responses to your spouse.

"Your environment...is an expression of an archetype."
— Carl Jung

The Four Archetypes, That Make up the Eight Relationships of Marriage

1st Archetype: Relationship to Feminine:

This is our relationship to and with the original mother or matriarchal figure while growing up. It is how we responded to our mother or dominant mothering force (grandparent, aunt); how we experienced her actions, reactions, and her sense of herself which informs, clouds, or inspires our experience and responses to all women — and to the general feminine qualities of intuition, emotion, nurturance, vulnerability, creativity, and patience within ourselves and our world.

This relationship to the feminine also incorporates and embodies our deeper longings and responses to the goddess spirit or the symbol and ideals of the divine feminine. In every human lives an intangible experience with the eternal yin, with this most ancient home, entrance point, and physical and emotional place of origin that are our mother.

Deida writes in *The Way of the Superior Man*, "The feminine in all her forms is the ultimate inspiration. All of nature is summarized in her body, her moods, her energy. However, if we don't understand who she really is, we will only fear and desire her. We will hurt her, negate her, exploit her and run from her." James loved and had a deep frustration with his mother. She was inexhaustibly creative but was not fully happy in her life and marriage. The incompleteness of that relationship — along with the emotional passivity and timidity of his father — led to his mom cajoling and browbeating his father.

She never fully addressed her inner, young girl need for her father's full attention through her post-depression era childhood. She needed a mature male force that could challenge her, one that would never change his mind just to please her.

James's father was a good, conscientious, and hardworking man, but his wife wanted him to strive for more, to push out more into his career. She outwardly settled for his modest, mission-like life, but this unconsciously stunted her giving of her fullest love and passion, and exacerbated a deeper longing for a masculine that could match and unwind her longing to release her creativity.

For James and his siblings, there was a palatable residue of the incomplete feminine desire and search for love within the psychological and emotional storyline of their home. That feminine dominance, almost bullying over the masculine, created a defensiveness in James that he never knew he had.

Magic and Aversion

For all humans, when we are not creating and feeling whole in our lives, we often turn to judging and criticizing. For females, the stunting of the creative energy, which is their core and gift, can lead to intensive judging, sarcasm, and pinching of those around them. James's mother was a bit of a pincher. That is why there was an active resistance in James to his wife's questioning and criticizing of him.

He began to sense that he cherished the magic and beauty of the opposite sex, experienced originally in the wonder that his mother held for him when young — but that he also reviled the cutting cynicism and subtle biting witnessed in childhood. In him there lived a dichotomous union of wonder and anger, respect and contempt, as well as a desire to both please and escape the mothering force.

It is important to realize that what matters is our experience with these four archetypes, how we relate to the female energy, in this case. Your siblings, friends, and indeed your parents may have completely different reactions to the same historical events. All your family members, including your mother, might completely disagree with your perspective, which often is the case. That does not matter.

What matters is the unlocking of how each archetype filters through into the present. What we wanted originally from each of these four ingrained relationships — what we received or did not get, how we trusted, loved, related to, ran from, cried for and eventually learned from a mother archetype — that is what we carried into our adult world and our marriage.

Three weeks after that session with James, when he realized his behavior towards his wife had washed down from his foundational early years with his mother, he started sitting in his living room at night when the family was asleep. Sitting in the dark one night, he drifted back to when he was eight years old. Like a movie scene, memories floated behind his eyes and in his heart. They became animated. They were not thoughts; they were happening in the present. While in them he found and sensed an old pool of sympathy for his dad, for all men. It was an unfolding of times back in his house when he was a boy. He could actually feel and sense the eight-year-old boy within his father's heart being overly mothered by James mom's domineering presence.

In other words, the forty-three-year-old James returned to the vibrations and sensations in the hallway and living room of his house in the Seventies and sensed the young boy yearnings in his then fifty-year-old father. He said that from this sensation — accompanied by a few tears of sadness for the lost, sad, and confused boy in him, and in all men — he knew why he always had a distaste for any kind of feminine mockery or sarcasm directed towards men.

Yes, all men have rich and unprocessed pockets of immaturity, and so they act like boys throughout their lives. James begrudgingly admitted this. But his frustration with the female archetype seemed to be in defense of his father, which he realized was also him guarding his own inner boy-self from that biting, mysterious, and divine feminine force. The matriarchal love and embrace he so wanted was also the force he pushed the hardest against.

The battle James was waging with his wife was him shadow boxing with these old, unresolved experiences and feelings: how he was mothered, how wives treat husbands, and what females meant to him. These sensibilities long predated his marriage, having nothing to do with his wife, and yet ruled so many of his reactions.

Her Dance with Female Archetype

His wife Paula's relationship to the female archetype, her mother, was different. She was always dutiful in her outward respect for her mother, following a long tradition in her culture of dogmatic honor of parents and ancestors. But that respect for her mother gave way as Paula became an adult, yielding to a distaste and condemnation of her mother's passivity and a lazy lack of assertiveness when confronting both her life and her husband.

Paula was deeply frustrated with how her father treated her mother, but ironically directed more of that resentment towards her mom. Why? Her mother allowed her husband to suppress and neglect her creative abundance. Paula then followed her mother's lead and allowed her dad to corral her own artistic urges. She realized her mother's life was not easy. But the victim-like passivity and the modeling of this female archetype during her formative years left a mark on Paula that read, "If you are a male, I will not tolerate any boyish behavior, especially the kind that holds me back."

Paula's dad loved her mom, but he was not mature enough to bridle his grumpy little boy energy, and too often he was inattentive and dismissive. Paula wanted her mother to stand up to him. She wanted her dad to grow up, not drink and smoke as much, but there was little she could do as the daughter.

She wanted her mom to work more at addressing and finding her own power within this broken marital field. But Paula's mom gave up and receded, avoiding the conflict which perpetuated and allowed the immature masculine to pervade the home. This created an edge in Paula, a thin tolerance for boyishness, accompanied with a resolve to defend the matriarchal domain.

Paula erupted when James questioned her spending. It awoke her defense of the feminine need to shape and create new things, which shopping is correlated to. She was pissed at her mom, deep down, for not owning her feminine. Paula was even more angry at her dad for not manning up, getting at his real mission beyond fishing, football games, and filling his unlived life with cigarettes.

"The search for freedom is the priority of the masculine."
— David Deida

Second Archetype, Relationship to Masculine

The second of the four critical, inevitable, immortal, and universal relationships that we all must recognize, peel back, and embrace is our relationship to the father or male archetype. This archetype, like the female, stores not only our actual and mundane experience of and interactions with our father. It also stores our deeply held beliefs, loves, hopes and fears around all heroes, soldiers, historical leaders and pioneers — and dare I say gods and deities.

Things like forcefulness, valor, guidance, caretaking of family, honoring of ideals and ancestral ways, strength, and vision are often conjured when we initially meditate on the word "father."

2nd Archetype: Relationship to Masculine:

How we respond to and what we experienced from our father, or the original, central male figure in our life when growing up, now informs and shades our reactions to males and the masculine qualities of directedness, assertiveness, purpose, challenges, discipline, and self-sacrifice.

Who your dad was to you, how you embraced, feared, or rejected him, and your general sensibilities towards and with men in general, informs how you currently engage your life. So often, we are not conscious of these sensibilities, but our partner will and does become very aware of how the current of the male archetypes seeps out from us.

The masculine way in the home, a.k.a. the father and husband, needs to be grounded in a sense of wholeness and completion. The male needs to feel whole. Moreover, the father/male grounding in self and the archetypical energy that he presents in his home is the framework from which his kids go out into the world. How he behaves socially sets the tone of how his kids interact and are attuned to their communities.

For many wives, this maleness can show up in their husbands as a boyish pride or acute sensitivity to criticism. "He may be all business and ironed shirt during the day," one wife quipped in a recent couple's session, "but when I question how he wastes time on the weekends watching sports, or how he defends his nosey, doting mother, he becomes the spoiled ten-year-old that his mom built."

Dad Ghost

James had witnessed such an automatic and frayed irritation in his wife with regard to her father that he joked, "It's like her dad is standing in the kitchen next to me as she yells, and he's been dead for like sixteen years." He knows Paula is very sensitive to any of his inattentiveness or seemingly innocuous moments of forgetfulness, especially when he forgets to tell her one of his friends will be stopping by the house for a drink. "I might as well have told her that zombies were a block away," he says. She tells him it's not his friends visiting that is the issue; it is a lack of respect for her. She wants the house, which is a reflection of her and the feminine presence, to look presentable.

"Her father was a real pisser towards her, her brothers, and her mom," he explained, "and I'm sure I deserve plenty of that old anger. But some of this stuff spilling out of her, the intensity, short fuses, just seems old."

He was starting to perceive that her mid-brain neurons, born and brewed back in the Seventies and Eighties, were calloused from witnessing an abundance of masculine obliviousness to and negligence of her mom's basic needs. Women, in general, want to be heard, understood, and to be offered their own flexibility with time and space. Ironically, all her mom wanted — what all women want — is to have their perspectives honored and not to be forced into taking action when not fully prepared.

Paula was not conscious of these basic, universal desires when she was young. These are not analytical concepts and psychological equations that teenagers can recite. She just felt, when she was young, that her father should have paid more emotional attention to her mother. But he did not, and that experience of male thoughtlessness animated and embodied her response patterns with the male archetype in her marriage. James received chunks of that feminine frustration as a result of what his father-in-law could not deliver.

In *The Way of the Superior Man*, Deida explores at great length the foundational, universal qualities of the masculine. He delves into the roots of this half of our species, how in their basic form, men tend to be mission-based. "The search for freedom is the priority of the masculine. For the masculine, mission, competition, and putting it all on the line — indeed, facing death — are all forms of ecstasy. Witness the masculine popularity of war stories, dangerous heroism, and sports playoffs."

Exploring the male archetype for men, married men especially, is a meditation and reflection on who our fathers are and were. How did they feel about themselves and their fathers? What was their comfort level with other men, with women, and what was their maturity level — which as we know is a measure of how aware we are of own our emotions and reactions? How much did our fathers own and take responsibility for every part of their lives, and what kind of confidence did they have when engaging the world and womankind? How willing were they to be open and vulnerable, and what was their disposition towards the matriarchs, their wives and mothers?

Heading Upstream

James had started this inquiry, up Conrad's river. He had begun to casually ask his parents more questions about their parents. He could not necessarily describe it. But he told me he had a vague sense that some of his deepest and basic inclinations, emotional inhibitions, and instinctual trepidations — especially and particularly around career and material abundance — emerged from events and moments even older than his parents.

Growing up, his family was comfortable in the middle class. The gap between rich and poor in the Seventies and Eighties was much thinner. Everyone they knew seemed like them, in the middle. He and his siblings never lacked anything. What he experienced, though, was an echo, an ancestral tendency or shadow of loss breathing within his father. There was a dialect of worry in his body language, words, and questions. There was a spirit around and towards money that seemed so thickly tied to basic survival, which he knew had roots in his dad's depression-era childhood. That made sense to him.

But James perceived that these sensations of loss in his dad were echoes of something even older than him. He wanted to understand these incessant bubblings of fear that seemed to have a life and consciousness of their own, that prevented him from relaxing into this life.

James realized that his reactions to his marriage, to his role of father and caretaker, the spending his wife did, and her calling him out, were all keeping this inherited, bio-magnetic dread and anxiousness alive in him.

"Intuition, by a strange sympathy, sees Reality in its totality, while thought chops it up into parts."
— Paramahansa Yogananda

Grandparents' World Still Alive

The disposition of the male archetype in James resonated with imminent and impending failure that he was inexorably passing down to his kids. This desire to change the generational course of this archetype compelled him to begin having long conversations with his relatives, going through old family photos, and meditating every night. During one of our intense counseling sessions, he described a dream where his grandfather showed up wearing a top hat and tails, but naked from the waist down. The setting was a stock and currencies market trading office on Wall Street in the Thirties. James could not explain the imagery, but he recognized the contrasting emotions of emasculation, exhilaration of speculating, fear, and anticipation.

In our next session he put it all together.

Just like everyone else, his grandfather lost everything on October 29, 1929. But James finally perceived that the electro-magnetic imprint from that loss in 1929 was the source moment and catalyst for his hidden disquietude. It was an emotional shadow of indebtedness that stirred a sense of his life being on loan. He always felt undeserving of money and bounty. It was right and just to sacrifice more of himself, give more and blood-let, just to earn his allotted share.

Many people and their offspring recovered from that

event, but many had not. His experience of the male archetypic was shadowed by that event. Had he inherited this dented self-worth? At times he could conjure an inner nobility — but in the light of day, his emotional self too often retreated to a peasant's disposition and allotment. He could not figure out why.

He wrote a story of what he thought his grandfather, Timothy O'Connell, experienced that fateful Tuesday. He wanted to write it out so that he could let it breathe. He extrapolated what both of his grandparents went through. He had read some of his grandmother's journal entries. He'd spent hours reviewing old photos and letters that were piled up in his uncle's basement. There were also sensations and intuition that stirred anciently in him through hours of sitting that seasoned his story.

Hard to Move On

This is what he wrote:

"Men are mules," thought Margaret O'Connell, as she walked home from work at about 7 p.m. on October 29, 1929. She had heard from her colleagues at the hospital, where she was a nurse, that the stock market had fallen. It had been dropping for a few days.

She could see and feel others' concern as she started her walk home. It was an uncomfortable sensation, but she worked daily amidst misfortune and sickness. Financial loss is painful, but it, unlike much of her patients' physical woes, would heal.

Margaret had a Gaelic passion that rarely flinched. She was in continual service to her family and community as a nurse and administrator. She shared her opinions and beliefs with a rigor and a smidgeon of feminine moxie that was emphatically ahead of its time. She knew things would get better. She knew her husband was going to take it much harder.

The air turned thinner for my grandfather as she walked through the front door. He was sitting in the living room. Stabs of gray regret pushed his shoulders forward when his wife Margaret looked at him, disappointed but not accusatory. She knew the look would not help, even though she had been telling him for months to sell everything. Adding to the pall was the fact he was even managing some of her family's money.

They both heard the echo of her pleas to sell their stocks when their eyes met, but he knew she would never replay those words or judge him. She knew he was steeped in enough disgrace.

Timothy had always seemed a man destined for bigger things. His grandfather was a farmer who had left Ireland sometime in the 1840's. Timothy was anxious to shed his family's long, rural roots, so he bypassed college and entered the local Albany banking trade in 1921. The years that followed were good for him and many Americans, especially those that lent money. He was a reserved man, judicious with his emotions and money, and easily discomforted by the belittling and skeptical glances of his non-Irish Catholic peers. His lack of a college degree exacerbated that doubt and insecurity.

He, like many Irish Catholic executives back then, felt like an outsider, warily elbowing his way into the boardroom terrain of the established Protestant and Jewish moneychangers. There was always a latent, almost gnawing sense in him that an accumulation of personal wealth would be a victory not just for his self-worth and his family's overall benefit, but for his culture and heritage.

He was not a banker at heart, though. Serving money, transacting for money's sake, taking it from one and giving it to another while taking a slice and pieces "that drop on the floor" (a term I saw written in one of my grandmother's letters) was his daily profession, but it never really filled him. He acted and succeeded materially like a banker, but not sure he ever felt like one. Deep down he was more interested in teaching and farming, taking care of more than just other people's money. But there was this compulsion in him to undo the sensibility of loss and defeat, the one that forced his grandfather to leave Ireland, the one that haunted him and his roots.

His industriousness, logic, and persistence brought him success, earning him much of the middle-class comforts and status. His dogmatic trust in numbers and reason, and belief that decisions should be made in congruence with what his peers are doing, prevented him from perceiving where things were going during the spring and summer of 1929.

His wife felt uncomfortable with all the comforts their community was enjoying. To her it seemed too good. She shared these feelings and her foreboding with him, but feminine intuition was not a language he understood. If he could not see it and it could not be calculated, he felt he just needed to keep going, staying longs stocks like everyone else.

But like it did to millions of others, October 29 utterly undid Timothy. The crushing exhalation of loss laid its waste on a nation, a world. He was forty-seven years old when his career disappeared on that fall day. The spirit of unreserved loss never left him. He never returned to the track of his life and bristled at the thought of sharing his misery. He brewed for long hours at home, like some boiling gin still.

His was always dressed in suit and tie. He was a restrained yet well-appointed presence in the home, riddled with emasculation, too sad and sensitive to seek help. He worked in mid-level, post-Depression era administrative jobs. By most standards these roles would be fine, but he always compared the wealth of them to the regrets of his life.

He whiled away his evenings listening to the radio, but all the Yankee game broadcasts in the world could never ease his deep-seated shame. It was as if the ancient ancestral wounds of his Druid and Gaelic kin, those who had been pushed to the damp corners of Europe's western-most shores when the Romans had tired of the battle, had re-emerged and were consuming him.

I sense my grandfather felt like a stranger as the sensation of ruin separated him from the world and life around him. It was a sadness that had an origin, but no name. It became a barren horizon for him, and like all parents who feel their lives are a disappointment, they silently constrict the wonder of those in their care

My grandfather never shared stories or spoke of

this event to his family. Even in the last years of his life, when living at a senior home, Timothy could not release the shame. Those are some heavy oats he carried, and some pretty heavy emotions that he left his kids to eat. For Timothy's family, regret seemed to be the main course at dinner.

That silence and regret was carried into my home. That is how the crash of '29 still lives inside my belly today. It is not easy (read impossible) to shake our roots, the feelings, sensitivities, and echoes of our ancestor's lives. This event and how it lingered in and consumed my grandfather are the archeology of my male archetype. It left in me a residue of smallness in the material world, a foreboding that I could never explain. But now I know that you do not have to actually experience a dramatic event for it to have a lingering impact. You just have to live with those who were around the event.

"A truth cannot be created, only perceived."
— Paramahansa Yogananda

Knowing the Archetype Brings Awareness

James swam back up to the headwater moment that created the bio-magnetic, psycho-emotional dent in the limbic body of his family, of his grandfather. His personal history was no longer just a thought, a black and white photo, or a few simple stories. His history was now alive. He had sat and felt the heaviness of loss that had been breathing in his bones for years, an amorphous weight that now had a beginning.

This emotion of loss and failure is not good or bad; it is the result and inheritance that he could now begin to understand. By reveling in this uncomfortableness and allowing it to surface and reawaken, by re-experiencing it through talking about it, by sitting quietly in it and writing about it, James began accepting it as a large strand of thread within the fabric of his life experience.

There is a reality of gifts and tenets to be revealed within the incompleteness of his grandfather's life and the accumulated uneasiness washing in James. It is access to this stored wisdom that James had been wrangling with for so long.

We need to consciously be consumed by feelings. On the other side of the tears and bodily ache that will overwhelm our logic is a truth — about what, who, and why we are, who our parents were and what we are supposed to learn from them. Yogananda says, "The reality that lies behind sensory perception and beyond the cogitations of the rationalizing mind, can only be grasped by intuition...a truth cannot be created, only perceived."

James was starting to perceive that his sense of his own incompleteness and material uneasiness, which became especially acute when his wife barked those cutting, demeaning comments, were signals to look deeper inside. He needed to stop unconsciously coveting what others had, to start filling more hours a week doing what he loved: coaching, taking classes, and preparing for more ways to express his desires. He had inherited a masculine archetype that relied too heavily on the reasonings of institutional norms, accepted social and cultural dogmas. It was the "get a job, have kids, and that was it" world that seemed to inhibit intuition and full communication with one's dreams.

But it was reason and simple acceptance, he felt, that got his grandfather into his personal giant, economic hole. Timothy O'Connell reasoned to stay long stocks when his wife's intuition told him to exit. James was done chopping. He was now imbibing, letting the sensations of his family's losses, regrets, and inhibitions fill his heart and belly in long, sitting sessions. He was letting the current of their lives and longings course through him, feeling this contraction deeply so that it could be expanded.

This physical manifestation, this perceiving, began to rattle his left brain, opening up this understanding that without loss, you cannot create space to expand into. He began to recognize knowledge within this conflict, that he had been limiting his life to what he thought it should be, what his relatives thought it should be, and not incorporating enough of what lived beyond these channels.

The Father Force

From our sessions and his at-home time sitting, James was amazed that he could now more clearly see how his and everyone else's behaviors and reactions were impelled by the unconscious flowing of their masculine and feminine archetypes. He had been stuck, caught in the unconscious eddy of fear that cut him off from his mission to do something additive to and with his community. It did not have to be big, just something that brought a currency of fulfillment and meaning. Dieda writes in *The Way of the Superior Man,* "The father force is the force of loving challenge and guidance. Without this masculine force in your life, your direction becomes unchecked, and you are liable to meander in the mush of your own ambiguity and indecision."

He had not conquered indecision. He discovered that it was passed down so he could use it to somehow rekindle skills and desires sleeping inside. He would leave the judging of what success was for others to do.

A Legacy of Pinching

One of my other male clients shared comments a few years ago, highlighting his culture's timeworn sensibilities of incompleteness. He was not mocking what was unlived in his relatives, he was just trying to tell a story. He wanted to write a poem about how we often resent other people's success when we are embattled with our own dented self-worth and feelings of lack.

He shared this handwritten with me in our last session:

"Yeah, my inheritance, it is like generations of injured self-worth. F' the British. All these old, ancient Irish inhibitions, only remedied by drinking, all fear-based, live inside me. Brutal. My mom, not really doing much, not creating anything. When we are not doing, we are dying. If we are not doing what we were made to do, we are judging and pinching other's ambitions because we long to be doing something ourselves. I don't know. I know criticizing though. I inherited way too much pinching from this long line of pinchers and it's killing me."

This client and James had both reached across and into the buried angst, the hollow lumps of longing, the weight of unfinished dreams in their hearts. They are releasing these feelings into their daylight-busy, thinking self. By listening to these sensations, they are loosening them. It is about allowing old sensations of sadness and joy, tears and clutching hands, shortness of breath from abject rage or fear, whatever it might be, to have the floor. Our rational self will then begin to trust that this uprising of emotions will not kill it.

It can and will be uncomfortable. But it elicits deep intuition of the life that is trying to arrive and be lived through you, the one that James is now breathing up. That which he feels and desires is beginning to befriend and merge with that which he thought and believed.

Integrating the knowledge of our archetypes and using this consciousness to grow and create becomes the real mission. Helping others is a natural offshoot as well, as you begin to notice everyone's story, how the intimate coalescing of our current life with our relatives' worlds is a universal fact. James was dumbfounded now at how knowing just a small piece of someone else's family history, a brief quip about a grandfather or a mother's upbringing, could clarify how his current life was so impacted by these seemingly long-gone lives.

One of his twenty-nine-year-old colleagues talked continually about wanting a boyfriend. She said she just could not find the right person. As she casually shared more of her background with James at a company party, and how much her father's indifference and disrespect for her mother killed the spirit of their family, it seemed she was being unconsciously drawn to men that mirrored that indifference. Perhaps she was avoiding relationships to stave off the discomfort.

Her mother's deep grief over her father's juvenile

detachment and bullying has incited a retreat in his colleague today. He felt she was trying to keep everything in and others out for protection, holding her life back. At some point the current will have to run.

Third Archetype:
Relationship to Relationships

The current psycho-emotional terrain of this beautiful, intelligent, motivated, and yet disheartened and sometimes lonely young colleague of James' shines some light on the third vital archetype.

3rd Archetype: Relationship to Relationships:

The relationship archetype is the tone, disposition, friction, love, and everything else physical and nonphysical that we witnessed while growing up in the marriage or relationship of parents or primary care givers. It sets our disposition towards and understanding of relationships and how they work.

That original dyad, that ongoing dance between the masculine and feminine that we observed and absorbed in our youth, becomes the lens and filter through which we view and operate. All the ways your parents treated each other, how they stretched their relational muscles, how they avoided, embraced, belittled, hugged, kissed, behaved in public, laughed, cried together, and parented, these all left an impression on you. How you engage your spouse, therefore, what you give to the marriage, and how you respond to "your environment...is an expression of an archetype," Carl Jung said.

Relationship Model Missing a Piece

Ironically, Dan, another counseling client, witnessed literally no interaction between his parents as his father passed away when he was four years old. For him the relationship archetype manifested as a continual search and longing for a male figure to be the father, but more importantly to be the spouse and partner for his mother.

His mother leaned too heavily on him to be her companion, directing mothering and spousal attention — as well as psycho-emotional desires — at him at early an age. He lost a piece of the frivolity and exuberance of his childhood as he sensed he owed his mother more of himself, carrying and owning some of the weight of her loneliness that would normally be the heart domain of a loving spouse. He rarely got to exercise and try his adolescent and early adulthood relationship skills, like going out on dates, getting his heart broken, being vulnerable, silly, and corny. These activities are important for young, more limbic-dominated teenagers.

Teens need to push out of and from their parents' house and sphere and try their impulses, experience the wounds, joys, relational losses and gains with their peers. But for this client, his domineering and withdrawn mother consumed his world. She guilted him into neglecting his friends to stay around the house and belittled his attempts to even show attention to girls. The unconscious little-girl, stuck in this forty-year-old woman's soul, was desperate to bond with a masculine, fathering entity that could cushion even some of her longings for the safety and warmth of a home-hearth. Men, she felt, were less afraid and more easily distracted.

She was so dependent on her son's affection that she killed much of his boy spirit, forcing him to move much earlier into adult-like sensibilities. He had to play adult at the ripe age of fourteen, but developmentally he was still eight years old. Being soaked in this relationship archetype unconsciously drew him into marrying a woman that was a bioelectrical, dispositional, and psychological match to his mother. His nine-year marriage was suffering along the same lines and ache.

Dan's wife held the emotional and financial power as he, without having any husband or father model, was a hollow man who had abdicated ownership of the family ship to her. He was afraid and angry at his wife, an anger that he knew was reserved for his mother. He had no idea how to set boundaries by lovingly challenging either his wife or mother with a "self-generated strength of truth," as Deida says in *The Way of the Superior Man*. Most of the time he avoided direct, honest dialogue. He had never processed and broke into his boyish vulnerability.

We have to crack the riddle of your relationship archetype. Dan needed to embrace the anger, fear, and regret that were infused in his experience of relating to others, especially towards women, so that he could more consciously embrace his marriage. By knowing the deep roots of his longing for male guidance and why he did not know how to be in a relationship, he would understand why others also unconsciously react. His relationship archetype contained a feminine force that impeded and forbade relationships. It was why he struggled to be present for his wife and two children.

One-Eyed King in the Land of the Blind

By knowing deeply the roots of our feelings, why the eight-year-olds inside of us laugh and cry, we become one-eyed kings in the land of the blind. Why? Because we then know why our boss and spouse are reacting. Truly intuiting and understanding self allows for such clarity when engaging others. We all have the exact same basic desires, the same mammalian and human needs for exchanging and relating to others. We just have to translate their reactions and words with our heart.

In our sessions, Dan began to plunge into how alone he always felt. He began listening in his silence, closing his eyes and going back to his kitchen table when he was in fourth grade. This softened his heart, which opened his senses up to the heart of the little girl inside his wife. She was asking, crying out for his affection, power, appreciation, and physical help, when she was scolding him for watching TV.

As soon as his thirty-nine-year-old self began to connect and dialogue with his inner fourth grader, the boy who used to come home to an empty house, he could feel the loneliness in his wife. They both experienced weak relationship templates growing up, but the sheepishness of whatever masculine he embodied was no match for the hurt and anger of her matriarchal current.

Until he acquired this consciousness, pushing upstream into his limbic past, his wife's rants were just an echo of his mom's tirades. Therefore, he was normally in resent-filled retreat. Their relationship was coming undone because of their relationship archetypes. He felt empty around his wife, like he did when he was ten. This led him to trying fill the aches, like a teenager, by flirting with other women and starting online relationships. This is a common, masculine reactionary refrain.

When he and I began our archeological dig into the well of his heart, he realized he was seeking some lightheartedness in his life, a place of play and puerile freedom that had escaped his youth. He never really intended on actualizing this freedom. He just wanted those moments when the shadows of his wife and mother were not dimming his passions.

As soon as he started to turn towards that boy in him, back to powerful emotional and actual images of his empty home, the boy and man in him started sharing their silence together. He imagined playing catch with his younger self. Sounds crazy, right? Well every night our dreams are doing this automatically.

When we sleep, our mid-brain awakens in the dreaming state and allows itself to release neuron signals more randomly. The frontal cortex rests, therefore, as Crick writes in *Of Molecules and Men,* in "shuffling of old connections that allows us to keep the important connections and erase the inefficient links." Good, holistic therapy does not wait for sleep to try to get the lessons and deepen our understanding of self. We can relax and dream-image during the daylight hours to bring a tear of openness that can change your life. I was helping Dan to reparent himself.

His inner boy's sadness woke him up to the latent joy and sadness that he and his wife both had. Once that bridge was made, the sadness did not go away, but it is no longer alone. It had been shared with another person, revealed to the reasoning, rational part of this thirty-nine-year-old father, man, and husband called Dan. The logic of the man meets the simple and profound perceptions of the boy. This awareness began to wake him up to all the parts of his life where he was afraid and unsure.

As he brought some of these insights to his wife, about how and why he retreated in many facets of their relationship, she began to sense his willingness to share vulnerability. She saw his ability to perceive, which made her less ready to belittle him. When a man brings out his boy and shows it to his wife — not to prove anything or looking for a pat on the back, but just to share his humanity and wounds — he creates the opportunity for a new level and sphere of trust in the marriage. A woman will only trust a man who will come to the altar of their marriage and challenge himself to become more, to own his actions, and share his mission for completeness so that she and the family will flourish.

Matriarchal Battle Lines

Our response to our embedded relationship archetype can impact not only how we behave with our spouse, but also how we address and interact with everyone else in our life.

One of the most powerful displays and manifestations of this relationship pattern is how a wife cares for and defends her home, really the spirit and dynamics of her hearth space. She is unconsciously and psychologically guided by how her mother and female relatives embraced and administered their power, or she resists and opposes those currents in order to better hold and serve her family. Either way, wives and girlfriends learn much of their reactions from their relationship archetype history.

So many marriages are stuck in this phenomenon, with the old reaction patterns "owning" each partner's behavior, starving the marriage of all its potential growth and maturity. Developmentally, behaviorally, many marriages resemble two ten-year-old's in relationship. As we saw earlier, almost two thirds of all marital fights are about the same thing, over and over. Our inner child is arguing with our spouse's inner child. That is the dynamic of many marriages.

If we do not unhook ourselves from the autopilot, child-like responses, we cannot release the marriage to its natural growth and ongoing stages. From our adult perspective, our youth seems like another lifetime. The rhythms and roots of our internal family myth are already indelibly etched in our heart by the time we enter college, the time we enter the workplace and begin configuring spreadsheets and balancing check books.

Whether we believe it or not, the human system is matriarchal. The healthiest relationships, though infused with the masculine power to animate and challenge, are organized, commanded, and counseled by the feminine qualities of receptivity, openness, and inspiration.

All of humanity's original cultures were ultimately coordinated by female elders. Theda Perdue writes in *Cherokee Women: Gender and Culture Change, 1700-1835*, "Cherokee women's close association with nature, as mothers and producers, served as a basis of their power within the tribe... the *matrilineal structure*—the oldest social organization known to man (woman?)."

Women learn and experience relationships from watching their mothers relate. Women will always defend their nests. Never have I seen this latent, ancient, and natural feminine defensiveness more prominently than when another woman encroaches a wife's home. In particular, when it is the mother-in-law.

There are probably a thousand books on this topic, but to me it is crucial to understand the filter through which women view each other within the marital domain so that both husband and wife can learn and grow. When the wife feels enriched and full in her relationship with her husband, she welcomes the mother-in-law's insights and giving of gifts. She is willing to open up the gates, then briefly share her mothering power because she already feels complete.

"Men are terrified of a woman's depth of love."
— David Deida

The Mother-Son Dance, in the Face of the Wife

The challenge arises when and if the mother-in-law, for instance, has not been able to loosen the apron string of her mothering energy with her son, the husband. Some moms struggle to let their little boys go. But her boy is now forty-two-years-old. Also, if the mother-in-law's relationship with her husband does not bring her the fullest masculine love, sustenance, and trust, she will unconsciously try to shift her son's attention back towards herself, away from *his* wife. This is a bad formula. By doing this, the mother-in-law breaks that sacred honoring of another woman's hoop, almost blindly and addictingly searching for a taste of that feminine power that she is not getting in her own marriage.

Whatever the mother-in-law is not getting from her

relationship archetype, she will continue to look for her son to provide. "Yearning for a way to release the love in her heart...giving love and receiving love," Deida writes in *The Way of the Superior Man*. This is when the unconscious behaviors of this husband's mom arrive. She pokes her views, judgements, and overcritical insights into her son's family dialogue, hoping her son, in particular, feels this as giving. She figures those opinions are love-based, and so to her it is giving, and in return she wants the adoration.

But so often, the husband's mother is not feeling whole and creative, so it is not from an authentic love but an unconscious need. She expects her son to side with her, like the obedient one he has always been. Deep down, her behavior towards her son's marriage can be an unconscious reenactment of the confusion and irritation living in her.

Never would the mother-in-law try to unseat her son's wife, even if for just one holiday event. Right? Maybe she would as part of that unconscious thirst to win her son back and remind him that she is his original matriarch-wife.

I believe many wives set out to want to embrace and love their mothers-in-law. They know there is always the boy in their husband who will seek some of the mothering wisdom, but most wives are willing to welcome their kid's grandmother.

One of my female counseling clients, forty-six-year-old Alison, talked about how much she tried hanging in there, attempting to respect her husband David's requests to have his parents spend the weekends. But the tension was too much.

Her mother-in-law was raised by a pincher, a criticizer and judger. That was not good or bad, simply her way of giving love, by imposing a dogmatic and misguided view. And that is exactly what Alison's mother-in-law unconsciously did in the early years.

Alison's mother-in-law was not happy, so her kids, really her sons, were her way of trying to sate that mothering creativity. She ruled her home absolutely, imbuing and commanding both the masculine and feminine currents within her marriage. She held both ends of the relationship archetype. All roads in David's house as he grew up went through Mom.

Therefore, that unprocessed and overstimulated masculine part of her, which was assertive, competitive, and unyielding, and her incomplete feminine — trying to draw the hoary, masculine adoration from David's soul — overwhelmed Alison. At one point, Alison told me she literally banished her mother-in-law was from the house, her kingdom.

Alison felt that her mother-in-law's desperate compulsion to give, assert herself, and acquire some control was strong. It was her psycho-emotional version of offering love, regardless if anyone was asking. Her presence at times caused an almost unbearable friction in Alison and David's marriage.

How Relationship Template Creates Behaviors

After a few sessions, Alison was beginning to see and sense all that was incomplete in David's parents' marriage. She realized that her mother-in-law's actions were not a personal vendetta against her. By turning inward, though, and looking at what she was insecure about in her marriage and life, Alison could see that her mother-in-law was triggering her own doubts about being a good mother, wife, and caretaker.

She had for too long logically fixed her attention on David and his mother as the problems, the two who were creating her angst and frustration around family events. But she started to see that no one could steal her joy if she could find it herself. Alison's mother-in-law was not weighing Alison's heart down and blowing out her candles. It was the remnants of her own incompleteness that were now therapeutically rising to the surface, as opposed to being released during another Christmas dinner.

Alison's rational side, that tough-minded perspective, could never find the solution. Her confusion, coupled with her anger, was why she originally exiled her mother-in-law. But by empathizing with the total home-life experience of her mother-in-law, in conjunction with David's awareness of his role and honoring of Alison's voice and needs, the matriarchal battle lines rescinded. Peace had settled delicately back in Alison's kingdom.

Fourth Archetype: Relationship to Self

4ᵗʰ Archetype: Relationship to Self

Our relationship to self is the most difficult of the four archetypes to fathom. If we have not allowed old sorrows and joys from our youth to bubble up, then our adult awareness has a limited perspective. One clue to where we need to focus our attention is the ninety-five percent of the actions and reactions in our adult life driven by the brain parts of which we are not conscious.

Building our knowledge and awareness of who we are and what we really desire, feel, and believe is an exercise in putting the rational self to sleep and listening to the whispers of your strongest desires.

This fourth archetype is ironically the only thing in our life that we can control. How we feel and react are the only experiences that we can know, control, or change. Everything else is out of our hands and regulation. This is why it is the most difficult to harness. Most people ironically spend the least amount of time working on this, the only thing they have power over.

Are you comfortable sharing your thoughts and feelings, or do you hide them? What has been or is your internal dialogue with self? If you could ask your heart three questions what would they be? Who did you pray to, speak to in your silence? How do you feel about yourself, especially when you spend long moments alone?

A mature, honest, and relentlessly unfolding marriage is built from understanding, answering, and fulfilling the longing for self, while allowing your spouse to augment, brighten, and enrich your journey.

We originally longed to be heard and understood by our parents, seeking a comfort, safety, acceptance, and simplicity in their glances. We unwittingly, unconsciously seek that in our spouse, but we need to find this acceptance first in ourselves before we can give and receive it in another.

Welcome to Self, the Most Ancient Traverse

Carl Jung says, "whenever we give up, forget too much, there is always the danger that the things we have neglected will return with added force." Jung goes on to say, "Deep down below the surface of the average conscience, a still, small voice says to us that something is out of tune." That is where you will meet your other, non-logical, timeless self. This is the part you need to complete your marriage mission.

When I first began sitting quietly, which seems like a thousand years ago, I was overwhelmed by tides of unruly sensations. A mix of sadness, relief, recognition, aloneness, wonder, and love rose from my chest and neck, and then finally soaked my face and forehead, all of which released a flood of tears. The most fascinating part was that the emotions did not seem directly tied or correlated to my current life circumstances or events.

I was living a fairly charmed, mid-Nineties life in London. Good job, great friends, the life of Riley. The more I sat alone and started working with a counselor, though, the clearer it became that there were two sides of me, two parts to this body-mind-life thing I call Bill.

One part carried me to and through work, ran spreadsheets, and organized my thoughts and actions.

Everything had a beginning and end. To my thirty-two-year-old mind and attention, life moved linearly. Things occurred and then that moment was gone. There would be emotions and sentiment around these blocks of moments, but once the event was over, the sentiment would fade as well.

Then there was another side that I found, or that found me. It was this opaque, out-of-current-time, a well of feelings that had never surfaced. It was a place, a locale where the heart grabbed the steering wheel.

Clearly, these two halves of me were not familiar with each other. They had no history together. They spoke different languages and sliced the world in different ways, with different bio-magnetic tendencies, skills, and goals.

Tale of Two Selves

Robert Monroe spent his whole life exploring these two sides. He reminds us in *Ultimate Journey*, "Human consciousness flickers back and forth between left and right brain all day." He explains the difference between the two and why they can be at odds. "Right brain perceives form and space, beauty, intuition, emotions, and has not changed for thousands of years. Our left brain, though, has become so entrenched in 'surviving' in the Earth Life System (making money, building things, destroying in the name of surviving) that it has resisted anything that interrupts this."

My thirty-two-year-old self struggled to make sense of these two worlds colliding. There was this profound boyish sentiment of sadness and fear, coupled with some ancient desire and longing for places, people, and sounds that just did not fit my white, middle class, suburban New Jersey background. It was like dropping my young adult self into a waking dreamscape, and it was up to the heart of the boy to make sense of it. I had no idea a successful, young businessman, senior sales executive, living abroad steadfastly in the adult world, could still be carrying the vulnerabilities of a ten-year-old.

This was my entrance into learning what the fourth archetype means. This is how I was introduced to my relationship to self. The exercise of sitting on the floor with my back straight, alone in my flat in London, became my classroom. I quickly realized how far apart the heart of the boy was from the beliefs and reactions of the adult.

The boy feelings coursing through my right brain reintroduced me to a curiosity and renewed wonder for the simple things and world around me. I bought a bike and toured the city, alighting that adolescent zeal for freedom, moving across parks and sidewalks at speed. I hiked mountains and traveled even farther abroad, wanting to touch more physically as I opened up more emotionally.

Without opening this door to self, I would never have found my wife and our marriage would never have lasted this long. Why? Because entering a relationship with the other part of self automatically allows you to hear, sense, and intuit this other half of others. Jane Roberts says in *Seth Speaks,* "A perception changes the physical, emotional, and psychological fabric of the human via the science of electrons in the body." It is like learning a new language. Our emotions communicate using the intelligence of the brain neurons in the stomach and heart, more than the neurons in the brain. We begin to sense another's motivations and inhibitions.

When I listened to my girlfriend with the heart of my eight-year-old, I could glean the soft desires of the young girl in her. It was much easier to get past and through the circumstances and adult plotline of challenges she was facing, and uncover what was driving her reactions. I was able to focus on her feelings because I had started paying attention to mine.

"She will point out your weaknesses better than a boot camp drill sergeant."

— David Dieda

Boy Meets Man

With my thirty-two-year-old self being re-introduced to the boy's heart, I started getting comfortable with being vulnerable. I no longer pushed against what my heart wanted to say. My newfound tears made me much braver. The natural trepidations and inhibitions of my young boy-heart — which at ages ten, twelve, or fifteen did not know how or was too ashamed to express — now had a willing adult presence. Instead of distracting myself with adult-world activities and dulling these aches, agitations, and pangs — drink, smoke, work, exercise, or anything else that kept them just far enough away — I opened to them. They then swept through me.

When men do not open themselves up to their boy-heart, they do not understand why their bodies ache and their knees throb. They do not know why they are grumpy, irritable, anxious, and often on the edge of a torrent of blind anger. They overeat and drink, hiding from the body sensations that want an adult who will listen. Heart attacks often have old, inherited roots of unconsciously, unexpressed hearts, the unprocessed and unexpressed longings and joys of boys inside all men.

Because men are not familiar with their hidden world of vulnerabilities, they bristle at a woman questioning them. When the feminine pokes at these raw emotions, but a man has not poked at them himself, he runs the other way. That had been the playbook of my dating life until I finally embraced this fourth archetype. A relationship would begin and seemingly flourish until I was asked to bring more to it. Then I would shut down.

Unconsciously, like all men, I wanted to share my weaknesses, loves, and joys with the feminine, or the mothering archetype. All men have that boy within that wants and needs to be embraced by the nurturing, universal her. After we conquer and battle whatever dragons we face in our daily, material adult world, we want to escape into the feminine acceptance, tenderness, and warmth. But if a man does not understand the dynamics of this natural, ancient, psychological pattern-archetype between the masculine and feminine, between his adult need to be strong and his boy-heart to be embraced, he will be forever terrified about showing weakness and vulnerability to the feminine. This is often why relationships fail: a man runs away and reviles the very thing that he longs for, the affectionate creativity and attention of the feminine.

Embrace the Terrifying

It is an incredible and common story. Man meets woman.

She embodies all that his unconscious boy-heart was looking for, the things that are beautiful, accommodating, accepting, and creative. The affection he feels for her bio-magnetically stirs though his adolescent loneliness, need for attention from mom and dad, and possibly an old wound from an adolescent love. Who knew those were still in there? We do now. The more he is with her, the stronger his new joy and old loneliness become, creating an inexorable tension. A part of him wants to throw open his arms and shed a tear of longing with her, emptying himself. But that fear of showing weakness is too scary.

Deida says in *The Way of the Superior Man,* "Men are terrified of a woman's depth of love....at the same time, men want nothing more in this life than to merge completely with a woman's devotional love and wild energy. Only as a man outgrows his fear can he handle a woman's tremendous love-energy without running." Until you practice being vulnerable with yourself, you will not expose these aches to your wife for fear of her being disgusted.

So often a man will feel so ashamed to be tender and show the misgivings of his boy-heart to his wife. "Once one's feelings are bound in shame, one numbs out," explains John Bradshaw in *Homecoming.* "Numbing is the precondition of all addictions because it is the only way we can feel." Or he does not know how to share these sensibilities, was never shown how, or never knew it would be helpful to do so. Often his wife has run out of tolerance and patience for his immaturity, his need for a pat on the back, or his inability to really hear and understand her. If she loves him, though, her inner drive is to challenge her man, to help him release the boy, to test him "with her darkest moods, over and over and over, until your consciousness is unperturbed by feminine challenge," Deida says.

It is nature, embodied in woman at the altar of marriage, that is relentless, at times illogical, destabilizing and mysterious to him. These times scare him, even re-awaken the timid boy inside. But these forces, if consciously and purposefully directed at him by his wife, are the gifts of the feminine. They are everything that his mother could never bring, most likely being afraid to bring them in fear of losing her son. The conscious wife is not afraid to lose him. She is looking to help him crack the boy-heart.

Many men are not brave enough to do this. As they did with any of the mother's challenging commentary or rules, these men end up retreating in the name of gallant masculinity and get their distance. "Women are crazy," is their unfortunate, ancient refrain.

The male desire to be embraced by the feminine never goes away, though. The fourth archetype demands that he step past the need for the mothering-nurturing presence and allow these goddess forces to wake him up, to shove him into the domain of the feminine which is the world of stored his feelings. Deida summarizes the ultimate experience of this path towards self for the man in face of the feminine: "Nobody will press your buttons or reflect your asshole to you better than your woman. She will point out your weaknesses better than a boot camp drill sergeant."

If he turns away from this force, the boy in him will search for the softer, mothering energy only, often in the arms of a younger woman, a hooker, or the use of pornography. If he settles for only the feminine energy that allows and discards the other half of her message that can destroy and unwind, he will often end up in the arms of a younger woman. A younger, forgiving woman will both embrace and ignore his boyish moods in her quest to find a man who is mature enough to fulfill her archetypes.

My newfound relationship to self created the foundation for a successful bond during critical early marital years. Finding the boy while single was one thing, but with three kids, a mortgage, work and financial pressures, and other life challenges, I had to summon more attention. After nine or ten years of marriage, I had stopped listening with patience and acceptance of her needs. I kept trying to fix and correct her moods. The flux of my career decisions and outcomes put dents in her trust in me, and instead of turning towards her for wisdom, I unconsciously cowered and dodged her guidance.

When I turned away from her glares, she naturally pulled her openness, trust, and love back. When the feminine cannot release her love into her life and marriage, she will find other places like shopping, eating, or judging others. It was on me to stop hiding and allowing the interference of kids, friends, social events, and the demands of suburbia to distract me from honoring her. The shift arrived after I began addressing my fears and sharing them with her.

The simple solution was returning to my vulnerability and showing it to her again. By going back to my boy-fears living in the adult, our partnership rekindled. It took ten years for me to see that we had lost the friendship. We had done so much of the heavy marital lifting:

parenting young kids, finding our place as a family in

a new town, weathering the machinations of in-laws, extended family, and long holiday nights. But we needed more. I needed to push to higher ground to the next level of my relationship to self — which was remembering that my inner boy needed and wanted a friend.

I had to quiet the dad, father, and husband voice which was trying to fix and solve all the family challenges, and begin re-dreaming our partnership with more respect and appreciation. At the most basic level, I started having more conversations with her that centered around her, not the kids, the dogs, oil changes, or next weekend's plans. I sincerely wanted to know more about her dreams and hopes, and as these discussions unfolded the storyline of our marriage shifted. We found the camaraderie, the silliness, and banter that was the original foundation. Life and ten years of marriage had worn those treads thin, but we found the passion of our inner teenagers which helped forge a new friendship.

"Deep friendship was the key, being well versed in each other's likes and dislikes."

— John Gottman

Have to Find the Friendship

Research tells us how important friendship is to the marriage. "Eighty percent of divorced men and woman said their marriage broke because they gradually grew apart and lost a sense of closeness, did not feel loved and appreciated. . . ," wrote John Gottman in *The Seven Principles for Making Marriage Work*. Women want to know their men are honestly striving to fully complete the life they seek. The size of this life and purpose are not the issue; it is the depth of the commitment that they watch.

I returned to my vulnerability, as did my wife, which brought a lightness to my presence, allowing her to express herself and her feelings. Our relational muscles flexed and were strengthened.

Remember, You are Married to Your Archetypes

As we stated from the outset, marriage is the arena for this confluence of our four archetypes to meet our spouse's four. The work in your marriage is go back into your four, in order to know why you are behaving and responding with impatience, indifference, fear, acceptance. You have to find the whys in you, not those in her.

The very measure of your current anger or frustration is merely the festering of the original unexpressed anger to one or more of your four archetypes. Because of the bio-magnetic heft of all those emotion-studded neurons that formed in your childhood, you are really married to your emotions and reactions. Therefore, your actual marriage can only expand and mature as far as you are able to unlock the wisdom, releasing those inner child inhibitions that live in your four vital archetypes.

CHAPTER 6
IT WAS IMPOSSIBLE TO KNOW

"To sustain love, a man and a woman must continually be marrying and divorcing, moving with, against, away from, and beyond each other, saying 'yes' and 'no'."

— Sam Keen

Your Brain on Marriage

It is physically and psychologically impossible to know how difficult a marriage is going to be. I will explain. But I want to normalize your experience so far if you are having challenges, frustrations, or moments of confusion.

There was no way you could have ever known what would unfold. Why? Because throughout most of the third decade of your life, from ages twenty to twenty-eight, biologically and electro-magnetically your brain is different than it is starting at the age of thirty. Your brain on marriage, when you said, "I do" during your twenties, is not the same brain even four or five years later, let alone fifteen years later.

There is so much going on with the neurons between and within your left and right brains over the course of your marriage that it is a wonder that any marriage survives. I am kidding. But the brain does undergo such powerful, developmental, mini-evolutionary phases and processes throughout life that I am shocked it is not discussed more.

Welcome to Your Crisis

These cycling, shifting and maturing neuron currents create and demand ongoing changes in our psychological, emotional, and spiritual sensibilities. The midlife crisis, for instance, is a natural and common experience and product of these anatomical changes. I had my midlife crisis early, when I was thirty-one. I unwittingly got a jump on that sucker. I enjoyed it so much that I am having another these days in my mid-fifties.

The late forties and early-to-mid-fifties crises are deeper, slower, and more intense than the psychological shifts earlier in life. I will not say harrowing, but big and heavy, like a glacier slowly and unexpectedly rolling into a quiet harbor town. It methodically pushes, upends, displaces, and consumes the docks, houses, boats, and everything else in its path. That sounds dramatic, but ask anyone who has been in or through one. It is a reckoning, a fierce, inexorable search for some kind of significance to what we are doing or have been doing for the last twenty years.

All of these life shifts, whether in our teens, twenties, or fifties, are caused by the melding, colliding and resisting forces of our left and right brains. Throughout our life, our brain biology continually calls up everything in us that we cannot touch — our longings, dreams, and regrets — so that they can be reconciled and integrated with our rationally formed thoughts, beliefs, and expectations. Life is an unending coalescing of these forces. The progress and development of our marital bond are a direct reflection of how we reconcile these neuron machinations.

These crises of the self, big or small, are expected,

natural, and part of the evolutionary construct of humans. But so many of us see these agonizing bouts and phases of questioning and doubt as failings. They are not. They are experiences of expansion that demand your time, attention, and ability to listen to their demands.

The word crisis is rooted in the Greek word *krisis*, which means to decide or interpret. That is what the timeless intelligence of our body chemistry is doing to us during these times. Our left and right brains are being blended. If you give up on these siren calls from within, you will give up on your marriage. Fatigue, fear, ignorance, and lack of will in the face of these transitional cycles of our inner lives will often cause people to punt on their spouse. I am asking you to hang on — it is worth the ride.

Takes Much More Than Love

Regardless of the changes our brains undergo, I believe that successfully sustaining and maintaining a healthy and mature marriage has little to do with love. Love is too hard to define and identify to be the deciding factor in such a powerful exercise as marriage. I have heard it said many times, "If you have love, the marriage will work." I do not agree. I have seen plenty of couples who love each other but whose marriage stopped. That is not a bad thing. I am just confirming my belief that it takes more than love.

Try this Love-Gut check:

- Close your eyes for a minute, put your right hand on your heart and focus all your attention on that space behind your rib cage.

- Imagine clearly seeing all twelve of those curved bones of your chest plate. Keep your attention there, on your hand on your heart.
- Welcome to the home of your heart.

Humor me for a few more minutes as we explore the intelligence and sensations stored under the hood.

- Now, with your hand still on your heart, take note of your next breath as you inhale into your nose.
- Notice your stomach and chest as you inhale. Try to hold the next breath right at the very top of the inhale, before you need to exhale, and then release it slowly out your mouth as your chest and stomach compress to the back of your spine.
- Repeat this for your next five breaths while you settle into a relaxed state.
- Keep your hand gently on your heart. Your heart likes this attention, whether you know or believe this.
- Now, quietly define, characterize, call up, and animate the word and concept of love. Use the relaxed motion of your heart to do the talking and visualizing. Keep your eyes closed.

Categorizing Love

Maybe you are feeling love as a longing for a grandparent that has passed and the joy they brought. Maybe it is an old, unrequited high school fling that cut you deeply, but you still feel giddiness under the regret. There was an innocence and simplicity in that adolescent love. Right now, as I do this exercise, I feel the soft pangs of a bond and appreciation for the Christmas gifts my three daughters gave me. These pangs are brewing a tear for a father's inexhaustible pride in the care and appreciation my girls share with me.

One of my other overwhelming experiences of love is in the memory of my dog, Sunny. He passed two years ago, but his patience and abiding affection for me floods my heart with warmth. His picture, a whole collage of photos, is three feet away.

Maybe you're conjuring of love held within an unrivaled friendship and union with your spouse, friend, sibling, or colleague. Love is in all of these, as well as being just a warm feeling, a sadness for days, friends, or family members that are no longer here. It could be in the sensation of wanting something more, or appreciation for what you have, knowing that someone is home or on the other side of a phone call. Or maybe it's plain old sex.

The point is that love is an experience, sensation, and perception, and there are a thousand ways to conceive it. But this incredibly powerful yet amorphous construct cannot sustain or hold two people together in a relationship for fifty years. Constructs cannot mend the resentment, frustration, anger, insecurity, financial issues, distrust, in-law issues and confusion that can eat away at marriages. Unfortunately, marriage statistics support this notion, as fifty percent of all marriages end in divorce as of 2018. If all we needed was love, that number would be different.

Love can be the fuel, goal, and passion that drives your work, studies, and finishing the yardwork. But a mature marriage depends on much more. It needs stamina, commitment, a willingness to be completely undone, a selfishness and selflessness, as well as a singular truth living in the bottom center of your stomach that says, "My life is better with my spouse in it, period." No other partnership or relationship in your life asks this of you.

Your marriage is a long story that must be constantly read, examined, felt, interrupted, laughed at, broken, lost, and wept over. There is a long history of memories and unconscious sensations stored in you and your partner, as we know. You have no idea of the heft of these memories and how you will react when your partner's inner story painfully spills on you. You are not supposed to. Why? Because the age at which we typically get married and the stages of human brain development that occur during these early phases preclude our ability to comprehend the intensity and shifts in our storylines.

The science of your brain and the developmental process called myelination is the culprit behind this changing plot of your marriage. Myelination is an epic shifting point that completely alters your interpretation and translation of your experience of life. It is an integration phase when the neuron fibers of the left brain blossom and strengthen, allowing them to more fully blend, merge, and communicate with the right brain. You had no idea that myelination was going to force you to adjust, tune in, hold on, and let go in order to make it through to the end.

The only thing you can do to stay within the plot of your marriage, the only time-tested, ancient exercise that answers all the marital questions is the one we have been propounding: to slowly teach your dominant, adult left-brain perspective the language of your right brain emotions. This is work done in your silence and in the counselor's office. Conscious sitting and listening alone and therapy are the only classrooms that can reconcile the blending of these currents. There is nothing logical about any of this.

"The more angry one person gets, the more sad the other. The more sad one gets, the more angry the other."

— Gahl Sasson

Unlikely Bedfellows, this Sadness and Anger

Cassandra Clare sums up, as mentioned in Chapter 1, the profound truth about marriage when she says in *City of Bones*, "To love is to destroy, and that to be loved is to be the one destroyed." You must open up and die to your childhood anger and fears. These are the mini-crises, times to interpret.

This is the irony and rub of being married, the pain within deepening the bond with your spouse. But only through the sadness, which is the surfacing of old hurts, can relief and joy be found.

What emerges from this inner work is a love and appreciation for self, for the crusade that you have been on throughout your life. All roads to completing your marriage, finishing up life with your spouse, lead through you and the exposing of your inner child heart through the mortar and pestle of marriage.

Go back to putting your attention on your breath. Take two to three minutes again and put your hand on your heart, count seven or eight slow breaths, and just sit quietly.

Now spend a few minutes feeling back into moments when you were an adolescent, when you felt lost, confused about life, or dispirited, as Laurie, James, and I have done. Feel those old joys and trepidation of adolescence. Press an old self-esteem bruise from a breakup or failure. Put your full adult attention into the middle of your fifteen-year-old heart, or whatever age you are feeling as you sit. You will know if you have penetrated that moment because your shoulders, stomach, and heart will thump or twinge. Your body will tell you when you have truly perceived and melded with your younger heart.

Those parts of you will no longer be separated. You will contact your experience of those moments right now. This is how you find your way home. Home is where and when you realize that you are a singular entity filled with a lifetime of unique experiences and emotions, moving in time. Many call this connectedness, oneness, or a union with God. This moves you to experience an acceptance of self. This acceptance incites a deep and quiet love for the most important person on the planet, you.

You loving you, or at least deeply appreciating your story, is the story of how your marriage subsists and thrives. Your spouse is a distant second on the list of key factors which will ensure success. Sounds New Age, but is not.

How can you really engage your spouse and your marriage, or another's desires, or know why your spouse rages at you if you do not know the most delicate and deepest pangs of your own heart? You have to desire your own growth within the arena of marriage because the self-undoing, the vulnerability, and destruction that Cassandra

Clare mentions is unavoidable.

Where Does this Come From?

You are going to tune into a channel that you had no idea existed, that you never imagined you would need to find. John, who we met in Chapter 1, started our first session together with a comment. "I know things are a lot different from when we were first married," he told me. "The kids, diapers, all the driving around, me being at work while she's home, all our stuff. But some of the things we end up saying to each other, some of the anger and fights, where the hell does this come from?"

He went on to say that his debates with his wife, Amy, were getting so loud. She hated how he avoided doing dishes and helping out with even the small stuff. He got so grumpy and frustrated with her irritable looks when he came home from work that he did not feel like kissing her. He told me he loves hugging the kids and kissing the dogs. "That," he says, "pisses her off even more."

Could John have ever imagined those words or that scenario when they were on their honeymoon or even a year or two into their marriage? As he continued to share his frustrations and growing resentment, I said that what he and his wife were going through is normal.

Just on a fundamental physical and psychological level, sharing space every day with another person is a biological challenge. Each of us wrangling with the ongoing weight of feelings, ruminations, desires, joys and insecurities. Each is carrying a personal cargo of unexamined and unconscious sensibilities and reactions. Placing someone within the same four walls is supposed to create major collisions. The natural and normal psychological and emotional gravitational pull on both bodies will always be active, impinging on each other's inner and outer orbits.

But there is much more than proximity that creates the inevitable confusion and unexplainable nuttiness of marriage. I said to John, "Even if someone like the priest or the entire wedding party had told you and Amy that the discourse of your marriage would be this intense, you two would've still gotten married." He agreed.

All three core challenges of marriage that were wholly unknowable — the constant proximity, intensity of our reactions, and the amount of indelible sensitivities that we carried from childhood — were built into the seed of your bond the day you married. These issues are not the real problem. It is the fact that the psychological, emotional, and behavioral changes that unfold over time in each partner seem to come out of nowhere.

They come out of nowhere because of the silent merging of our left and right brain neurons during the myelination phase, one that begins in our mid to late twenties and early thirties. This developmental phase begins to crack our sensibilities, like two inner oceans colliding.

"Our left brain finds meaning...by rendering the world more orderly and predictably."

— Iain McGilchrist

A Car Accident and Your Marriage

It is important to review again the contrasting ways that we view and experience the world. Our adult attention relies on the logic of neocortex, while our sensation of it lives in emotion-infused right brain.

The neocortex, the youngest part of your divided brain-self, organizes and analyzes. When we see an accident on the highway, for instance, our left brain quickly deciphers which lane to get into as traffic backs up. It sorts out the logical next steps, finding another lane and not getting hit by some texting driver who does not see the backup. The electrical wiring of our neocortex is pattern seeking, in this case instantaneously looking for encoded images of prior accidents that we have witnessed and then making a logic-based decision. The output here is, "Change lanes and move on."

Our left brain is da bomb. It gets stuff done. It builds computers. Writing in *The Master and His Emissary: The Divided Brain and the Making of the Western World,* Iain McGilchrist says the left brain "finds meaning...by rendering the world more orderly and predictably. It helps us feel safe, reassured and in control...attunes to what is happening right now."

In contrast, the right brain is old, ancient, 100 million years old. It is instinctual. Our right brain is a bundle of tissues and nerve cells that sit on top of our neck and spine, intimately wired to our heart and solar plexus. This network stores sensations, emotions, and memories in the form of bio-chemical and electric charges coursing through the neurons of our stomach, heart, and mid-brain, and is continually sending these feeling-impulses up to the left brain to be processed. McGilchrist says this pre-historic right hemisphere "perceives the world holistically, in a raw and unmediated way."

As you drive by that accident, your right brain is

brewing up feelings of sadness or remorse for those in the car, concern and empathy, or even frustration and angst for now being potentially late for work. It is not trying to make a decision about anything. It is just experiencing the scene, wading through whatever memories the experience of "car crash" inspires. Meanwhile, your left wants a result, is pushing against any sentiment, and wants action.

Left Avoiding Right

A random highway accident and your marriage are, well, fairly similar. One is the collision of two objects moving into the same space from further afar, culminating in a sudden confrontation. A car accident, on the other hand, is... (just kidding). Marriage is also two objects bouncing off each other. Add in kids, neighbors, in-laws, bosses, and mortgage payments from the outside world, along with our visceral responses to these influences, and the analogy works. Our interactions with our spouse will become accident-like.

Two married people clashing is not the issue or problem, though. The issue is that our logic-seeking left brain constructs our world by thinking through it, while our right brain is feeling into it. Our left is designed to avoid the emotion-studded world stirring below it. As Robert Monroe explains in *Ultimate Journey* there is "a basic battle between our left and right sides."

Within each of us, therefore, are these divided lives, two completely different dimensions within, filtering, responding, and competing for resolution in completely different ways. In *The Right Hemisphere, Brain Research Laboratory* we learn from R.G. Joseph that our right hemisphere is "dominant over the left in regard to perception, expression and mediation of almost all aspects of social and emotional functioning...and appears to maintain a realm of conscious-awareness which is completely different than from that of the left."

The Human Development Bombshell

The real bombshell — the tsunami of all cosmic, human development jokes — is that during the early years of your marriage, that crucial stage of adult brain development, myelination, has not begun. It does not start its full expansion until our late twenties to early thirties, all the way up to our mid-forties.

It is a turning of the page of our late adolescent body and soul. Sara B. Johnson, Ph.D. writes in *Adolescent Maturity and the Brain: The Promise and Pitfalls of Neuroscience Research in Adolescent Health Policy*, "This growth and maturation phase of your brain's anatomy, called myelination, which continues into your forties, is the body's critical physiological stage of integration of the two distinct and separate halves of the brain."

This integration phase is the most crucial transition period of life because the only way to evolve and become a mature, wise, conscious adult and spouse over time is to reconcile and balance the two competing parts of your being. Remember, your left brain is reason based, commanded by the frontal cortex that sits on top of the mid-brain tissue of the right brain.

Nature has designed these two sides to be separate in its attention to efficiency. In *Left vs. Right: Battle in Brain Discovered,* Robert Britt writes, "It allows the two sides...to become specialized, increasing its processing capacity and avoiding situations of conflict." Mother Nature thought she was doing this to help out with "situations of conflict." Clearly, she was not married long to Father Nature, since our left and right are in continual conflict.

Bioelectrically, your left brain is constantly retreating from the strong, sensation-saturated impulses from the right. Robert Monroe reminds us in *Ultimate Journey* that "our left brain cannot categorize love, friendship or inspiration." Your left brain just wants to control and organize impulses and emotions, but it is our emotions that store the whys of life. Why we behave the way we do, why we respond, laugh and cry, why your girlfriend dropped you like a hot rock. All of these questions can only be answered through the perceiving and intuiting of our sensory perceptions.

When your girlfriend dropped you like a hot rock, your rationalizing functions filtered and processed the event with action. Unless you really wanted to learn and grow from this, your rational side just wanted to take back control from the competing energy of your wounded heart. It is great at impulse management, therefore driving you to stuff the hurt away with some booze, focusing attention on outside forces that were the causes of the breakup, and then taking action by going out to meet another girl. This hurt could last for so long, using the left-brain game plan, that for the rest of your life you have a small vendetta against all women because of this event from tenth grade. This is not uncommon.

According to this deduction-based plan, a new girlfriend will distract you from any hurt, making the old one jealous, which in turn could get her to want you back. It's unlikely that is accurate, but to the prefrontal cortex, that is the plan, the basic procedural steps and reaction to a common life event.

This speaks to the limited perspective and scope of understanding when we use the linear, time-based lens that is focused on survival. The left operates to protect self and survive by moving on. Car accident, steer clear, move on. The issue is, using this rudimentary girlfriend-breakup example, the likelihood of this event repeating is high. Why? Because it is only by taking stock, by showing your rational self the truths behind the desires and feelings that caused the reactions and breakup, that a new awareness can emerge and evoke new behavioral response.

Robert Monroe says about the left-brain perspective, "We are only partially successful using an incorrect standard of measurement." If there is very little incorporation of context around understanding what was behind the breakup, there is no learning. Only by jumping down from our prefrontal cortex and into our heart and stomach — to re-experience the deep-seated desires and motivations of our own actions — can we fathom the actions of others.

Interestingly, part of the word experience has the Latin root *peril* within it, which means test or danger. While your left brain would rather run from any kind of trial or hazard, allowing your intuition to get involved will incite new insights on self, relationships, love, hurt, and more. That is integration, when the language of our anger, joy, and longings is introduced to our rational self.

This is the beginning of adult maturity and consciousness: perceiving the roots of our feelings, fully owning our reactions that emerge from these feelings, and then allowing our left brain to organize and coordinate this new attention and perspective to adjust future behavior with these new insights. This is the process of ROAR discussed in Chapter 3.

Robert Monroe summarizes this equation of human growth and maturity in *Ultimate Journey*, the processing within the brain structure that elicits self-awareness: "The left brain takes an idea, information, or inspiration from the right brain and puts it into action." Without this merging, we see the world with a narrower lens.

The Rub? Your Marriage Started Pre-Myelination

If you are like many of us, you dated, courted, and got married sometime between the ages of twenty and thirty-five, the general timeframe leading up to and into the early part of the myelination epoch of your life. This means that the collection of events and discord in your marriage during these early years happened while your brain was more adolescent than adult. The research is not saying that you were not mature, intelligent, and worldly. It is the fact that your capacity to draw psychological and emotional insights and context had not begun to expand.

The reality of marriage during this timeframe is completely different than the one during the later years because both of you have not fully incorporated the perceptions offered up from your inner worlds, the feeling knowledge that the right brain brings. Therefore, what occurs in these early years should be used more as data points for your experiment of marriage. Do not put too much weight onto what you did or did not do or say because you were developmentally more adolescent than wise adult.

My wife often recounts dumb things I said or did in year four of our marriage. "I never intended to hurt you with those comments about old girlfriends, sweetie," I would say. "I was just an imbecile and immature, and had not learned what it means to really honor and respect your feelings at that point." That was the truth. My thirty-three-year-old self and my just-starting-to-myelinate-neurons had no capacity, experience, history, and context to draw from so that I could behave any differently. My fifty-two-year-old brain considers my thirty-three-year-old self a very young adult, dare I say a kid.

Too many people become overwhelmed in these early myelination years. They start building their case on their long-term commitment to the marriage based on words and actions fired off during this earlier marital epoch. Writing in *Time*, Belinda Luscombe says the average length of a marriage that ends in divorce is less than eight years. I am sorry, but that is just when it starts getting good, when we are becoming neurologically adults. Your late adolescent brain has not grown up. You have not given your inner world the chance to review, opine, and reengage your spouse with fresh self-awareness.

"Earliest experiences remain within each of us. Our whole existence is based on the vitality and the dynamic experiences of our very beginning."

— Ludwig Janus, MD

Valentine's Day Massacre

My very first *Valentine's Day* with my wife twenty-two years ago is the perfect case study. By 4 p.m. that afternoon, after an otherwise ordinary day, she walked to me as I sat reading the paper. She lowered her head in disgust, after surveying the tables in the living room, and uttered four words that still echo in me every year during the second week of February. She simply asked, "Where are my flowers?"

"Shoot, sweetie, I didn't think you wanted them. I never gave flowers in the past. Growing up, flowers were never important in our house," I said with more than a hint of sheepish fear.

"I care. I want flowers. I am not your mother, asshole."

Nothing more needed to be said, ever. Valentine's Day in our house, for the last twenty-one years, has plenty of flora. The lesson from this first-year event is not about flowers and chocolates, though. It is about the long, interpersonal, memory-infused history and experience that my wife had from her youth. Flowers represented thinking of someone else, about giving, recognizing, and being honored and appreciated. Flowers now became the mechanism that triggered her frustration, which is really sadness and hurt turned outward.

The legacy of showing affection and availing love to another, the one that I was lugging around from my youth and early adult years, was purely pragmatic. My pre-myelination, misguided belief was, "I told you I love you, you know I love you, why would I waste money on a dying plant if you know I love you? That is what everyone else does, not me."

It takes years for our human hearts to really open, and the well of experiences of a thirty-two-year-old's heart is not nearly as deep as that of a forty-seven-year-old's. If you do not give the biology of your body and brain time to unfold through this extended and unwieldy myelination phase, you cannot offer the wisdom it has set out to uncover.

Even though I changed my habit on Valentine's Days ever since, it took me at least three to four years to really understand the feelings and nonphysical weight tied to sharing gifts with my wife. It is a timeless act of sacrifice, with a trace of vulnerability as the giver of something that was once mine but is now the others. Yes, even Costco flowers carry this much significance.

And it is only in the later years of marriage when our logical brain, which wants to survive and therefore spend less money, can realize this. Our divided brains merge during our mid to late thirties. Merging is what occurs by meditating as well, as the left and right sides actively coalesce through our thirties.

Flowers of any kind were an expression and symbol of love for my wife, an emblem my brain and heart had to learn. If I had factored too heavily her scorn and subsequent browbeating of me during this Valentine's massacre, as the years went on, it would have been convenient for me to use her belittling actions as excuses to withdraw from her and the marriage.

The left brain wants to get control back. "Why be committed to another," say our executive functions, "when they make us feel like crap?" But my commitment and desire to expose myself to me — to embrace the discord in the arena of marriage and try to learn from the early, maddening marital interactions — allowed me to lean into the discomfort. I could have just allowed her reactions throughout the early years to be the basis of moving apart.

But I used our outer dialogue, the arguments, love-making, rants of disappointment, grunts of impatience, whatever it was, as fuel for my inner communication. I would take my sadness and hurt, aroused by her, to spark deep meditation and therapy sessions that always revealed the story and context behind my feelings and her reactions. I was not content with just the first and apparent narrative in any given blow up. I did not trust that my anger or fear for instance, in those early years, began with my wife's actions towards me. There had to be a much longer trail back to my childhood.

In other words, I jumped into the myelination phase in my early years of marriage and pushed my right brain, inner child sensitivities and vulnerability onto my young adult perceptions. I knew I could not know my wife unless I knew the landscape inside my heart. M.D. Bramlett and W.D. Mosher report for the Centers for Disease Control and Prevention, "Sixty percent of marriages for couples between the ages of twenty and twenty-five end in divorce, compared to only 24 percent divorce rate for those marrying after 25 years of age. Also, the average age of first-time divorce is thirty years old."

Do not blame your discomfort on your spouse during these early years. Look inside first. Take the hit and realize it was your brain's fault. Ride it out. Let myelination offer your inner sensibilities up to your rational self so that you can understand the meaning.

High School Level Books, PhD Curriculum

We cross the marital threshold with high school math and English books as resources, and by the third and fourth years of marriage we are in a PhD level curriculum. The left brain is slowly going to be asked to tune into the more unruly neuron signals stirring within our emotional world. You and your marriage are still in the early adult cycle. There is a sense of being stupefied within this new arena.

It is like the two worlds of an athlete. There is all the preparation and work during the hours of practice. But then comes the rigor and demands of game time pressure which are completely different. Marriage is game time. You add a new baby, which many of us do, and the discourse accelerates. John Gottman writes in *The Seven Principles for Making Marriage Work*, "A child is a grenade...you set off an explosion once a child is born and marriage is never the same."

Half Syndrome

Upon entering marriage, we all suffer a bit of what I call Half Syndrome. We have developed only half our interpersonal, psycho-emotional capabilities. Our rational self is still young, naïve, even slightly self-assured. If we have enjoyed early material success in our burgeoning careers, if we applied our intellectual and executive talents, taken business risks, traveled, and built ourselves a professional dominion, then there is a logical and well-founded sense of accomplishment during our twenties and thirties.

We feel like adults. We perceive ourselves as card-carrying adults, having probed, tasted, and gathered many of the fruits of the adult world. But this perception and self-concept sits in a false dawn. Alexandra Sifferlin writes in *Why Teenage Brains are So Hard to Understand* that our reliable left-brain apparatus has governed all our "decision-making, planning, sober second thoughts." It has so far guided our successes and failures throughout this early adult phase. It has been a fantastic tool, helping us expand the physical and some of the psychological boundaries of our life.

There is a maturity, but it is thinner. It is without that deeper, brain-neuron history of your left being overwhelmed by the right. The uprooting of your intellect by the unraveling reactions in you and your spouse is the wisdom you will need.

That is the basis of this Half Syndrome deficiency. It is the natural limitations of the separated brains' halves. Issues in the marriage, from this still-limited lens, become things that you think you need to solve instead of patiently wade through. We are skeptical of all the fiery discourse, and our overreactions seem irrational and baseless. There is a reason why the U.S. Constitution precludes an adult under thirty years old to become a U.S. senator. The founding fathers, like all the early cultures, somehow knew that the trail towards full maturity begins well into our thirties, during this phase of brain development.

Twenty-something

The early years should not be used as the foundational reality of your marriage. Meg Jay writes in *The Defining*

Decade, "When we graduate from school, we leave behind the only lives we have ever known, ones that have been neatly packaged in semester-sized chunks with goals nestled within. Suddenly, life opens up and the syllabi are gone...It can be disorienting. The twenty-something years are a whole new way of thinking about time." We are initiating our powerful maiden voyage into the adult world, reforming and reorganizing our adolescent sensibilities.

What it takes to enter marriage is completely different then what it will take to travel through it, downstream with kids and jobs for the next fifty years. The criteria and psychological lens we use to determine who we court and marry has none of the scope and depth that our later years will provide. It does not mean, by any means, that those early decisions were wrong or misguided. It does not mean we are with the wrong person. It means you had a powerful, more rational, less emotionally seasoned hunch that impelled you to choose a person that you thought was perfect. Regardless of whether or not the marriage eventually works, strap yourself in and do the inner work that your life and marriage want you to do.

Career Achievements Uncorrelated to Marital Success

So often, though, especially because or if material success was tasted during your twenties and early thirties, we believe our marriage should work like our career has. We get caught in the vortex of if-then scenarios that are still shadowed by our adolescent nature, more twenty-something and less emotionally mature. If I addressed a slowdown in sales at work, for instance, by refocusing sales goals, hiring and firing new staff, and uncovering new target clients, then why can't my wife and I figure out a plan to stop bickering? Why can we never agree on how to address a crying infant or correct sloppy manners at the dinner table?

There is almost a haughtiness or dismissiveness towards the emotionality of the marriage-scape, emanating from our left-brain mentality. Robert Monroe says in *Ultimate Journey* that the left-brain perspective is dismissive, that it tends to regard the right with contempt.

Therefore, as we continue to use tools like logic and reason to address our relationship, tools which work in all the other areas of our life, we lose patience. Your adolescent-like expectations need to be thrown out. The lingering teenager inside of us, the one that we carried into our marriage, needs to open his heart. Gottman says in *The Seven Principles for Making Marriage Work* that you are not expected to know that "respecting each other's deepest most personal hopes and dreams is the key to success." In time, you will.

The true essence of who you and your spouse are, which manifests like the tree from the sapling, will eventually be revealed. Our deep-seated emotions are supposed to well up and impose their discomfort on the just-so perceptions of our evolving, still too logic-focused mind. Those are the signals from the relationship that a new phase has begun. But just as Gottman alludes, it is the separate dreams buried in each of you, revealed only by a time-softened heart, that have to be allowed to surface. The very act of holding these back is the death knell of your relationships and your ability to complete this life.

"In evolutionary terms, it became advantageous to our long-time survival to form complex relationships."

— Dan Siegel

Barnacles of Resentment

I often share with young couples in my counseling practice that the awareness gap between their left and right brains was at its widest during their early years of marriage, especially as their first child was born. This means that seemingly minor reactions, comments, or gestures directed at the other might have fomented unconscious feelings of hurt, disgust, or resentment that the adult mind no longer registers.

As I sat in therapy with my wife seven years into our marriage, she recounted a comment I made about her mother in our second year. I had no recollection, but she replayed the entire scene, including where we were sitting and my exact words. There is nothing more powerful than the feminine recall when the masculine has acted the fool.

I told her that I had no intention to hurt her. It was just a flippant, immature comment that I would never fathom making now. But she had connected my comment about her mother to her own heart and sensibilities. My rational self, back then, framed and experienced this opinion solely as commentary about her mother. My opinion of and disposition towards my wife was a million miles away from any characterization of her mother.

The point is that our left brain is young and dismissive of the emotionality of early marriage. It does not absorb and store information like our limbic, right brain apparatus does. In this vignette, my wife's perspective embodied the powerful, memory-soaked right brain that had stored and held old barnacles of resentment and frustration towards me for five years.

All kinds of feeling stuff get dumped into the marital stream early on. Our reactions then get quietly stored in the emerging, more communicative and myelinating right brain that our left has no idea about. I, in this story of course, represent the left brain. If my wife and I had not jumped in and pulled that barnacle of resentment off the dock where it had been stuck for so long, it would continue to grow and slice us apart.

We all need to learn to use the early years and our recollection of them as training, as learning this new dance. Do not blame the limited left brain, or your husband in this case, for the ignorance early on. If he is willing to do the work, then the weight of those old comments will lessen.

Not surprisingly, marriages fail due to two major reasons: lack of commitment and arguing too much. Bramlett and Mosher report for the CDCP that these are the most common reasons given by divorcing couples. We just need to be committed to unearthing what has been deposited early.

Impelled to Mate: Universal Forces

From a sociological and behavioral perspective, as we enter early adulthood, we begin to move towards what the great developmental psychologist Erik Erikson calls intimacy versus the earlier, more adolescent state of *isolation*. Erikson describes these stages in his seminal theory *Eight Stages of Life*.

After we have developed a sense of self in adolescence, we are ready to share our life with others. However, if other stages have not been successfully resolved, young adults may have trouble developing and maintaining successful relationships with others, writes James S. Fleming in *Erikson's Psychosocial Developmental Stages*. Therefore, it is important to lean into the emotional discomfort of this phase. Because we are carrying a kingdom of unprocessed emotions from our early twenties, we must allow a seasoning of our inner experiences in order to understand the true challenge of marriage.

It takes more than love.

Deep rooted emotional events are stuck below. Dad belittling you after striking out to lose the game in sixth grade baseball — and the ensuing, sunken feeling of uselessness, that quietly sleeps inside your midbrain — has created a thick, neuron groove in your memory. It has its own storage space soaked in disappointment. Erikson said that we must have a strong sense of self before we can develop a successful intimate relationship. These pangs of disappointment will not reach the height of their discomfort in you until age, your marriage, and your myelinating brain thrust them up.

During this myelination cycle we are also latently and unconsciously impelled to mate. It is as if we are turning back from the open seas of our risk-taking, late adolescent days and towards the shores of our home, any home, searching for a place to begin something of meaning with someone else. We are beginning our adult life story and myth, just like Odysseus in Homer's *Odyssey*. He and we, in our thirties, heading home. That is part of psychological and developmental current that Erikson's isolation to intimacy is referring to.

Even deeper in this well of self, there is a primal urge to create. For all living things, creation means reproducing one's DNA. This is the most basic instinctual and non-rational force that drives us into marriage, another reason not to beat yourself up for mistakes and confusion within the arena of your marriage during this timeframe.

The Hindus tell us that there are three cosmic forces in the world: preserve, destroy, and create. They call these The Trimurti. These primal energies impel you to bond, as if there was no choice. They are calling everything.

Beyond even this three-fold cosmic pull, we are inextricably impelled to bond with another person because our brains are wired to attach. Unconsciously, as we enter our mid-twenties, there is an ancestral, electromagnetic call to bond, an ancient, cellular, and eternal drumbeat for a merger. Dan Siegel writes in *Relationship Science and Being Human*, "The repeating patterns of communication we have that link us together in families, communities, and societies actually shape the structure and function of the brain. It seems that from the beginning of human evolution, our relationships and the myriad ways that we communicate within them...allowed us to not only survive, but ultimately to thrive."

And as we begin the climb towards our third decade, regardless of any ruminations or thought-doubts bellowing from our rational self, the evolutionary impulses to get married are going to win. "In evolutionary terms, it became advantageous to our long-time survival to form complex relationships within groups of extended families," says Dan Siegel in *Relationship Science and Being Human*. It is as if our right brain, which will get louder, is whispering to our left brain to move forward, take action. We are impelled by the right, but trying to hold it together with the younger left brain.

Saturn Returns, Asks for More

Throughout history and cultures, this timeframe when myelination kicks in, was often called the *Saturn Return*. It was the demarcation of leaving our youth behind and entering the true psychological state of adulthood. It was directly correlated with the planet Saturn, which takes twenty-nine and a half years to make a full orbit around the sun. As it is above, so it is below.

Forget about astrology and horoscopes, and just recall the basic physics of electrons and gravitational influences. We know the moon effects tides, for instance, by pulling the oceans toward it. *Continuous Planetary Interaction Theory* by Tony Waterfall tells us "Every planet in our solar system has an ionosphere where electrons join and release elementary particles. The spins of the electrons are...influencing other electrons to change."

We are made of the exact same stuff as planets. "Ninety-seven percent of your body is made up of the elements shed from stars over the last 4.5 billion years," said Elizabeth Howell, in *Science & Astronomy*. Our bodies are tiny planets, sitting on top of a big planet that is circling around other planets. Whatever is happening out there, beyond our Netflix movies, neatly groomed lawns and thoughtful setting of life goals, is being absorbed by us down here. Each planet has its own varying, elemental characteristics. Each radiates with a unique tone.

Saturn, in the pantheon of energetic forces, is historically characterized as the great task master, the bringer of order and discipline, the teacher of limitations and responsibility. It is a powerful rock of iron–nickel, surrounded by a metallic hydrogen. It is truly a force to be reckoned with and not to be taken lightly.

Saturn was symbolized as the sickle, the farming tool that finishes off the harvest as it cuts the grain. The sickle is the perfect representation of discipline and limitations as it imposes its sharp edge onto the growing stalk. The lifecycle of that plant is complete, thanks to the swing of that tool. With its extreme cold and dry nature, Saturn imposes its formidable inclination to finish and persevere so that everything gets done within the allotted timeframe.

The minute you were born, Saturn was sitting somewhere in the sky. Then, twenty-nine and a half years later, it is there again, in the exact same place. Whether or not planets and moons have distinct characteristics that influence things thousands of miles away, there is something electromagnetically relevant about this return. There is a quiet, very subtle sense that it is time to do something more, or at least an inkling that time is poking you to stop waiting and start doing.

This phase happens over years, from our late twenties well through our thirties. Unfamiliar pangs or longer doses of doubt and uncertainty mist up. Out of nowhere, we intuit a shadow of those expectations we set when younger. We begin to weigh our current life achievements with our head and heart, using a scale established well before our heart knew how to get involved. Father Time, embodied in the direct and less forgiving nature of this

Saturnal guidance, activates a drive to make changes.

This is just another reason why this timeframe creates such wonderful challenges and surprises. Saturn return, myelination, and the mammalian impulses to mate all coalesce as you are just beginning to have kids and continue your career. It is a perfect storm.

I got lucky, though, because I was not married when my Saturn Return phase kicked in. Sitting on Europe's largest financial trading floor back in the mid-Nineties, Lady Myelination and Governor Saturn wafted through me like jilted lovers.

I was thirty-two. My love life stunk because I was completely unable and unwilling to be honest and vulnerable. I did not know the angry boy in me yet, the one who wanted to open his heart to women but feared being dismissed.

The boy in me that my wife would wake up three years later was, at this point, still hiding from life and relationships. My left brain had built a sturdy wall of material abundance and distractions to keep the music of the mind loud enough to drown out the longing of that boy. Vulnerability was coming after me, mostly in the form of the long faces of disappointment and frustration of my girlfriends who kept walking away.

When this brain development phase hit me, the computer screens and flashing stock and bond prices, that had captured my adoration for eleven years, in an instant no longer told a story. They became just numbers. All the psychology of the game — the movements, the shifting news and headlines and all the market reactions to these events — seemed less important. When I was twenty-seven, though, those prices were my life.

Out of nowhere, during this first life cycle break, it felt like a close friend from high school had moved away. There was a subtle, stilling emptiness in me. The spirit of meaning and familiarity that I had built with and around my job in finance began to fade.

Something felt off. It was not just a thought or an idea. It was like drinking something and becoming slightly queasy. Not sick, just a bit of an ache. My activity at work, which had deep meaning months before, now felt hollow. This was my entrance into the transitional hallways of myelination, just as Saturn began to loom in my sky. This phase became the gift that opened me up to world of feelings. Without this phase, I would not have found my wife, as I would not have been able to hear my heart or hers.

The Wonder-ish Years

All couples debate and overreact to each other. My wife responds curtly, for instance. Instantly, I resent her dismissive tone. It seems excessive. Deep in the swirl of my mid-brain, below the current of this relatively innocuous discussion, a flash of my grandmother belittling my grandfather forty years ago stabs my awareness. I am now charged by her seemingly disrespectful tone, even though she might just be tired or preoccupied with figuring out if the kids are dg their homework.

What has arrived, via the current topic of money and groceries, is the unconscious presence of the immature, often spoiled ten-year-old inside of me. His silent grudge towards women is awakened. It was sleeping just under the surface, just below my reasonably mundane interaction with my wife. The entire scene of this kitchen discussion shifts to me wanting to lash out at my wife's disrespect and insolence. She is the one making me feel small, hurt, and angry, right? She is the only other person in the room, so who else is to blame? This, dear reader, is why marriages fail.

They fail because I want to release my deep, unconscious current of frustration around a global topic of women disrespecting men, hurling it onto the messenger my wife. But the conflict is mine, not hers. It is between the divided lives inside of me, between how I consciously and rationally thought during the early part of this kitchen discussion versus the pile of old feelings and yearnings that my emotional self is still soaked with.

We are unprepared and naïve to the concept of cohabitating with our spouse over a long period of time. We are oblivious to how triggered we would become throughout the discourse of marriage. What's more, we never knew how much unconscious material was sleeping in the shadow of our adult sensibilities.

A Test Site

Whether it is the return of Saturn, myelination, or our instinct to form a bond and create, our early adult years have to be used at the testing site for our marriage. We should call them the Wonder Years, because you wonder how we made it through them. I look at how I parent, perceive, and appreciate my wife, kids, and extended family now versus the lens of what I could see and perceive when I first got married. I might as well have been another human being.

CHAPTER 7
SIT! EVERYTHING ELSE IS AN EXCUSE

"In other words, all our perceptions and thoughts are colored by emotion."

— Frijof Capra

John Sits

After another of our sessions, I started encouraging John to start sitting and listening to his heart. "Meditation?" he asked.

"Yup, just find a quiet place in your house. I actually sit in our walk-in closet," I told him. "As soon as you start doing this you will loosen up sensations inside the chest and throat. At some point, a memory-emotion will rise up from the stomach area, cross back through your heart, and a tear will form."

He looked confused. I told him to just try it, that it was hard to describe and explain. He and I had a session three weeks later without Amy, and he told me that something opened in him when he meditated one evening.

He said it was very weird. After about ten minutes, it felt like the back of his throat and shoulders warmed up like a summer evening breeze from the days when he was a kid. Suddenly, it was like his heart opened up to an image of him waiting for his mom to come home when he was young, waiting on some porch stoop as the sun was setting. But no one arrived that day. This was the only way he said that he could describe the sensation. It was like the middle of his throat and bottom of his heart were lonely and starting to get heavier than normal. He said it was something that just wanted to come up that was going to bring a tear.

What was happening with John was that the linear trail of the day-to-day thinking part of his brain was getting quiet, like falling asleep at night. His current life stuff was fading out, though he was wide awake, while his organizing, adult thoughts were slowing down. He had sat long enough so that most of the back and forth rhythm to his thoughts stalled.

Physiologically what happens after ten minutes of relaxing with our eyes closed is that the pineal gland at the top of our head starts secreting enough serotonin and melatonin that the spinning electrons in the cells in our brain slow down to about eight to twelve cycles a second, mentions M.D. Khalsa in *Meditation as Medicine*. When we are wide awake, our brain cells are cycling at about sixteen to eighteen cycles a second.

The Oldest Path Back to Self

All John was doing was allowing his limbic right brain that stores memories and sensations to pass through the thick walls of thought and daily activity. Our right brain "perceives form and space, beauty, intuition, emotions plus everything else the left brain cannot understand or categorize," said Robert Monroe in *Ultimate Journey*. When we sit and breathe, though, the right takes the stage while the left sits in the audience.

As Monroe further explains, there is a basic battle between our left and right sides. It is hard for our rational mind to explain love. It is like trying to put friendship and a passion for cooking into a spreadsheet. One has lines, the other has curves.

Joseph Campbell said, "The chief aim of all religious teachings and ceremony is to suppress...the sense of ego and develop that of participation." Sitting, merging these two sides, this is the only way to begin the personal hero journey. John, our suburban, corporate lawyer-knight, has seen for the first time his first mid-sized dragon. That dragon was an old sadness and broken heart of a boy many years back that somehow created insecurity and anxiousness in John about expressing his feelings, especially to women (in particular his wife). To share his feelings meant revealing vulnerability, which was not encouraged while growing up.

So many psycho-emotional memories and dragon-experiences live inside John, in all of us. There is possibly the angry grandfather, the depressed aunt, the loves and divorces throughout generations, the battle scars from dividing grandparents' assets, or just the general and seemingly emotional chaos that families contain. All of this would soon be coming up in him. Big stuff.

Since college, John had to formulate, analyze, and materialize his thoughts and beliefs in order to earn money. We have all been doing that nonstop. There has never been a reason to slow that down. Memories of fourth grade cannot enter the door of our conscious mind unless we slow it down.

In his dating twenties and early thirties, John would often pour his wounded heart out. He would overwhelm his girlfriends with passion, scaring them along the way. Or he would casually and confidently draw girlfriends in with his charm and playfulness, but never let them further into his life. When the music stopped, during those quiet times alone with a woman, he often just wanted to run away. This dragon of longing, which formed the basis of his insecurity, plagued him. He never really understood why this series of girlfriends all told him the same thing, that he was running from something. He was about to find out that their tears were really just a reflection of his unexpressed ones.

As weeks went by, he continued to sit. He would come into our sessions and he could identify the roots and history of a specific feeling, one that he had now introduced to his adult lawyer's brain. I knew from there on, John's life was going to change, his emotional intelligence was going to break new ground, and he and his marriage were going to mature and evolve. He was going to understand the behaviors of his wife with a clarity that he never thought imaginable. That was still months and years down the line, but it had begun.

GM Betty, Kitchen Elder

Recalling that session with John, long memories of GM Betty, that stove from our early years of marriage, seep out. She was like that old, resolute tree by the river or in your backyard that has witnessed everything, the endless current and every season's death and rebirth. She heard and watched the boy and man in me, the girl and woman in my wife, and knew if we kept coming back to the hearth, kept carrying our heated longings and joys back to each other, we would break ourselves and our marriage open.

I think of how naturally innocent we were, how little we knew. Raw and young, just as the science of myelination was quietly waking our childhood memories, we began the long search for out adult selves within the container of marriage there. It was as if Betty was the elder reminding and pushing me to work on understanding the sadness and joy my wife was creating in me so that I could recognize the hurt and delight in her. Great Elders and wise women do not need words, their presence is the reminder to go further, to move towards the heat and risk awakening the pain.

The love I have now for my wife is so different than what it was then. The years, the experiences, and the debris we have confronted alone and together, like rings on a tree, have built layers of appreciation for and awe of her. She pushes me away and calls out the right path. I know her mood before the door closes when I come home. I see the little girl in her reactions and trust the precision of her intuition. This progression into adult love only emerges from starting and continually coming back to the heat and alter of marriage. My recommendation? Stand in the fire in the wisdom of what is burning you, in front of your own Betty, whatever locale that symbolizes your heart and hearth. She was the place of our beginning. Consider where is the hearth of your marriage? Where is that origin?

Thought Your Brain Was Smart? Think Again

Our body knows everything. Our stomach knows that our parents were not deeply happy growing up, that our work colleague is immature and spiteful, and that we would rather be taking an art class than staring at the TV or doing laundry. But the roots of this story are much deeper than just some gut feeling about life and self.

Our stomach and solar plexus live, breathe, behave, respond, and experience our life almost completely separately, distinctly and independently from our higher neocortex. Who we are in our gut is not who we are to our adult self.

Our solar plexus at the top of our stomach has the largest bunch of nerves and neuro-transmitters in the body, and as reported in "Complex and Hidden Brain in Gut Makes Stomachaches and Butterflies," in the *New York Times*, "nearly every substance that helps control the brain like serotonin, dopamine, and norepinephrine" are found in the stomach. There are brain proteins in our stomach, ruminating, remembering, and learning in the stomach, right next to yesterday's dinner.

One Life, Two Worlds

Do you understand what that means? There is a brain, a disposition, comprehension, and consciousness in your stomach that responds to and generates its *own* feelings and motivations, quietly assessing, worrying over and about its environment. She, your tummy, has been there all along at every single, monumental, psycho-emotional juncture in your life, and she has stored every feeling. At your first kiss, she was fluttering and unhinged. When your girlfriend ditched you in tenth grade because of the comments you made, your stomach neurons turned empty and hollow.

That emotional dent was probably filled in with ice

cream and bagels. But until there is a reckoning, until the feelings of emptiness and hurt are allowed to be re-expressed, re-felt, and unfolded, then a hurt will always live there.

Or, as another example, when you failed that final in college, she (your belly) constricted and blanched with overwhelming sensations of loss and self-loathing. Here again is where the body and head storylines separate. Your rational, psychological response to failing that test in the beginning, was similar to your stomach's. It was a potpourri of loss, anger, and frustration for not studying enough, leaving your conscious self embarrassed and even sheepish about your intelligence. As the months and years unfolded, though, as you left college, got a good job, and activated your materializing skills, that miserable test score was a punch line to your hallmark, self-effacing jokes and tales about the frivolity of college days.

To your conscious self, that event held no more significance. It was just a pale memory about some chemistry test from the Eighties. But to the memory-infused nerves and peptides in your stomach, that sense of loss and misgiving lingers and is only about two deep breaths away from alighting a cascade of fear and doubt that is as bright as the moment you got the test back.

Just the thought of a test could stir a lump in the stomach. With the deeper and often recurring emotional events of our life, like familial relationships and the discomfort they can bring, the biochemical reactions continue to churn and spin far away from our adult realizations.

Adult Forgot the Teenager Lives in the Belly

Close your eyes for two minutes and just put your attention into your stomach. Feel her. She is living, remembering, and collecting the unmitigated and unabridged truth of your life. Physical, biochemically generated sensations are the authentic, undivided truth of every single human moment. Thoughts are derivatives of these physical sensations. In *Seth Speaks* we learn that "Feeling and emotions create thoughts, thoughts create your beliefs. A belief is a thought done over and over."

Close your eyes and fathom that last sentence again, please. "A belief is a thought done over and over." If you just keep thinking about your resentment about your spouse, thinking that one politician or race or sex is better than another, and that sitting quietly is a waste, than you have your belief. So, your thirty or forty-year-old self has moved long beyond that tenth-grade moment, having kissed that experience goodbye. But the soft hurt still lives in stomach time, and therefore, still gently and faintly informs your thoughts and beliefs about yourself.

Your forty-year-old self, if asked, would not recognize or believe this emotional dent still lingers. Watch, though. When a similar kind of event occurs today, the neighborhood ladies somehow do not invite you to bunko, or your spouse innocently questions why the kitchen is so messy, that lump of rejection is awoken. The conscious thought of being left out ignites those old, authentic enzymes of sadness and hurt. Our true beliefs about who our adult selves really are were formed by the mechanisms of our youth-based emotions.

Sadness and hurt become anger in the adult. But we

know what is underneath and below the frustration. It is heartbreak and a desire to be included and held.

Buddha Belly

How important is the belly, what scientists now refer to as the second brain, to our life, marriage, and to reminding and waking up the truths about ourselves and what we are carrying around inside? How crucial is it to find a way to open and release these old stored experiences? Well, the basic practices of Buddhism, as immortalized and symbolized by the Buddha's large belly, are to breathe deeply into the solar plexus.

When we breathe into our stomach, extend it out during the inhale and press it back in towards the back of our spine on the exhale, magic happens. The entire body is powerfully transformed. In Sarah Novotny's paper "The Science of Breathing," slow belly breaths "reset the autonomic nervous system...slowing electrical action currents which synchronizes neural elements in the heart, lungs, limbic system and cortex." What happens is our heart rate slows, which in turns generates serotonin that seeps into your rationalizing brain's sector, easing its normally jumpy, skeptical, and resistant construct.

The punch line is that your adult sensibilities, those that always want to move forward in time and not back, out and not in, are given the chance to wade into the neuron current of those tenth-grade emotions. In this sacred locale, induced by simple breaths, sitting quietly alone, you perceive the emotional reality and language of how that feeling of loss from that failed test still somehow weighs you down.

When your husband makes an innocuous comment about watching the household spending, your adult attention registers a mild caution, so you scratch off a few Target runs. But to your stomach world, a quiet torrent of fear and worry from fourth grade, when your dad lost his job and the electricity was cut off, rolls in. You reach for some food to soothe those nerves, but granola or cheese will never undo or resolve this fear.

That is where I am taking you, to that place where these two worlds meet and become one.

"To weep is to make less the depth of grief."

— Shakespeare

Circling Around the Center, that First Therapy Session

As discussed in Chapter 1, my first counseling session was with Dr. Moore's. I did not know this one-hour therapy session was my crossover point, the doorway to these two inner worlds colliding where boy meets man. We all have one, two, or twenty-five throughout our life, that deeply uncomfortable, long, threshold moment.

Job loss, marital issues, parents passing, or just something being off inside of us, are all inflection points, where and when we either keep pushing outward and avoid the dull aches, malaise, or sorrow, or we stop, close the door, sit down with our back straight, and just sit and listen. These threshold points are when our inner and outer worlds are at their widest points, when our heart and stomach-based desires and longings are the most distant from our adult beliefs and expectations. Some recognize this psycho-emotional gap as the basis of depression.

It was the mid-Nineties. I was thirty-one and a pretty successful research sales trader, working at a big American investment bank in London. Like I said, you have probably heard this kind of tale before. I would not have known a neuron, cortex, limbic brain, or Buddha belly if they were sitting next to me, also waiting for therapy. I was not ready to know, feel, or experience more about myself — but there I was, anxious, restless, and confused.

I kept thinking as I sat in that first therapy session, "Maybe right now I turn back, no, run back to the safety of my apartment and to the knowable, empty, unexamined and dimly lit, rationally-based life I know so well." I was either too cowardly, tired, or anxious to run.

So many stories had been told in this office to this therapist Dr. Moore. She had surely heard them all. Was it even worth sharing mine with her? Was she really listening? She was old school with her ponderous desk. Maybe I would just spin my current life tale so it all seemed good, she buys it, and then I could get out unscathed. No harm.

At least I had my healthy, inherited cynicism to keep me entertained, that voice sent down through the generations that placed that chip on my shoulder, saying I knew better. If we never find the deeper wisdom and peace stored in our inner worlds, the result is normally a sarcastic defensiveness of the world and the opinions of others. That voice of disquiet likes to discredit and undo the voices and overtures outside of us. It is a natural reflex. If we doubt and disrespect ourselves, then the chip we carry seeks to chip away at someone else's life force. It is a learned trait.

My generation, raised in the Seventies and Eighties, absorbed the unconscious, timeworn dispositional tones, accents, and psychological constructs of Depression-era parents. It was more of a grin-and-bear-it world we grew up in, a natural progression from parents born during and into the heavier days of a world war. It just seemed logical to dispel comments or insights that were asking for more self-awareness, for more looking at one's feelings and how they impacted the environment. There were not a lot of self-help books circulating back then.

There was probably a long line of male ancestors that should have tried a bit of therapy. The path that led me to the chair in front of Dr. Moore was seemingly lined with the unexpressed losses and longings of those who came before me. Maybe all of us would benefit.

Heart Whisper

All I know is that my heart, the heart of my third grader trying to sing something, trying to hold or grab or touch something or someone else, was ready. But my naïve, overconfident, analytically minded and inflated masculinity, as well as my adult sense of self were not. The thought of being alone, sitting quietly alone, stilled and floored me. I knew the gnawing restlessness was not going to dissolve unless I did something about it

With ten minutes left in that first session, as my body and thoughts exhaled more and softened, the first tear in seven years welled. It was the warming and longing in my heart-belly drifting up, meeting the cool, detached reasoning of my young adult self. The egoic self above the neck was white knuckling it to keep the yearnings of the boy out. It was like a tropical storm where the heat rises and meets the cold upper air, creating rain, forming that tear.

It was going to rain a lot more.

Young Adult World and Job

There had been nothing more satisfying to me over the prior ten years at my job than studying and strategizing market movements with my global, money managing clients. Our job was to connect clients with the global securities markets.

It was physically and mentally demanding, but also compelling and stimulating, to try to recognize, anticipate, or sense when a bond, stock, currency, or commodity was making a move. If you studied and took notes, listened and watched prices closely, and felt into the psychological and behavioral storyline of the changing numbers, those prices would whisper their next movements. It was like seeing a storm before others even knew it was cloudy, or lunging quickly forward just in time to catch that wave when surfing.

For so long, it never felt like a job. Yes, there was the obligatory suit and tie, but to a man-boy in his mid to late twenties, that was sacred garb, a uniform that allowed entrance to the phone banks of the trading desks. Each change in price told a story that impacted the story of all the other prices. Why is gold going down when the Germany 10-year bond is going up? If Japanese inflation is lower, what does that mean for US stocks and French three-month bills? In Jack Schwager's *Market Wizards,* he writes that one client described investing by saying, "When you really get involved, the screen almost reaches out and grabs you."

"To make money in the markets, you have to be willing to get in the way of danger."

— Michael Steinhardt

What Investing Reveals of Self

Working in finance was like working on a global puzzle. The pieces were made up of political edicts and policy decisions, economic data reports, corporate earnings and headlines, central bank money flows that coalesced into prices. Our intuition drew us to our most insightful and profitable trades, but it was logic that contained our feelings and overreactions and managed the risk.

The market was always right, and she never cared about what you felt, wanted, or longed for. How often did she take off in that direction you knew she would, that you had felt coming for days, but on which you had not taken action? You were afraid. You were not quite sure, afraid of taking the risk while she turned from you and accelerated more, just as you thought you could grab and leave with her one more time.

Those market moves you miss incite an ache that is worse than when you were dead wrong and took a loss. You are left cold and frustrated like missing that last commuter train or the final flight of the night because you'd dallied. It was an ancient speculative curse to sense a move with your gut and intuition, but not hand over the perceptions to your higher, analytical brain so it could parse and assess how much risk to take.

Your feelings must share the decision-making with your reason.

Many people believe that choosing the direction of the market is the key to successful investing. It is not. It is about choosing how much money to risk once you surmise the direction, and then determining when to get out, when to get back in, when to leave this trade behind and move on — to maybe buy or sell more, or even when to take an opposing position to balance the risk.

The game is not up or down; it is the hundred other decisions once the first one is made. Each one demands that you somehow, some way trust, believe, and accept your process based on your responses to the data and yourself. It is you versus price, your conviction and judgement versus the current market quote, which is the distillation of two thousand other traders' decisions.

One of the industry's all-time great money managers and speculators, Michael Steinhardt, said, "to make money in the markets, you have to be willing to get in the way of danger." To him and many other traders, it was financial warfare. But the enemy was never outside of the screen or beyond a desk. Like golf, investing and speculating is a singular, relational battle between two objects: every part of you versus the current market price on the screen. Those are the only two entities involved.

This probably sounds esoteric or maudlin, but for those ten years, my clients and I were having personal relationships with each market we watched and acted in. Money was the scorecard, doctor, and therapist telling us the overall health of our relationships.

Another titan of Wall Street, Bruce Kovner, pioneered strategies that measured the relationships between all the different bonds floating in the markets. He talked about how visceral and impassioned the experience of investing can get. In *Market Wizards*, he talks about the Heisenberg Principle, which states that if something is closely observed, odds are it is going to be altered in the process. That is, the more we impose our attention, thoughts, feelings, reactions, losses, love, hate, anger, and exuberance on headlines and market prices, the more we impact these. The more energy given and offered to a thing, the higher the likelihood of that thing changing.

If you followed the narratives emerging from each price change, you could truly sense coming market tides. Seemingly out of nowhere, though, the prices stopped telling a tale and became just numbers to me again. Watching, staring, waiting, and expecting those price changes, almost in an instant became a shallow, uninteresting exercise. The problem was, at this point in my life, they were my whole life.

Plotline? Lost.
"Are You Sure You Want to Do This?"

Not caring about things other than the market and my job was becoming uncomfortable. A malaise had gingerly and faintly seeped into my days. I had begun to wonder what she, the market, her prices, and her gifts of profits meant to me. The screens and her patterns were calling, but I had no more emotional attention to give her. Working on Europe's largest trading floor at the time only exasperated my inner disquiet. The sea of ringing phones and shouting salespeople made me feel even smaller, emptier. The less fulfilled we feel, the louder the outside world rattles.

Yes, I know now that meaning refers to "a nonphysical reality inherent in the relationship between a symbol and that to which it refers...a way to make sense of our existence," as it says in JC Crumbaugh's "An Experimental Study in Existentialism." Meaning emerges when we keep asking the bigger questions even though we do not know the answers. I did not know that in my thirties, though.

Remember, my brain was just starting to myelinate. It had been a relatively long stretch for me, over the preceding ten years, of *doing* all day balanced with very little feeling. A muffled, unexamined heart will eventually come up for air. I had been staring at only one relationship, my career in the financial markets, at the expense of all other potential relationships.

I had been living in this little world of work, only participating in moments, events, or activities that I could easily get into and out of without much emotional turnover. I was removed and detached from other people's inner stories and dramas because I had not even peeked at my own inner myth. That was probably going to be scary.

Dr. Moore then asked me, in the middle of our session, the world's greatest question. It had only one real answer. She knew I was struggling. She was trying to slow me down so I did not fully unravel right there. "Are you sure you want to do this, Bill, keep asking these questions?"

"I'm not sure," I said, even though my sarcastic inner voice seemed to be whispering, "How much is this session going to cost us?" I really was not sure. But I did know, having sat long enough in her office, that I was more miserable than I thought.

I know now that if there are long doubts, pauses, regrets, and grief in our experiences of our relationships and marriage, then this kind of sitting is the exact spot we need in order to find relief and answers. Your desire to know more keeps you reading this book, and it will draw you further into the vague and unsettling place of your feelings. But your thoughts want nothing to do with this landscape. They figure a solution is just around the corner. With another aspirin, jog, job, meal, or self-help article, all will be well.

Feelings Stick Around Long After We Thought Them

Think of the mixture of emotions, the normal love, guilt and anger towards family members, office managers, religious zealots, and politicians we encounter. When these frustrated thought-feelings seemingly dissipate because you blithely go back to surfing the net or unraveling a spreadsheet at work, the bio-magnetic sensations of guilt and anger do not evaporate.

Like a mid-summer rainy mist bathing your lawn and bushes, feelings and sensations nestle themselves in the tiny neuron cells along the mighty heart-midbrain, the electron highway. Your muscles, neck, shoulders, heart, forehead, every sinew silently is soaked with a longing or desire for dad to hug you, or that girlfriend not to have broken your heart, or that job or investment not to have gone sideways. Silent but big are these old sensations. You need to hear what they are trying to tell you.

Every headache and lower back spasm — the body chirping, old memories unconsciously weighing us down

— tries to tell us something. Fritjof Capra, a brilliant physicist and feeler, reminds us in *The Web of Life* just how pervasive and inescapably tied our emotions and memories are to our body and thoughts: "Scientists have observed that the central nervous system which connects sensory organs with the brain is enriched with peptide receptors that filter sensory perceptions. In other words, all our perceptions and thoughts are colored by emotion."

Every hurt and joy, every little want or dent of loss that never got filled, explained, reconciled, or just fully let go of, somehow lives and tugs at us like my dog Smokey does at dinner time. He scratches my chair, just like an anger towards your mom powders your response to your kids and spouse.

We now see that there is a world of entire life experience and mythology embedded in our body neurons, all of it completely foreign to our organizing adult attention. When I left Dr. Moore's office that night, I decided I was going to learn how to sit quietly, alone. I found a class with a teacher that had been sitting quietly for nine years. Nothing has been the same since.

Only Solution, Sit

Why sit? You and I can avoid all the feelings, hoping they just go away and our marriage gets better. But sooner or later, this lifetime or next, whether you believe it or not, you are going to have to just sit still, close your eyes, and listen to your heart. It is the oldest and only way to know what is really going on in your life.

I have sat for seven thousand hours since that first therapy session. This is my whole message: getting others to sit for as long as possible. Everything else I have ever written or talked about — every other concept, idea, truism, exercise, story, quip, and scientific data point — are just filler and delivery mechanisms for the one and only exercise that will actually change your life, as well as the trajectory of your response to and experience of your marriage.

No need to chant, no incantations, mantras, thoughts or things to avoid, no clearing of the mind, no emptying of anything. Just sit and listen, maybe a few deep breaths. Listen to what? Your heart, period.

If you fall asleep, great, it means you are tired. Bored, anxious, riddled with lower back or knee pain, rescheduling your day, about to cry, remembering how angry you are at your spouse, choosing tomorrow's outfit, or just begging for this sitting to be over? Perfect, right on schedule. Just come back to the chair or cushion again when you muster the courage.

No More Excuses

Sitting might be the hardest thing you ever do. I get it. You might not be ready.

Everything you do during your day that distances and prevents you from doing this one simple thing, though, is an excuse grounded in fear. Fear of what? A fear and reluctance of truly knowing, understanding, owning, and taking full responsibility of every single emotion, action, and reaction in your life.

You are just minutes away from allowing this life to pour up and out. A part of you knows it. If you are still reading this, then you have a curiosity: a part of you that instinctually knows that something is missing.

Our highly charged left brain "get it done" adult rhythms are kind of afraid of all those amorphous pangs living deep within our emotion and memory infused, amygdala mid-brain. In the same way as described in "Amygdala Hijack: When Emotion Takes Over" on healthline.com, my frontal lobes "really wanted to override the amygdala, and respond in the most rational, appropriate way." Sitting in front of the therapist was rational. What was going to unfold in the coming weeks was far from that.

"The first step in the acquisition of wisdom is silence, the second listening, the third memory, the fourth practice, the fifth teaching others."

— Solomon Ibn Gabirol

Land of Vulnerability

Our adult mind actually acts as a dam to hold back other perceptions. Think of how much we do to avoid remembering, especially those deeply visceral life moments of an old friend who is gone for instance, a hug we always wanted, or a hate or love we never expressed. Some of these old experiences are like our scarier dreams that we would never even consider going back in to. Please feel free to hop off here, but what you will find if you stick around will change your world and your kids' kids' life experiences as well.

During our youth and into adolescence, our thoughts and feeling sway, mingle, and surge. Everyday Mentor's website tells us "the amygdala and prefrontal cortex battle it out for control over behavior—until the prefrontal cortex eventually takes over." As adults, that battle is just quieter, its aches and pains more subtle, instead of crying at our parents' feet when we are bored or tired.

But the feelings live on, embedded within heart and stomach brains — and what lengths do we go to today to not cry or feel too much? How hard do we avoid sitting still, in silence, so that our heart world does not open and speak its mind? You and I will eat, drink, run, work, argue, read the paper, watch TV, listen to music, take the kids somewhere, walk the dog, talk on phone, text, have sex, talk about other people, check the sports page, masturbate, smoke a joint, uselessly and aimlessly surf the internet, and do a million other things other than sit quietly in a dimly lit room.

The actions all seem innocuous. But what are we avoiding? You and I both know we are pushing against something, something big and kind of scary. Carl Jung based his career on the search for self and recognized how difficult it seems at first: "People will do anything, no matter how absurd, to avoid facing their soul."

Growing Up Sucks

Sitting is the only classroom. Are you willing to become a student to your life and marriage? You must perceive yourself as student in relationship. That is why so many fail. Solomon Ibn Gabirol says that the first step as student in the acquisition of wisdom is "silence, the second listening, the third memory, the fourth practice, the fifth teaching others."

A few weeks after that first session with Dr. Moore, I

sat for the first time, sober, in a room, eyes closed, in the company of perfect strangers, guided by someone who did this every day for, it turns out, the last nine years.

We did a few deep breaths with our hands on our stomachs. This makes sense to me now, but it did not then. She guided us to focus on our stomach. Slowly, I could feel a soothing pool of humility, a heaviness in my shoulders. It was similar to when I was on a fishing boat off the Florida Keys, miles offshore. The further out we headed, the closer we came to something bigger, more portentous. The continental shelf and its playful turquois water were giving way to a ponderous, deep blue current. It was the mighty Gulf Stream, over 2,600 feet deep in places, with one million cubic feet of its water flowing past that shelf every second. There is an ominous tone to that part of the ocean.

The longer I sat, the more I sensed something, sensations that felt bigger, heavier, and impending, just off in the distance. It was similar to those darker gulf-stream currents. There was a fathomlessness. My seemingly important thoughts about my current life stopped sticking to my brain. Thought sensations were not staying in my forehead, but drifting into my ribs.

My teacher's voice in that room seemed far away as she continued to talk us through slower breaths. The clatter of expectations for next week's meetings, the aches surrounding my mostly off-again relationship with my fifth girlfriend in two years, and the question about where my Nineties life in England was going all felt very briefly like someone else's issues. These thoughts were like my three dogs when I pour their food: quiet, poised, expectant, anxious and unsure.

Heavy Fullness, Unplugged in London

By the end of that class, I had sunk into a heavy fullness that felt like some large, curved edge was near. I sensed a soothing pool of humility darkening blue around me. What I experienced in the final fifteen minutes of that class was a moment of subtle interruption of all things linear and obvious to me. I would have laughed if someone said that a complete undoing and redoing of my life was going to ensue.

When we opened our eyes, it took a few minutes to rev back up. That edge was gone and it was time to take a cab home. Before I made it to the door, though, the teacher came up to me. I believe she could sense a subtle fracture in my look, an unsettledness.

"Remember, Bill, all Eastern thought is based on not knowing, saying I don't know," she said. "Western thought is about defining something, everything, about having an answer. The further you go into I don't know, the wobblier it gets." I had no answer. I thanked her and left.

Two weeks after this meditation class, I came home from work and decided I would try sitting alone. More of that graying dullness was washing through me. "F-it," I thought, "I am not going for a run, having a drink or eating anything. I am just going to sit."

I put my pillow on the ground. I faced the inky, chimney-lined skyline of central London. Squeaky brakes outside did what they did best outside, slicing the wet night. Just another night in the ancient town. Not a big deal that another body begins to sit for the first time on his own. This city has seen it all. Ancient Gaelic warriors thousands of years ago gathered around fires, calling in the spirits to guide their walks and hunts. Just around the corner a week before, another Roman site had been found during the excavation for a new building. This one dated back to pre-Christ times.

Sitting is the oldest human exercise. In Eric Jaffe's article *Meditate on It*, we read that "A couple hundred thousand years ago, early humans huddled around campfires to meditate and partake in rituals, which strengthened the mind's ability to connect symbols and meaning." As I began to slow my breath, I felt something. If there was ever a time in my life that something could spill, it was right then. My neck and shoulders tensed up, as if something was trying to come up and out of my chest.

Without any thoughts attached to them, a wash of feelings surged upward. There was no content to these emotions; they seemed to be just circulating in the air in my room. The pressure at the back of my neck and head was building, uncomfortable to the point where I was not sure I could keep going. But I did. Then tears streamed down my face, but I was not sad or happy. It was like my adult sensibilities were just watching, listening, and feeling a cracking of my self.

Weeks later I wrote in my journal about this specific moment when tears started to flow. It felt like the emotional part of me, over the last ten to twelve years, had been parched like some endless desert valley, scorched by ceaseless sun and wind. But as my thoughts drifted down into my heart, a stirring, gap, or shift of some kind ensued, and a drop of rain soften that desert floor. "To weep is to make less the depth of grief," wrote

Shakespeare in *King Henry VI.*

Then the clouds, I mean tears, really opened up and exploded as my body shook like I was being choked and hanged. Some part of me just stayed with it. Again, there was no content or story behind or inside these heaving sobs. They were crying themselves, leaving my thirty-one-year-old out of the plot. At the height of these bodily convulsions, I passed out.

When I woke up in the dark, there was sense of utter peaceful exhaustion. I had some trepidation, though, because it somehow felt I was not alone. Then, like in a movie, an audible whispering voice clearly and succinctly said, "Welcome back."

Holy acid trip! How far had my imagination taken me? How far off the reservation had I traveled? Suddenly, and I get goose bumps as I write these words now, I sensed and felt that I was sitting in the middle of a circle of stately wise, female Native American elders who were chanting an ancient, guttural, and mesmerizing song. Right there in my Chelsea apartment. Did they take the tube?

I can hear this chant right now. We read in *Seth Speaks*, "In moments of solitude you may become aware of some of the other streams of consciousness...hear words, see images that appear out of context with your own thoughts. According to your educational beliefs, background, you interpret these in any number of ways."

Was all this coming from inside of me or around me? Was I awake or dreaming? Was I alone or were these apparitions sharing my room? It was dark and quiet in my room, but a reunion was taking place. That is, for the first time, I sat alone and just listened to my heart.

Nutso, Right?

To many readers, this might seem like some drug-induced, psychotic schism. Morning headlines read, "Commodity broker hear voices, sheds a tear in Central London. No casualties reported." Actually, there was one victim, my entire sense and perception of time, self, feelings, the past, and who I really was or was not. No biggie.

It is probably what Eratosthenes felt two thousand years ago when he planted a stick in the ground in Alexandria to see what angle the sun's shadow would take. When he saw that its angle was different than the one the sun cast in the city of Syene to the south, he realized the world was curved.

When I woke up in the dark that evening, my life experience was curved. Now I must convince you to do the same, to be willing and courageous enough to trust not only me, but any current sense of boredom, longing, and a desire to make changes in your life. Trust that there is much more to the linear, this-then-that, good-bad perspective which your adult thoughts are handing you.

Yeah, right. Sit and chant and visualize, blah blah, and my husband will stop being an idiot, my parents will stop driving me crazy, and my kids will do the dishes which will make me happy and my marriage will miraculously blossom. I get it. You want action, you want others to understand you and not talk back or disagree with you. You want less stress, more time, less anger, more forgiveness.

When you see what is in store for you inside, once you get through the first few painful old memories, or the boredom, and wait for the movie to start inside, things will shift. But I am not expecting you to believe that, yet.

What I Found, What You Will Find

As the days and weeks unfolded, and I continued to sit, the experience of opening something deeper and crazier continued. It was like going up into your parents' attic to see boxes and trunks you never knew were there. It would take you years to go through them, but you decide to do so.

I have sensed a thousand insights since my first evening, as will you too. The single most powerful and important truth, whether you believe it or not, is that your physical adult heart is the heart of the child still living inside. This silent, roaring, childhood-soaked, electromagnetic muscle stores every single dream, memory, joy, and fear that has ever existed in you, your parents, their parents, and everything else that has ever glanced across your intuition.

In order to know the extent of your frustration about your husband, you will need to measure and re-feel your love and hate across your archetypes and that original male figure in your life.

Much Deeper Possibilities: You are the Hero

Nothing you ever do will release the power, wisdom, and possibilities that are stored in your heart like sitting alone with your back straight. No pill, exercise, class, degree, song, lecture, podcast, book, or religious sermon can even come close. Just sit and wait. Put this book down and close your eyes. Keep your back straight, though.

Steve Jobs had one book next to his bed his whole adult life. It was *Autobiography of a Yogi* by Paramahansa Yogananda. Guess what that main message of that book is? Just sit. How strongly did Jobs, one of the world's most prolific creators and successful entrepreneurs, believe in the transformative power of sitting quietly? At his request, every mourner who attended his funeral received a wooden box. Guess what was in that box? *Autobiography of a Yogi.*

You are reading this book and others like it because, like me, you want more, desire more, want to see your marriage and relationships become more. You do not have to know what to do next once you sit. Sitting will guide you.

The most powerful forces in your universe are the inner sensations, that boyhood love for the freedom felt while bike riding and climbing trees, that girlhood excitement about the same things, as well as flowers, story-time, and grandma's old magazines. Those are the feelings that will bring you back to the life waiting for you today. Everything else, any other place you turn your attention to — because you are afraid of touching and feeling your child-based sensibilities — is an utter waste of time and breath.

Your ability to be in a mature relationship has so little to do with the other person and everything to do with your ability to sit silently and listen, know, unwind, and apply the emotions that are stored inside of you. Nathaniel Branden in *Breaking Free* has issued a similar call to arms. To all of us who struggle to allow the kingdom inside to be brought to the surface, to our rational self, he says, "No pain is so destructive as the pain one does not face — and no suffering as enduring as the suffering one cannot acknowledge."

What you are going to see, though, is that this story about "deeper possibilities," about this passage of opening the human heart through this timeless and simple exercise of sitting, is not only old, but both personal and universal. I am not talking about my story, about sitting one evening in London. I am talking about your story, about your life that seems pedestrian and ordinary compared to the great hero stories you may be watching tonight that Hollywood tells and sells.

"Where we had thought to travel outward, we shall come to the center of our own existence."

— Joseph Campbell

Every tale of adventure — *The Odyssey*, *Braveheart*, the *Bible*, *Mulan*, or *Don Quixote* —seems so exciting, so real, death defying, otherworldly, and so utterly eternal, mysterious, foreign. It also feels external to your world. You experience these characters with your adult, rational perceptions as legends, people who have gone to the brink in some battle with something dark-ish and returned, having achieved something bigger than themselves. It is the hero journey template.

These stories appear to be about others, but are in fact just myths and allegories written for and about you and your fully unleashed heart-story. This sounds dramatic and almost silly. You say that there were actual Huns and the British that had to be fought, so that is not allegory. Yes, I get it.

But from your released heart's perspective — from the inner planes of longing, sorrow, from the purview of the tears and smiles generated from the fully-erupted sensations of childhood dreams and memories, reached through the passage of deep sitting — every single adventure story is exactly like yours. When you psychologically and bio-magnetically leave the unlived life of your rational adult self and meet your child-heart longings in the chair in your home office, you will see relatives, places, dragon-like things, and lands. They might seem foreign at first, but then become recognizable as yours, your family's and community's. You might not physically fight a Hun, but emotional exertion will be similar.

"If the person doesn't listen to the demands of his own spiritual and heart life, the person has put himself off-center," Joseph Campbell said. "Psychologically, the dragon is one's own binding of oneself to one's ego...must re-associate himself with the powers of nature, which are the powers of our life, from which our mind removes us."

When you commit to your heart's world, you will realize you have been looking in the wrong direction. You have been searching outward to escape and travel psycho-emotionally into the worlds of other people, transporting yourself during a two-hour movie to other places and times. You do this so that you can feel, remember, and believe again, even for a moment, in what you want, love, and trust.

The hero epic inspires, but what I know and am pushing you to experience is that when you turn inward and dive into the bewildering, nail-biting, confusing, and emotionally unruly realm of your heart's memories, that inner eight-year-old's world, you will find your real life there. Campbell says your sitting quietly is a passage back to forgotten feelings, is the "jumping-off place...where we had thought to travel outward, we shall come to the center of our own existence."

Rational No Match for Heart

What is happening when we sit in a chair with our back straight and eyes closed? How can this simple, seemingly innocent, non-action exercise be so altering and create so much drama? It is simple math. Rollin McCraty says in *The Heart Has Its Own 'Brain' and Consciousness* your heart generates an electrical current that is sixty times stronger than your brain's current, while the bio-magnetic field it produces is five thousand times stronger than the head's.

Think of—I mean, feel that. The raw electric power and energy of your heart muscle is five thousand times stronger than all the fleshy wiring and neurons stored in your brain. The heart is an electromagnetic muscle, a punchbowl, a warehouse that collects, absorbs, holds, and stores its goods using electricity. It is beating silently, literally ignored and forgotten by our conscious self, until we find the chair.

What many people misunderstand is that mental and emotional stress are not caused by the electricity of emotions coursing through their heart, head, and nervous system. The stress comes from the resistance our adult, rational left-brain mechanisms put up. It is like having a nightmare and waking up relieved at dawn. Your rational self is ready to begin its day, unsullied and so thankful to have cast away from that inner, dream place of confusion and fear.

That is the basic template of the human conscious, the waking self versus the deeper unconscious self. The challenge, though, is that this unconscious piece of us is not gone. It is just waiting below.

The Best Part

This is where it all turns. This is where and when we understand how important it is to return to the stories that our heart is aching, literally dying, to tell us.

Think of what we call the unconscious. It is all our feelings, every single one ever felt, which our mighty heart is storing. Your heart has been holding your love for chasing butterflies since you were seven years old and those soft memories of your childhood dog. You see an old photo of her or watch that dog food commercial where the dog ages, and a wistfulness seeps up from your chest, an ancient human longing to share and exchange warmth with another mammal that stirs way below our thoughts.

Then a tear wells up which is that child's heart-want in you for a dog's undivided, all-consuming, smiling and wagging love. That want is completely foreign and out of time and place to your current adult needs of cleaning the garage and finishing your taxes. The loving memory of your dog, a broken heart from eighth grade prom, or the regret from passing on a job twelve years ago are all part of an intimately woven life and world of yourself breathing inside the cells of your heart. Nothing in life has occurred without an emotion driving it.

It is how I ended up in Dr. Moore's office, impelled by a discontent that turned out to be the same one that plagued my grandfather. My thirty-one-year-old self, of course, did not know that, but in the hours of long sits that I did following that first one, he actually started coming back to me in my dreams.

Your heart is a brain and has a consciousness that is not unconscious; it is just so foreign to your adult self. It is pulsating and operating outside of adult time. *A General Theory of Love* tells us that "sixty-five percent of the cells in your heart are neural, identical to your brain. It is composed of some 40,000 neurons, and has its own neurotransmitters and proteins, allowing it to act independently of the cranial brain."

When Nietzsche said, "the child is far from being buried in the man...on the contrary its rules him absolutely," what he is alluding to is that from a cellular level, your fourth grade self is not only alive inside, but has desires to be held, heard, understood, and to create and play.

When we were young, the two parts of our brain were better pals compared to when we began to leave adolescence. Our emotional and organizing sides lived easily together as we were being cared for by others, by our parents. We did not need our rational like we do as adults. Our experiences were more fanciful, more naturally receptive. And then our inner world changed. During adolescence, the amygdala and prefrontal cortex battle it out for control over behavior — until the prefrontal cortex eventually takes over.

The hypertension that doctors talk about is the buildup of unexpressed heart electricity that really is a measure of how far apart these worlds have become. You must stop ignoring your heart twinges — those magnetic, intelligent pulsations that manifest as boredom aches from a meaningless job, the indifference and discontent with a spouse who cannot pour his or her heart out, the bolts of rage and anger that seem to be about traffic and unpaid bills. These twinges are really from the deeper story of feelings from the original and old child-time moments, before our brain worlds divided.

Broken Heart-Disease

Now that you know how strong the electricity of these feelings are deep within the neurons of your heart, meditate for a second or two on how much tension exists there. A heart attack comes after the long hours of wear and tear of erratic and disordered electrical heart currents ravaging the memory and cognition centers in your mid-brain.

In a *Lancet* paper, Dr. Ahmed Tawakol says that all of this "increased activity in the brain, specifically in the amygdala, is predictive of cardiovascular disease. It also illustrates a path from emotional stress to heart disease." The dramatic impact of the electro-magnetic divide between our heart and head is important to address, so much so that the medical field now uses electric currents, called pulsed electromagnetic field therapy (PEMF), to try to counteract the pressure that our unexpressed, child-heart is under. If you sit for long hours, you probably will not need PEMF, though, because you are going to unleash the frustration and joy you feel towards your parents.

Why We Come Back

The Hindus say there is a three-fold reason why we come back as humans: consciousness, awareness, and bliss. Our purpose is to take all that is not physical and unknown about ourselves, stored in the domain of our desire-infused heart world, and bring it into the material plane. That is, we need to be conscious of what our heart is telling us, of why it is beating so strongly.

The heart, this independent, mysterious and intelligent harbor of experiences, knows that it needs our rational side to release its messages. Consciousness is converting, translating, and intuiting the roots of why we feel, hate, love, and want, and putting these roots out into the world. Our life is an endless opportunity to create, which is the unraveling and revealing of the language currents of feelings. In order to fully complete your life, you must know, perceive, and unwind the original moments from your past that created your feeling reactions.

The adult who scorns his emotions, who runs from the pain of early memories, leaves these to be examined at another time, dare I say another lifetime. And if you get to your deepest feelings, you will know the reasons why others react, pout, hate, and fear.

This raising of consciousness, this waking up at the altar and intersection of your heart and adult attention through the rigors of sitting alone, is the basis of what we now call emotional intelligence. When we re-experience the natural and normal sadness of our inner child about that fifth-grade summer that was long gone by October or the longing for freedom to just climb a tree or get that undelivered hug of our emotionally distant father, we break open an empathy towards ourselves. By feeling it again, we understand where it came from.

We can see that sadness is okay; it is just part of the fabric of living. By not feeling it, it lingers as a hurt or anger. It comes out as today's much deeper frustration with a job or spouse. But when we open to it and put our adult attention into it, we do what we could not do as a child. We recognize it as just another verse in the heart song.

The elders of many Native American tribes had a ceremony they called lamenting, an exercise in which they danced and sang and chanted until they overcame themselves with emotions and tears. That was their Peloton, their hour or two at the gym, where they celebrated the preciousness of human life. By lamenting, they embraced and processed all that was sorrowful, so they could better recognize the preciousness of land and animals around them that sustained them. To feel this sadness makes the joy of living ten times better.

Knowing Darkness

Carl Jung agreed, saying, "Knowing your own darkness is the best method for dealing with the darknesses of other people." I continually encourage my counseling clients to stay with opening the heart.

When you know your own impulses — like when I found the boy-heart defensiveness toward the feminine — I realized that women I knew and cared about could easily trigger this in me. As soon as I wallowed in my childlike longing for and resistance to the feminine, I could then catch it when I first got married.

I, of course, have done a lot of dropping of the proverbial ball in my twenty-three years of marriage. I have caught my inner frustration during arguments, but still adolescently expressed it in dumb comments. When you own what you feel and wade into its watery roots, though, you begin to see how little others can impact you and your sense of life.

You see their stuff coming at you, anger right there and then, but you know it is rooted in days long ago because so is yours. An empathy and emotional intelligence will emerge, kind of like having the answers to the test in eleventh grade. You know what is inside your book, and all the life-test questions are pretty much the same, just different people expressing the exact same core emotions.

A mature adult has high emotional intelligence. She has wrestled long hours with the joy and tears of her inner child, can see the fragile child in her mother or friends, and even though she will continue to exclaim and expel her emotions onto others, she always has a sense that each outburst is another layer to watch and learn from. That is when our life really starts.

I wrote a few lines years ago about maturing, about bringing your inner child with you into your life:

We will only have to do it again, another lifetime. Let your emotional right brain storm your rational, left brain by sitting alone for long, long minutes, over and over. Like beaches erode and give way to the tides, let yourself be undone by your own emotions.

Pain will give way to relief. You will know where the longing comes from, and you will move closer to right now,

*this moment, not from it. This is what the storm is for, this
is how you understand, this is where your life begins. Oh,
to finish this life up fully, the unraveling dream.*

*"Change happens in the boiler room of our emotions— so
find out how to light the fires."*

— Jeff Dewar

Got Tears?

Expounding on what really stirs us is the magic of
meditation. Go listen to Joni Mitchell's "Circle Game" song,
rummage through old black and white photos, remember
the passing of your grandfather, or watch that dog food
commercial again, the one where the dog ages. Now go
and take one of those moments and bring it to your sitting
chair and be alone with the feelings for thirty minutes. We
both know that tears will flow. That is the point. That is
your homework, that is the magic.

Those emotional tears emerge from the lacrimal
glands behind the eye generated from signals powered
from the heart into the limbic mid-brain. It is the mind of
the heart helping the entire body reduce stress. In *Crying,
The Mystery of Tears*, we learn that "Eighty-five percent
of women and seventy-three percent of men feel better
after crying. Emotional tears resolve ambiguity. Some
hypothesize that crying is the body's way of shedding
stress hormones like prolactin."

You might get wildly bored and just go back to your
phone and the confused ache of a less than satisfying
relationship. Eventually, you will need to come back,
though. At times, it will be harder than a root canal. But

this is the only way. I say stop blaming a lack of time or money to go see a counselor, stop blaming your mother-in-law for making you miserable and the holidays lousy. In reality, it is all you. Those feelings of inadequacy are being woken up. Your spouse is not a liar or fibber or the culprit for stealing your joy and love. Something went missing long before, which is creating this.

Just when you thought you really knew how powerful your heart is and what your mission in life is, your heart is about to reveal an even more profound side. It beats to a rhythm tethered to a timeless world filled with images, sensations, and shadows that could fill a library, which, of course, the hearts of humans have been doing since time began.

But beyond the sensations and reconciliations of this current life, your human heart is intimately connected to your reptilian brain at the base of the skull, the part that makes your heart beat and your blood flow, the brain that still lives when somebody is brain dead. This prehistoric, neural membrane sitting at the base of our brain stem is 150 million years old. It is slow to evolve. It guides all our instinctual impulses like eating and procreating.

Feel how far back this part of us goes. You will have to close your eyes and really relax into this next concept. It is not one your rational mind will initially embrace. But, as you access the physical, neuron-laced currents of your heart that have lived, cuddled, wallowed and been showered by the ancient impulses of a body organ that lived in the shadows of dinosaurs, you will realize that you have access to unfathomable knowledge and experiences. If Dr. Emily Sterret is correct when she says in *The Science Behind Emotional Intelligence* "our feelings began in our reptilian brain, millions of years ago," then the beating of a drum can transport us to a wisdom about time and places that time cannot withhold.

You will realize that, and you — in the face of your job's immediate deadlines, your kid's college invoices, and the devolving of socio-economic and political landscape one Tweet at a time — are just a part of a super long thread of lives. You are the result of all that have come before you, and their lives have been electro-magnetically stored in these lower brain pieces.

This access to much older times is how I seemed to find, in the well of silence, the unexpressed longings and joys in households of relatives that I never met. Every family, every home has currents of missing emotional pieces. They are not good or bad, just blocks of unlived wants.

One counseling client's dad watched his brother die in front of him way back in the Twenties. He realized that ache of loss, from an event a generation before he was even born, still lived as a chemical peptide storm of longing and loss in him. It will continue to live strongly down into his kids as well, unless he turns and faces that gargoyle of pain. Once faced, the charge of loss dissipates. It still lives like a virus in his children, but with much less unconscious weight. In *Energies of Transformation*, we learn that the ancient Kabbalah teachings tell us when a person sits and awakens the energy of the heart, that alights the spine, seven generations forward and back experience the growth and awareness. It is because everything has emerged from what came before it — and the groove or rut of each inherited emotion is based on the intensity of its frequency.

Those born into the Depression Era had the weight of the physical experience of loss and trauma from the economic woes and insanity of World War II. The next generation, mine, born in the Sixties and early Seventies, never touched war or deprivation, we just felt its frequency in our parents. It can live as a trepidation about ill-winds that will be coming, or a tireless and critical sensation of lack, like it will never be enough.

Christopher Bache in *Lifecycles, Reincarnation and the Web of Life* frames this concept of today being a collection of a lot of yesterdays, and that the only way to alter tomorrow is to reconcile your inheritance. He says that "you are an aggregation of life experiences stored in the limbic body — you keep coming back in a feedback process." I am not asking you to believe in the continuation of life, of reincarnation. Many religions do not see it that way, and I honor and respect that. It is vital, though, that you recognize how today can change your experience of tomorrow.

I see our reptilian brain as a connecting device to places and times very distant. How many hours on my cushion did I hear the whispers and chants of Native Americans, did I witness in dream-like, waking moments the battles and celebrations of events no history book fully revealed? Many hours, many scenes.

I could feel the dislocation of a great grandfather who married for love out of and against the customs of his family, then realized that I had done the same thing. That was a heart impulse he sent down to me one hundred years before I met my wife. We repeat all that was missing and embraced by our ancestors until we align heart and head, the adult and child heart that must sit and dance together. This is the road home. "It is by going down into the abyss that we recover the treasures of life," said Joseph Campbell.

"His crude energies of love and aggression are being broken from their primary sphere of reference and reorganized for manhood."

— Joseph Campbell

Hero Journey is Your Story

Sitting turns your adult attention to the palpitations of the ancient heart that is tethered to a family mythology, your family's story. This is completely unnerving. I used to come home from ten hours of work on a busy trading floor, put on my sweatpants, and sit on the floor in the dark. What started to happen is that I could feel-recognize the confines of rules, perspectives, beliefs, apprehensions, joys, sorrows, and the cultural and sociological norms that my parents and ancestors grew up in and were tethered to. I could see so much more of the whys about what they thought and understood to be absolute truths, but also began to feel an expansion of their truths through which I could emerge.

I embrace religion. I embraced the rigor of Catholic beliefs, only in a form that does not necessarily include a singular, transformational human. I feel everyone is resurrected. Everything and everyone can hear and has access to the frequency of the mighty original word, spoken and representing god, Aum, Amen, or Ameen. These three words are the Hindu, Christian, and Islamic versions of the exact same word for the sound you will hear in deep quiet.

Through the long hours of reading and sitting, as I witnessed my inner unraveling with all the tears and muscle spasms, I knew this was an exercise, a passage away from the normal psychological, emotional, and spiritual framework of my cultural upbringing. To fully leave home, you must break the frequency umbilical cord. It does not mean blaming and accusing and denigrating anyone else's beliefs. It means becoming your own, taking the gifts of all that was unlived and trying to live them yourself.

Every ancient culture had this belief that the adolescent must grow up. To grow means to turn and break the heart, soften the body so the heart truths emerge. Joseph Campbell pioneered the term for this, the *Hero's Journey*. You must put the rational brain to sleep, so to speak, and awaken the heart. He wrote, "On the psychological side...the boy is being carried across the difficult threshold from the sphere of dependency on the mothers to that of participation in the nature of the fathers...by means of intense psychological experiences...reorganizing all the primary imprints and fantasies...his crude energies of love and aggression are being broken from their primary sphere of reference and reorganized for manhood."

The leaving home, being torn apart by dragons and other warriors, and returning to share wisdom is the oldest and only story that has ever been told. Some are expelled from paradise, others sit under a tree or get nailed to one, while others slay dragons or run from wicked witches. It does not matter. When you sit, you are going to see that these are just psychological expressions of your heart starting to feel the beat and perceptions of your eight-year-old's experiences, which initiates you into reliving memories. Then, when your now eight-year-old daughter cries or laughs, you know what she is feeling.

Every Hollywood movie adheres to this sequential framework of unfolding: departure, the call, initiation, the abyss, etc. George Lucas worked with Joseph Campbell to fully develop the hero's journey for *Star Wars*. You must start yours right there, right now where you are.

No need to watch *Braveheart* or *Gladiator* for the eighth or ninth time to become inspired. You will join the ancient cultures when you sit firmly on the floor and wait for currents to take you back, out, and around. The Assyrians, Egyptians, Celts, Greeks, Tibetans, Gnostics, Christian mystics, Freemasons, and Jews all had their rituals to subject a normal, daily state of mind to induced relaxation via song, drum, breath, and dance. In doing so, they were circulating light, blood, tension and attention into and through the solar plexus and heart. Bam, that is all it takes.

Campbell said, "The chief aim of all religious teachings and ceremony is to suppress...the sense of ego and develop that of participation." You wait, though, because it still does not make sense. One male client began to sit longer than I thought he would, and he said the sadness he felt in his deceased grandfather's heart was like a dragon chasing his joy. The insecurity and anxiousness in him manifested in a rage on the football field, plus an obsession with his looks. These were masking a child's desire to be recognized and liked, and not to feel empty.

Death-Rebirth in the Suburbs

The original name for this book, the one that I started when my hair was brown, was *Death-Rebirth in the Suburbs*. Every culture had their exercise and term for breaking the young adult. It was called cosmic humiliation, the exercise of breaking oneself down. It was an essential psychosocial ritual. Native Americans called it becoming "lower than an ant," which is the same kind of rite of passage or experience of growth that the Christians call the spiritual poverty, Islam calls Faqr, or the Balya of Hinduism. It is the condition of those who realize that in relation to the ancient truths, carried in the heart and lower brain channels, each of us, even in the lavishly appointed, manicured lawn-lands of suburbia, are as nothing.

The natives call meditation and dancing and chanting "crying for a vision." It is just like a purification rite of the Inipi. There are the whirling dervishes and all the other cultures that had their ways of churning up the feeling world. This is a way of praying that is very important, the center of their religion from which they receive and perceive self as part of everything else. Every man can and must cry for a vision or lament, and in the old days they did it all the time. "The only true wisdom lives far from mankind, out in the great loneliness, and it can be reached only through suffering," said Campbell.

Many have heard the flowing of the blood within and across their ear drums when sitting long hours, as well as the frequency of some kind of sound. The ancients called this universal sound, this whirling of electrons, *Aum*. It is the sound from where we get Amen. It connotes and warbles like water. Hence the baptismal rites of some religions, whose original source was not actual water being poured from someone else that held higher rank. Water is the physical symbol for the sound heard in silence, a hum, as well as the tears of our child-heart opening. Google the word Amen.

I believe there was a man, avatar, healer, shaman, and psychic named Jesus who was undone by the Romans. I also believe that the Bible is a great and timeless hero's journey, a story-poem written and interpreted by smart men and women across the years. But right now, via your heart, via a tear, a resurrection can and will occur, regardless of what any poem says. If I wait for someone else to show me, then I never finish this life.

When the Bible says "son of man," it is a recognition that if we limit our awareness to how we think, touch, taste, or experience life, using only our five senses and intellect, then we are bound by the linear time frequency created by us men and women. This is not a bad thing. There are some great cars to buy and overpriced coffee to drink. We need and want these things. But these physical constructs are determined by humans. This is what "son of man" means, tethered to manmade things.

But when the Bible says, "even so must the son of man be lifted," and when Jesus says, "I am in heaven," there is a more expansive reality and lesson in this part of the poem. When we sit, break open, hear and feel the dream-memories of our earlier days, there is a shift away from the fleshy, manmade world and into the non-physical, eternal feeling world. The lifting is the experience you have of being connected to things beyond your human flesh. The "son of man," your rational conceptions, become sons of God. Right here, right now, no need to wait.

Yogananda writes in *The Yoga of Jesus* that the Hindus had already written the expression "I am in heaven," called *nirvikalpa saadhi*, long before the Judaic-Christian Bible was written. Christ and his consciousness are part of the long thread of myths, like the Hindu's Krishna. You say tomato, I say ketchup. You get what I mean.

The point is every culture, every faith, every movie, and every tale ever written is about what you are going to do right now, release your limited adult attention to your part of the eternal storyline. Look no further than that lonely chair in the corner of your bedroom and let it hold you. Join the long line of sitters.

Get Thee to A Cushion

Every minute you wait shows that you are rightfully scared to open up old hurts. I understand. Many will continue to resist and deride my singular obsession with sitting alone. Your avoidance, to me, hints at your clinging to a teenaged fear at your core. You still do not really want to listen to mommy or daddy, and not sitting is an expression of that resistance.

Go find a big closet, though, sit down in the dark on a cushion with your back straight. Do not lie down. Sit up, and let the body ache and throb with old pains and boredom and anxiousness. You will feel an emotion you have not felt in a long time and you will want to shed a tear — and if you do, you will water the soil of generations of your offspring for the next two hundred years and beyond, says the Kabbalah.

In the time it took you to read that sentence, a hundred thousand homes across the U.S. were just riddled with a partner "by-passing" his or her reasoning functions and unconsciously acting out his inner child. Therefore, a hundred thousand more relationships just took another sucker punch.

So Basic, So Easy, Here Goes

Let me try it again. I am going to tell you what you need to do in order to begin to understand why you are not feeling complete in your marriage and life. From there, you will know where to turn next:

- Just sit quietly alone for twenty minutes every day, in a chair with your back straight, feet on the ground, and eyes closed
- Listen to your heart, stomach, back of neck, forehead, and top of head, in no particular order
- While sitting in this position, slowly inhale into your nose while pushing your stomach and belly button out into the room, towards the wall you are facing
- Hold your extended stomach out into the room until you have inhaled all the way. Your shoulders have probably lifted a bit as you inhale deeply and push your stomach out
- Now exhale out of your mouth very slowly, making a sound like huh while squeezing your belly back in, actively pulling your stomach back towards your back bone
- Do ten of these deep, slow breaths. Once you are done with these ten, just sit and listen to your

stomach, heart, back of your neck, forehead, and top of head.
- That is it. Mic dropped.

ABOUT ATMOSPHERE PRESS

Atmosphere Press is an independent, full-service publisher for excellent books in all genres and for all audiences. Learn more about what we do at atmospherepress.com.

We encourage you to check out some of Atmosphere's latest nonfiction releases, which are available at Amazon.com and via order from your local bookstore:

Great Spirit of Yosemite: The Story of Chief Tenaya, nonfiction by Paul Edmondson

My Cemetery Friends: A Garden of Encounters at Mount Saint Mary in Queens, New York, nonfiction and poetry by Vincent J. Tomeo

Change in 4D, nonfiction by Wendy Wickham

Disruption Games: How to Thrive on Serial Failure, nonfiction by Trond Undheim

Eyeless Mind, nonfiction by Stephanie Duesing

A Blameless Walk, nonfiction by Charles Hopkins

The Horror of 1888, nonfiction by Betty Plombon

White Snake Diary, nonfiction by Jane P. Perry

From Rags to Rags, essays by Ellie Guzman

Giving Up the Ghost, essays by Tina Cabrera

Family Legends, Family Lies, nonfiction by Wendy Hoke

What?! You Don't Want Children?: Understanding Rejection in the Childfree Lifestyle, nonfiction by Marcia Drut-Davis

Peaceful Meridian: Sailing into War, Protesting at Home, nonfiction by David Rogers Jr.

ABOUT THE AUTHOR

I have spent the last thirty-two years in the financial field, building relationships with my investing clients. Since 2006, when I earned my *LCSW*, I have been studying, teaching, and counseling relationships in my evenings and weekend therapy practice. Find me at www.wholecounseling.com.

A few highlights from my last twenty-seven years:

- Successfully navigated, so far, the challenges and joys of marriage and parenting three daughters
- Lived and worked in the financial field in London, England for six years
- Travelled to forty-six countries, so far
- Read 125 books on spirituality, history, mythology, and the science of human development
- Have sat quietly for 7,000+ hours

I graduated from *Middlebury College,* VT in 1986 with a BA in English, and earned a Master of Science degree from *Columbia University School of Social Work,* NY in 2003.

More Background on Bill

- Bill believes that working on yourself, which will automatically improve the dynamics of your relationship, is the most important thing in life. He writes, "What we do right now in our relationship echoes down through posterity, changes who our grandchildren's children become."
- Bill's career spans 30+ years in the financial field as a research sales and capital markets executive, having worked in New York, London, Stamford, CT and now Austin, TX.
- Back in 1997, while living in London, England, after having spent eleven years in the financial field, Bill took a work hiatus and enrolled in a language immersion program in Merida, Venezuela. His goal was to learn Spanish and to continue studying and researching the customs, ethnology, and psychology of local communities
- Using this experience of living and working with locals, Bill began developing a basic model for applying universal and holistic approaches to human development and self-awareness. It was simple; slow down and relax the rational, left part of the brain to gain access to the emotional, right side of the brain. The right, feeling-based limbic side of the body and mind hold all the answers to why we feel and behave the way we do
- In 2002 he enrolled in *Columbia University's School of Social Work* master's program. As part of this curriculum, Bill became a member of the social services staff at North Haven, CT's *Veterans*

Hospital where he worked with WWII, Korean, and Vietnam War veterans and their families.

- This experience catalyzed his desire to further research the science and physiology behind more interventions that address and reduce the deleterious effects of PTSD and stress–related symptoms surrounding trauma. Most of the conventional interventions he witnessed were not positively improving our veteran's lives
- After earning his MSW in 2003 he became a director at *Domus*, one of Connecticut's most progressive youth focused, human services non-profits. He led their juvenile justice program called *Avenues*. With the help of his colleagues, he introduced practices and curriculum that incorporated a more integrated approach to educating and supporting students, families, and program staff
- This program earned the *State of Connecticut's* highest marks in youth retention and development. With this practical and clinical experience, Bill then launched an evenings and weekend counseling practice, working with youth, adults and couples
- The basic principle underlying his work is compassionately direct: create an environment for clients to go much deeper into their feelings so that they can fully understand what these emotions are trying to teach them. The wisdom and guidance we all seek is stored within our feelings.

CPSIA information can be obtained
at www.ICGtesting.com
Printed in the USA
BVHW031321211020
591527BV00011B/54

9 781649 218681